CHILDREN, SPIRITUALITY, RELIGION AND SOCIAL WORK

D0153835

To John, with love and thanks

Children, Spirituality, Religion and Social Work

Margaret Crompton

Ashgate

ARENA

Aldershot • Brookfield USA • Singapore • Sydney

Published by
Ashgate Publishing Limited
Gower House
Croft Road
Aldershot
Hants GU11 3HR
England

Ashgate Publishing Company
Old Post Road
Brookfield
Vermont 05036
USA

British Library Cataloguing in Publication Data
Crompton, Margaret, 1941–
    Children, spirituality, religion and social work
    1. Children – Religious life 2. Children – Services for
    3. Children – Counseling of
    I. Title
    362.7

Library of Congress Catalog Card Number: 98–70340

ISBN 1 85742 377 1

Printed in Great Britain by The Ipswich Book Company, Suffolk

Contents

Acknowledgements

I thank all the people whose contributions enabled me to research and write this text.

In order to relate this discussion of spirituality and religion firmly to everyday life and practice, I met practitioners in a number of settings (including both local authority and voluntary agencies), who generously gave time and shared ideas and memories. The interest they showed in the topics gave me encouragement essential to completing what proved to be a huge, and often exhausting, task. Except for Martin House (see Chapters 13 and 16), agencies are not identified, to protect confidentiality.

The Central Council for Education and Training in Social Work generously gave permission for me to develop ideas and to quote from papers which first appeared in the training pack *Children, Spirituality and Religion* (Crompton 1996).

The following publishers gave free permission for substantial quotations from the following publications: Chapman and Hall for Hill (1994), the Children's Rights Office (CRO) for CRDU (1994), Routledge for Sinason (1994), and The Children's Society for Bradford (1995).

Valerie Sinason and Janet West commented on drafts of Chapter 12 and gave permission for quotations from their publications (Sinason 1994; West, J. 1996).

Jo Gooderham gave me the opportunity to pursue study of the topics which are discussed below and provided perfect editorial support, always answering my fussy questions quickly, and reducing anxiety with calm, sensible advice. Kate Trew continued this editorial support with efficiency and sensitivity.

John Crompton advised, chauffered, corrected, discussed, read, shared adventures and supported me with patient love.

Foreword

Children of spirit

Ruby Bridges was 6 when she braved hostile mobs, the only black child to claim her right to attend an integrated school in New Orleans (see Chapter 3). She responded to hatred, threats and insults with cheerfulness, determination and compassionate charity, forgiving her persecutors in accordance with the example of her religious and spiritual leader, Jesus, because: 'When he was dying, he asked God to forgive the people who were killing him' (quoted in Coles 1984, p.xiii).

For Ruby, religion and spirituality were the unquestioned fundamentals of everyday life. As a Christian, her spirituality was expressed through religious forms of worship and language. However, spirituality is not necessarily associated with religion. Neither is it the prerogative of children with a command of verbal communication. Edward (aged 2) was described as 'oozing spirituality', exhibiting 'all the capacities and predispositions of an individual who has an awareness of the spiritual dimension of ... life', and able to experience 'ecstasy, totally absorbed in and drawn towards realities outside himself' (McClure 1996, p.9; see Chapter 3).

Such delight may be submerged by busy-ness and pressures, yet can be nurtured in apparently inimical circumstances. Joanna (aged 10) found spiritual refreshment in an imaginary garden, contrasting with her gloomy, noisy home life, where she could think about God and seek a better life (Nye 1996, 2/16 and 17; see Chapter 3). However, for some children no garden, physical or imagined, can relieve the agonies of spiritual distress, even despair. One girl spent the years between the ages of 8 and 11 in a religious crisis associated with fear of both death and life, causing severe panic attacks which no one noticed (Robinson 1977, p.111, see Chapter 4).

Yvonne Stevenson (1976) endeavoured to demonstrate religious devotion by wounding herself (pp.43–4; see Chapter 4), but far more common are the wounds inflicted by adults. Neil Charleson was sexually abused in a residential school for children with learning difficulties (Charleson and Corbett 1994, p.168;   see Chapter 12). A 13-year-old girl was sexually assaulted by a vicar for whom she was babysitting (Kennedy 1995b, pp.3–4; see Chapter 12).

Not all assaults are physical. A nurse fed pork to a Muslim baby because it was too much trouble to order permitted food (see Chapter 12). Roksana (aged 9), also a Muslim, suffered guilt and anxiety because, in order not to draw attention to herself, she ate food forbidden by her religion (see Chapter 10), thus betraying both her mother and Allah (Ahmed 1986, p.59). Amit Tal (1975) (aged 11), living in the midst of war, cried: 'O why the immense hate?/Why shouldn't there be Peace?' (see Chapter 3).

Spirituality, whether or not expressed through religious belief and observance, can be respected and nurtured in every setting. It is integral to the whole child and to the whole of everyday, every-minute living and dying. 'Maria' died after a life of physical weakness and suffering due to incurable illness which could have been identified *in utero*. However, as she told hospice staff who loved her and admired her great spirit, she was opposed to termination of pregnancy on the ground of genetic risk for, if her mother had made such a choice, Maria would have lost the chance of life, which she relished (see Chapter 13).

These and many other children may be found in the following pages, illustrating the importance of really attending to the whole person.

Background

An Indian proverb describes the individual as 'a house with four rooms, a physical, a mental, an emotional and a spiritual', advising that 'unless we go into every room every day, even if only to keep it aired, we are not a complete person' (Godden 1989, p.13).

This proverb provided the title for a chapter exploring spiritual aspects of counselling in relation to children in an earlier book (Crompton 1992). Expecting to find little material, I was encouraged by the range of sources and ideas available in both professional literature and fiction which offered enlightenment about spiritual experiences of not only children but also practitioners. Brian Thorne (Director, Centre for Counselling Studies, University of East Anglia), for example, wrote of his recognition of 'a capacity to express tenderness both physically and spiritually', 'a tenderness that moves the soul while embracing (sometimes literally) the body'; acknowledgement of his spiritual self enabled him to bring his whole self into counselling encounters (Mearns and Thorne 1988, p.37; see also Crompton 1992, p.114).

In 1964, Noel Timms (a social work lecturer, later professor) had identified that although 'perhaps in religious belief and practice ... a person's values are most clearly apparent ... the relationship between religion and casework has received little attention'. He proposed 'A new appraisal ... based on the assumption of the importance and significance of religious belief and feeling in human beings' which should not 'be hidden away or dissolved by analysis' (cited in Moran 1968, p.94; see also Crompton 1992, p.114).

In 1992, it seemed that such an appraisal was still awaited, that the significance and importance of religious belief – and, I would add, spiritual experience and well-being – were still largely obscure. Brian Thorne's acknowledgement of his spirituality had a confessional element, almost a 'coming out'.

Two important documents were published in the early 1990s but perhaps had limited distribution among social workers. The National Children's Bureau *Taking Care* pack noted the problems of theological language when associated with abuse which 'might have an effect on the child's spiritual life' (Armstrong 1991, p.18; see also Crompton 1992, pp.115–16). The National Youth Bureau published a survey on the spiritual development of young people which included a summary of the attitudes of youth workers: some, for example, believed spiritual development to be 'an integral part of youth work, quite independent of any particular form of religious belief or organized religion' (Garrett 1990, p.1; see also Crompton 1996, 4/6).

Following publication of *Children and Counselling* (Crompton 1992), I became interested in pursuing study of children, spirituality, religion and social work, and was delighted to be invited to contribute to a conference at the Centre for Research into Spiritual and and Moral Education, Plymouth University, where I began to learn about the immense interest in these topics among teachers and education-based academics, and the amount of work being carried out on them.

As I was preparing to write a book on these topics, I was invited to tender to produce a training pack for the Central Council for Education and Training in Social Work (CCETSW). Following a conference of Christian childcare voluntary organisations in 1993, the CCETSW and the National Council for Voluntary Child Care Organisations (NCVCCO) had become convinced of the need for training materials 'relevant to practitioners of a range of faiths or no faith working with children and families of a range of faiths or no faith' (Roskill 1996, p.v). Materials in the training pack (Crompton 1996) comprise papers on seven religions, commissioned to provide information on aspects of particular relevance to children, young people and families, a paper on spiritual development, a reprinted paper on 'Religious persuasion and the Children Act' (Seden 1995) and copious materials and ideas for practice-focused training activities. In 1995, The Children's Society published *Caring for the Whole Child: A Holistic Approach to Spirituality* (Bradford 1995), to which reference is made in both Crompton (1996) and the present text.

The experience of commissioning papers, editing and writing this material strengthened my interest in the topics, which was confirmed by three piloting conferences, two with practising and experienced social workers from a variety of agencies, voluntary and statutory, day, field and residential, and one with students on a university MA course. It became clear that consideration of spirituality, religion and social work stimulated an interest to delight Brian Thorne and Noel Timms. More recent work with staff of a large voluntary agency, training student teachers specialising in theology and preparing for placements in social care agencies, and discussions in connection with the present book have further indicated the importance of these matters and interest in them.

My own background lies in Christianity – an Anglican girlhood, followed by many years without attachment to any denomination, then (and presently) membership of the Religious Society of Friends. Inevitably, my own background and beliefs must be evident in the text, but this is not a book about Christianity: the essential theme is respect for the whole person and nurture of spiritual well-being, whatever the beliefs and philosophy of the individual.

Writing about spirituality and religion is fraught with problems, not least the spiritual exhaustion resulting from engaging with such topics as abuse. Clearly, no book, however scholarly and detailed, can represent every belief, every approach, and this text offers only brief introductions as models and to offer a stimulus to practitioners' further study based on individual children and families.

The comments above indicate how this book endeavours to combine my own interests and development of study and understanding with the requirements of social work practice and attention to the whole care of the whole child.

Intention

This book seeks to expand, extend and deepen ideas and materials from the CCETSW training pack, with particular reference to everyday practice in settings associated with social work, and to introduce a further range of materials and topics.

For example, a number of ideas about and definitions of spirituality, from a wide range of sources, are discussed in Part 2 in order to offer practitioners access to the breadth and depth of this concept. No single formulation is presented as definitive, for, as will be seen, concepts of the spirit/spirituality depend on beliefs about, for example, religion, the meaning and nature of life, and/or the existence/destiny of the soul. It is expected that practitioners will use the material on this and other topics to develop awareness of and clarity about their own beliefs and those of the children with and for whom they work.

Despite legal and official acknowledgement of rights to spiritual and/or religious nurture, the very complexity of these topics may inhibit practitioners from devoting the attention which would ensure fulfilment of those rights. Practitioners responsible for training may feel that scarce financial and time resources cannot be spared for such matters. Yet those who attended the piloting conferences and training days mentioned above expressed great interest and found the topics of importance, both to themselves and the children for whom they were responsible.

The intention of this book is to propose ways in which religion and spirituality are of importance in social work with and on behalf of children in a range of settings, including day, foster and residential care, and home-based individual and family work. The material and ideas are relevant to practitioners in voluntary and statutory agencies and establishments, and in settings concerned with medical, psychiatric, offending, educational and other specialisations.

A number of practitioners in a range of settings contributed experience and ideas, for the intention at all times is to demonstrate that spirituality and religion are essentially aspects of the whole, everyday person, with implications for well-being in ordinary, everyday life and practice.

These topics often inspire anxiety: for example, after a girl had informed two social workers that she had become a Christian, one told her Christian colleague: 'I'm glad you were there, I wouldn't have known how to respond.' No doubt this social worker would have 'known how to respond' to revelations of abuse or offences and other matters of which she had no direct personal experience (see Chapter 11).

A further intention is to contribute to the literature on communication with children. Although the focus is on spirituality and religion, the underlying philosophy at all times is on essential good practice, on listening, attention and respect. If practitioners do not profess a religious belief or feel comfortable with the vocabulary of spirituality, they none the less have a responsibility to care for and about the whole child in the context of the whole background.

Matching Needs and Services (Dartington Social Research Unit 1996), for example, encourages planners to take 'a rounded view of the whole child and to gather information about every aspect of his or her life.' (p.24). While neither religious nor spiritual needs and services are mentioned in the Dartington document, 'a rounded view of the whole child', in the context of family background, surely includes attention to these aspects of life which are, to many people, fundamental.

It is not suggested that religious and spiritual experiences are always welcome or beneficial. Indeed, the concept of spiritual distress in relation to children seems to receive little attention. However, spiritual experience is by no means all a matter of wonder, love and joy. If spiritual/religious experience can contribute to the well-being of the whole child, it must, by implication, also be involved in abuse and neglect. An essential intention of this book is to explore some ideas about harmful aspects of the topics.

Sad, even tragic events need not lead to spiritual depletion, for growth of the whole person depends on engaging with, learning from and balancing the whole of experience, from despair to delight, from frustration to fulfilment.

The book is intended to stimulate interest, and to encourage further exploration by practitioners who, like the children and families with and for whom they work, represent every kind of belief and attitude from hostility to devotion.

Format

This book is arranged in six parts, of which Parts 1–3 present ideas and information about spiritual and religious rights, spirituality, and religion, constituting a broad and brief introduction to these topics. Parts 4–5 apply these topics to two areas of practice: abuse and neglect, and death and bereavement. These areas have been selected because they are important in themselves, and as models for similar approaches to disability and offending, for example. Part 6 suggests two approaches to communication in the context of religion and/or spirituality which serve as models for other forms of communication and applications.

Groups of questions and suggestions are included throughout the book. These may be used by individuals or informal groups, or in training programmes to help focus material and ideas on everyday practice.

The style of individual parts is adapted to the kind of material presented.

Part 1: Spiritual and religious rights

Chapter 1 discusses some relevant Articles in the United Nations (UN) Convention on the Rights of the Child (1989). The Convention (ratified by the UK) requires recognition of children's rights to spiritual and religious freedom, nurture and well-being. For example, every child has the right to: 'a standard of living adequate for ... physical, mental, spiritual, moral and social development' (Article 27).

These rights are reflected in the Education Reform Act 1988 and the Children Act 1989. Although legislation about education refers to spirituality, legislation relating to care and upbringing refers only to religion. Similarly, Department of Health (1995) *Looking After Children* questionnaires anomalously require exploration of religious but not spiritual well-being. While it may be supposed that 'religious' includes 'spiritual', there is no provision for the spiritual nurture of children who profess no religious belief.

Part 2: Children and spirituality

Chapters 2–4 explore definitions and models of spirituality, spiritual development and well-being, with attention to distressing as well as desirable experiences in childhood.

Religious belief usually implies an integral concept of spirituality. However, association with a religion is not essential to such a concept; for example, a comprehensive definition was formulated by the British Humanist Association (see Chapter 2). Although it is often considered that the whole human comprises body, mind and emotions, the existence of spirit is perpetually debated. The holistic approach implies respect for and attention to the whole life of the whole person; difficulties are inevitable when the one who cares and the one who is cared for hold differing views about the constitution of the whole person. These chapters introduce approaches which may contribute to discussion and understanding of various viewpoints.

Part 3: Children and religion

Chapters 5–10 introduce five aspects of religious belief and observance with particular relevance to children. Children are legally entitled to spiritual and religious nurture, just as they are entitled to physical and cognitive care. However, attitudes towards religion vary from hostility to devotion, indifference to enthusiasm, rigidity to universalism. Practitioners may dislike the beliefs and observances of children for whom they are responsible, yet every child has the right to religious respect and encouragement. These chapters offer information and ideas about religious belief and observance which are of importance in everyday care.

Part 4: Spirituality, religion, abuse and neglect

Chapters 11 and 12 explore effects on the spirit and/or religious belief of sexual and other forms of abuse, and of abuse deliberately associated with religious observances, including oppression and ritual abuse.

Practitioners encounter effects and expressions of failure to nurture or actively, even deliberately, to assault spiritual and religious well-being. Whether or not they are comfortable with the vocabulary and concepts of spirituality and/or religion, responsibility for the whole child requires practitioners to attend to these aspects of life and vulnerability.

Part 5: Children and death

Chapters 13 and 14 introduce ideas about dying, death and bereavement in the context of a children's hospice and hospital (including attention to siblings), and of suicide and abortion.

Another focus of practice in which attention to matters of spirituality and/or religion is of special importance is bereavement, dying, death and other types of loss. Practitioners sometimes consider that death has little relevance for children with whom they work, but these chapters indicate broad and deep implications.

Part 6: Communicating with children

Chapters 15 and 16 offer one model of communication and one model of practice focus. One intention of this book is to encourage development of communication with children. As the emphasis throughout is on religion and spirituality as inherent in attention to the whole well-being of the whole child, so excellent communication about religion, for example, enhances total communication between child and practitioner. Only one form of communication (story) could be explored here, but practitioners are encouraged to apply ideas about such other forms as art and music. Chapter 14 relates particularly to Part 3 and Chapter 15 discusses some methods of communication in relation to the practice focus of Part 5.

Note on vocabulary and conventions

The intended readership comprises people who care for and work with children in any setting associated, in the first instance, with social work agencies and establishments. The book is also intended for use in training programmes, whether in-service or organised by an academic establishment.

Material is drawn from social work and other disciplines, and it is hoped that practitioners in educational, medical and penal services, for example, will also find it of use. It would be clearly cumbersome to write 'carers, practitioners and students' throughout the book, so 'practitioners' will be used to refer to all readers. Similarly, 'children' refers to children and young people, aged from 0 to 18.

Vocabulary associated with religion is rich and complex; individual words are often spelled in various ways, depending on the language of origin. For example, words used here which originate in Hebrew or Arabic are not only translated but also transliterated into the conventional Latin script of the English language. In most instances, the spellings used in this book are based on those in *Dates and Meanings of Religious and Other Festivals* (Walshe and Warrier 1993).

There are many ways of referring to a collection or gathering of people who profess the same religious beliefs and fulfil the same religious obligations; 'religious congregation' is used here.

Many religions require and/or encourage attendance at a designated place (in the UK, usually a building) for participation in some form of corporate worship. This may be a purpose-built, dedicated building, a rented hall or a private house, indicated here by 'place of worship'.

For many people, the word 'faith' is powerful and expressive; it is used rarely in this book, but may for some readers be interchangeable with 'belief'.

'God' indicates the proper name of a deity, as appropriate. 'Deity/god' indicates a general reference to a divine being.

Interviewed contributors are identified by their first names, with their permission, or by pseudonyms chosen/approved by them, indicated by being enclosed in quotation marks.

Part 1

Spiritual and religious rights

1 Spiritual and religious rights

Rhetoric or reality?

> The way a society treats children reflects not only its qualities of compassion and protective caring but also its sense of justice, its commitment to the future and its urge to enhance the human condition for coming generations.

Javier Pérez de Cuellar (Secretary-general of the UN) made this statement in 1987 during the drafting of the Convention on the Rights of the Child. In 1989, after adoption of the Convention, he said: 'the UN has given the global community an international instrument of high quality protecting the dignity, equality and basic human rights of the world's children' (quoted in UNICEF, 1995). In 1990 the World Summit on Children was attended by 71 heads of state and government (including the UK) who pledged: 'The well-being of children requires political action at the highest level. We are determined to take that action. We ourselves make a solemn commitment to give high priority to the rights of children' (quoted in CRDU, 1994, p.xi). However, seven years later, Caroline Hamilton (Director of the Children's Legal Centre) found that 'Much of the rhetoric on children's rights is just that, rhetoric' (Hamilton 1996, p.1).

Although the Convention was ratified by the UK in 1991, in 1994 the Children's Rights Development Unit (CRDU) commented:

> It would be good to report that in the UK the obligations of ratification were being taken seriously, that there was an open commitment to giving high priority to the best interests of children throughout the political agenda. Such a priority would require a careful audit of the state of UK children and the law, policy and practice which affects them, and energetic implementation of the duty to the Convention to make its contents widely known, 'by appropriate and active means', to adults

3

and children alike. Discrimination in children's access to basic social, economic, health, and education rights would be openly acknowledged and properly considered when decisions that affect them are made.

Sadly, none of this has happened. (p.xi)

For example, Article 42 requires States Parties 'to make the principles and provisions of the Convention widely known, by appropriate and active means, to adults and children alike'. However, as the CRDU (1994) notes:

In relation to the duty to disseminate the Convention, it has been put on sale in government bookshops, circulated to local authorities, and a few hundred leaflets distributed. Nothing has been directed at the UK's 13 million under 18 year-olds. (p.xi)

Moreover:

There has been no attempt to place Government policy as it affects children (and most of it does) within the context of the Convention. In a growing number of countries, governments have moved logically to appoint ministers for children and independent ombudspeople or commissioners with statutory powers. In the UK, such proposals have been rejected by the Government as entirely unnecessary. (p.xii)

While acknowledging positive contributions of the Children Act 1989, this review finds that 'It has no influence at all on many services and many aspects of most children's lives' (CRDU 1994, pp.xi and xii).

This analysis of the UK's responses to the Convention found, in relation to the social and economic rights:

a very clear dissonance between a professed commitment to children's welfare, and the effective implementation of that commitment. There is evidence that in some very fundamental ways things are getting worse, not better, for many children. Article 2 ... insists that the rights ... must be implemented for all children without discrimination on any ground. Yet it is clear that whether for reasons of poverty, ethnicity, disability, sexuality, immigration status or geography, many children are denied fundamental rights in the Convention ... [Black children] are more likely to experience difficulties in gaining access to health and social services ... [which] often fail to address their particular cultural and religious needs. (CRDU 1994, p.xiii)

A number of Articles refer to religious or spiritual rights (but not to both in one Article), and others are informed by concern for religious/spiritual welfare (Bradford 1995, pp.5–8 and 16–20). Key provisions can be summarised under four headings, all of which may be seen as relating to spiritual and religious rights:

- **survival rights**, from the child's right to life through the most basic needs, including food, shelter, and access to health care.
- **development rights**, or all those things that children require in order to reach their fullest potential, from education and play to freedom of thought, conscience and religion.
- **protection rights**, requiring that children be safeguarded against all forms of abuse, neglect and exploitation.
- **participation rights**, including the right to free expression, which allow children to take an active role in their communities and nations (UNICEF 1995, p.2).

This chapter focuses on the concept of rights in relation to children, religion and spirituality in the context of the Convention under eight headings, most of which are taken from the relevant Article headings in the Convention.

Attention can be given here to only a few of the 54 Articles (of which 1–42 relate directly to children; the remaining Articles define the responsibilities of governments). The text of the Convention, together with 'Know your rights! Children's rights in plain English' (1995) a leaflet by Alexander Nurnberg (age 9) is available from UNICEF (see 'Useful Organisations').

The rights of the child

The Convention defines 'child' as: 'every human being below the age of 18 years unless under the law applicable to the child, majority is attained earlier'. The UK applies this only following a live birth.

The concept of 'children's rights' was formulated by Eglantine Jebb (British founder of Save the Children) and formalised in the first Declaration of the Rights of the Child drafted by the League of Nations in 1924. The 1959 UN Declaration of the Rights of the Child asserts that 'mankind owes to the child the best it has to give'. Work on the 1989 Convention on the Rights of the Child was initiated by a proposal from the government of Poland in 1979, the International Year of the Child (UNICEF 1995, p.1).

A 'right' is defined (*Oxford English Dictionary*) as: 'what is just, fair treatment; justification, fair claim, being entitled to, privilege or immunity, thing one is entitled to; authority to act in a specified way'.

Not only 'the rights but also the responsibilities of the child to respect the rights of others, especially the rights of their parents' are defined (UNICEF 1995, p.2). The Preamble to the convention states that 'the child should be fully prepared to live an individual life in society ... in particular in the spirit of peace, dignity, tolerance, freedom, equality and solidarity'.

This is summarised by Alexander Nurnberg (1995) thus: 'Your *rights* are about what you are allowed to do, and what the people responsible for you have to do for you to make sure you are happy, healthy and safe. Of course you have responsibilities towards other children and adults to make sure they get their rights.'

On Article 42 (above), he comments: 'All adults and children should know about this Convention. You have a right to learn about your rights and adults should learn about them too.'

However, it may be difficult for adults to learn about and understand not only the letter but also the spirit and practical implications of the rights (and responsibilities) described in the Convention. Although the concept of 'rights' is (apparently) easy to define, it is less easy to apply in everyday life. It may be even less easy for individual practitioners to develop their own responses to and ideas about the linked concepts of 'rights' and 'children'.

People concerned with the care and welfare of children are inevitably involved in the paradox of 'child-as-vulnerable-citizen' and as 'citizen-with-unenforceable-rights' (Harris 1995, pp.34–5). If children's rights are defined as unenforceable, the whole concept and structure of 'rights' is undermined and must collapse. If, as seems likely, that is the case, what rights have children to redress, and what responsibilities have adults to repair the damage?

QUESTIONS

- What do you think about the concept of rights?
- Do you think it is appropriate to design rights especially for children?
- Do you agree that 'mankind owes to the child the best it has to give'?
- Do you think children are 'citizens-with-unenforceable-rights'?
- Do you think children's rights can be respected and fulfilled?

SUGGESTIONS

With colleagues and children:

- Discuss one another's ideas about the questions above.
- Define children's rights.
- Compile a list of children's rights for your own agency/ establishment and discuss how these could be fulfilled.
- Compile a list of adults' responsibilities.
- Compile a list of children's responsibilities.

Article 27: Standard of living

1 States Parties recognize the right of every child to a standard of living adequate for the child's physical, mental, spiritual, moral and social development.

You have the right to a good enough 'standard of living'. This means that parents have the responsibility to make sure you have food, clothes, a place to live, etc. If parents cannot afford this, the government should help. (Nurnberg 1995)

This wide-ranging, umbrella Article is numbered 27, half way through the convention. Articles 28 and 29 (education) do not mention spiritual development at all, although personality, talents, mental and physical abilities are to be developed to their fullest potential. Article 19 (protection from abuse and neglect) refers only to physical and mental assault. Reference to spiritual development or well-being is found in only three other Articles: 17 (Access to appropriate information), 23 (Disability) and 32 (Child labour).

The vagueness of this Article, not least in referring to largely indefinable concepts of development, leads to questions about approved standards of adequacy in spiritual development. How, and by whom, is this defined? Do children contribute to such standard-setting and definition?

It can be argued that spiritual development (or well-being) cannot be considered as separate from all and any other aspects of life. The child whose physical and/or mental well-being is neglected is disadvantaged spiritually.

QUESTIONS

- Do you think it appropriate that spiritual development/well-being is included only in Articles on disability, standard of living, labour and the media?
- Do you consider that the standard of living of children known to you is adequate for spiritual development and well-being?
- If so, what does this mean?
- If not, what changes are needed?
- Do children known to you consider that their standard of living is adequate for spiritual development and well-being?
- If so, what does this mean?
- If any aspects of the standard of living are not adequate, how does this affect children's spiritual well-being?

SUGGESTIONS

With colleagues and children:

- Discuss one another's ideas about the questions above.
- What is the standard of living familiar to children who are with their own families and/or in day or residential establishments? Discuss how this contributes to, or detracts from, children's spiritual well-being.

Article 12: The child's opinion

1   States Parties shall assure to the child who is capable of forming his or her own views the right to express those views freely in all matters affecting the child, the views of the child being given due weight in accordance with the age and maturity of the child.

2   For this purpose the child shall in particular be provided the opportunity to be heard in any judicial and administrative proceedings affecting the child, either directly, or through a representative or an appropriate body, in a manner consistent with the procedural rules of national law.

Whenever adults make a decision that will affect you in any way, you have the right to give your opinion, and the adults have to take you seriously. (Nurnberg 1995)

Article 13: Freedom of expression

1   The child shall have the right to freedom of expression; this right shall include freedom to seek, receive and impart information and ideas of all kinds, regardless of frontiers, either orally, in writing or in print, in the form of art, or through any other media of the child's choice.

2   The exercise of this right may be subject to certain restrictions, but these shall only be such as are provided by law and are necessary:

a   For respect of the rights or reputations of others; or
b   For the protection of national security or of public order or of public health or morals.

'You have the right to find out things and say what you think through speaking, writing, making art etc, unless it breaks the rights of others.' (Nurnberg 1995)

The CRDU (1994) found that every group of children and young people consulted:

felt that adults did not listen to them, respect them, take them seriously, or value what they had to say. They felt this in respect of their personal relationships with parents, in school, in foster- and residential care, and in the outside world in relation to the media, politicians and policy makers. There is a general feeling among many young people that childhood is characterised by low status, little power and almost no control over the outcomes of their lives. These views were echoed by many of the professionals working with young people. (p.xiv)

Among the professionals to echo this view is Andrew West, who concludes a summary of research by Save the Children Fund (SCF): 'Children are not heard even when they speak and have no impact, yet their abilities, simply of description and analysis alone, cry out for much more response' (West, A. 1996, p.8). From interviews with 80 recent care leavers and 21 staff, West's study identified a 'void between the views and experiences of children and adults' corresponding with 'the location of power'.

In the same *Community Care* supplement on children's rights, Caroline Hamilton (1996) notes: 'The most frequent comment received by the Children's Legal Centre national advice line from parents is "no one is listening to my child". Children ask: "When will I get a chance to speak" or, for example, "They never take our view into account."' (p.1). For example, in 1996 the debate about reinstating caning in schools enjoyed an airing. Politicians and parents, teachers and even 'the general public' were invited to comment, but few, if any, children's voices were heard.

Ann Jeffreys (1996) (a Children's Rights Officer) refers some problems with implementation of children's rights to misunderstanding and fear by social services departments: 'that [officers] were being appointed to ensure that children always got what they wanted; that they would raise children's expectations falsely; or that they would force young people to be involved in making decisions they did not really want to make'. Rather, she defines the role of the Children's Rights Officer as: 'to ensure that children and young people are receiving services to which they are entitled and that their voices are heard. There is no power in our role; this rests with the young person.' Officers were told constantly that young people were 'not being listened to by social services departments'. One element essential to improvement is 'direct work carried out with young people individually or in groups, which makes them realise they are actually being consulted about their own conditions' (p.5).

If children find that they are not listened to, that their views, even when expression is permitted, are not respected, Article 13 loses much of its force, for freedom of expression means nothing if that which is expressed is ignored or discounted. This is fundamental to discussion of rights in relation to spirituality and religion, which must imply respect for and attention to the whole child.

QUESTIONS

- Do you consider that children known to you are enabled and encouraged to express their views freely in all matters affecting them?
- Do you consider that children's views are expressed in judicial and planning contexts?
- Do you consider that children's views are given serious attention?
- Do you consider that children receive and are helped to understand and interpret all information and other material necessary to help them contribute to decisions?
- Do children known to you consider that their views are well-informed, expressed and attended to?
- In your experience, is there a 'void between views and experiences of children and adults'?

SUGGESTIONS

With colleagues and children:

- Discuss one another's ideas about the questions above.
- If children do not consider that they receive adequate information and help to understand it, identify ways in which this might be improved.
- Identify ways in which children might be enabled and encouraged to express their responses, ideas and views.
- Identify ways in which adults might be enabled and encouraged to respect and attend seriously to children's communications.
- If there is 'a void' between children and adults, identify how and why this can develop and how it can be constructively crossed.

Article 14: Freedom of thought, conscience and religion

1   States Parties shall respect the right of the child to freedom of thought, conscience and religion.

2   States Parties shall respect the rights and duties of the parents and, when applicable, legal guardians, to provide direction to the child in the exercise of his or her right in a manner consistent with the evolving capacities of the child.

3   Freedom to manifest one's religion or beliefs may be subject only to such limitations as are prescribed by law and are necessary to protect public safety, order, health or morals, or the fundamental rights and freedoms of others.

You have the right to think what you like and be whatever religion you want to be. Your parents should help you learn what is right and wrong. (Nurnberg 1995)

Article 2: Non-discrimination

1 **States Parties shall respect the rights set forth in the present Convention to each child within their jurisdiction without discrimination of any kind, irrespective of the child's or his or her parent's or legal guardian's race, colour, sex, language, religion, political or other opinion, national, ethnic or social origin, property, disability, birth or other status.**

2 **States Parties shall take all appropriate measures to ensure that the child is protected against all forms of discrimination or punishment on the basis of the status, activities, expressed opinions, or beliefs of the child's parents, legal guardians, or family members.**

You have these rights, whoever you are, whoever your parents are, whatever colour you are, whatever sex or religion you are, whatever language you speak, whether you have a disability, or if you are rich or poor. (Nurnberg 1995)

The CRDU notes that:

Children under 18 do not have a statutory right to choose their own religion in England and Wales or N. Ireland. In Scotland, children have the right to choose their own religion at 16. It is discriminatory that children in different parts of the UK have uneven access to these rights ... While legal reform is essential, full implementation of children's rights in this, as in many other areas of civil rights, will only arise through a change in attitudes towards children and a shift in the prevailing widespread and powerful belief that parents 'own' their children and have the right to control their *spiritual* as well as their physical activities. (1994, p.11)

This radical and powerful comment challenges understandings of 'parental rights', extending concern to the inner, essentially private worlds of children.

The experience of a 13-year-old reflects and reinforces the observations on Articles 12 and 13 above: 'Children and young people should not be forced into deciding on their parents' religion. We have our own views but sometimes we go to church because my parents are Christian, but they never ask me if I am.' The CRDU (1994) refers to the 'Gillick' principle, based on a court ruling that children have the right to choose their own religions when they have acquired 'sufficient understanding at the latest at 12' (p.11).

Articles 12(1) and 14(2) associate implementation of the rights therein described with 'the age and maturity' and 'the evolving capacities' of the child. Concepts of maturity and models of development relating to any aspect of life are fraught with difficulty, dissension and debate; those regarding matters spiritual and/or religious are, in terms of these provisos, perilously diverse (see Chapter 2). Alexander Nurnberg's confident and hopeful summaries may reflect the spirit of the Convention, but they fail to detect the reality implied in the wording.

Assessment of 'the evolving capacities' is to be made by parents and those *in loco parentis* in accordance with not only Article 14(2) but also Article 5, which requires States Parties to: 'respect the responsibilities, rights and duties of parents ... to provide, in a manner consistent with the evolving capacities of the child, appropriate direction and guidance in the exercise by the child of the rights recognized in the present Convention'. What rights have children whose assessments of their own capacities and maturity differ from those of adults? 'You're only a child' is a powerful terminator, and prevents adults from even seeking to discover children's opinions, assessments and preferences.

QUESTIONS

- Do you consider that children have freedom of thought, conscience and religion, including the right to change religions or to have no religion at all?
- Do children known to you consider that they have these freedoms?
- Are you aware of ways in which children may experience disadvantage, perhaps bullying or persecution, because of religious adherence and association?

SUGGESTIONS

With colleagues and children:

- Discuss one another's ideas about the questions above.
- Identify ways in which children may experience disadvantage because of religious belief, or lack of it.
- Think of ways in which children lack control over their religious and spiritual lives and propose ways in which this could change.

Article 20: Protection of children without families

1   A child temporarily or permanently deprived of his or her family environment, or in whose own best interests cannot be allowed to remain in that environment, shall be entitled to special protection and assistance provided by the State.

2   States Parties shall in accordance with their national laws ensure alternative care for such a child.

3   Such care could include, *inter alia*, foster placement, *kafala* of Islamic law, adoption or if necessary placement in suitable institutions for the care of children. When considering solutions, due regard shall be paid to the desirability of continuity in a child's upbringing and to the child's ethnic, religious, cultural and linguistic background.

If you do not have any parents, or if it is not safe for you to live with your parents, you have the right to special protection and help. (Nurnberg 1995)

Article 30: Children of minorities or indigenous peoples

In those States in which ethnic, religious or linguistic minorities or persons of indigenous origin exist, a child belonging to such a minority or who is indigenous shall not be denied the right, in community with other members of his or her group, to enjoy his or her own culture, to profess and practise his or her own religion, or to use his or her own language.

If you come from a minority group, you have the right to enjoy your own culture, practise your own religion and use your own language. (Nurnberg 1995)

Bradford (1995) notes that:

freedom of devotional spirituality ... refers to the informed choice of a child or adult to practise, deepen or develop his or her religious devotional life in a particular way. This will probably include a combination of acts of devotion in common with others of the same faith community, together with a rule or pattern for private and personal study, prayer and meditation, and social concerns. (p.17)

Implied also are observances and practices associated with, for example, food and dress (Bradford 1995, p.16). For children whose preferred form of worship differs from that of adults with whom they reside (whether or not these adults are their parents), this requires that those adults should be well informed and should respect, enable and encourage fulfilment of religious obligations.

This has particular implications for adoptive, day, foster and residential carers. The Children Act 1989 (England and Wales) requires that where a Care Order is made, the local authority 'shall not cause the child to be brought up in any religious persuasion other than that in which he would have been brought up if the order had not been made' (Section 33: 6a). The local authority is required to give 'due consideration ... to the child's religious persuasion, racial origin, cultural and linguistic background' (Section 22: 5c).

Department of Health Guidance (DoH 1989a) comments that:

> each child is, *as far as is practicable*, to have an opportunity to attend such religious services and receive such instructions as are appropriate to the religious persuasion to which the child may belong ... [and] be provided with facilities for religious observances for example special diets and clothing. (p.4)

'As far as is practicable' suggests that local authorities might not need to endeavour too strenuously to provide 'an opportunity' for children to fulfil religious obligations and develop education and understanding within their religions.

However, the *Looking after Children* questionnaire (Department of Health 1995) does ask 10–18-year-olds (with an equivalent question about 5–9-year-olds, but not about younger children):

> Do you belong to a particular religion?

> If so, do you have enough opportunities to attend religious services?

> Do you have enough opportunities to follow the customs of your religion (eg festivals, prayers, clothing, diet)?

And, perhaps both most important and problematic, it asks:

> Who will help you take further action if needed?

The inclusion of 'enough' questions in this context seems inappropriate, and at the very least requires that the enquiring practitioner should have considerable knowledge and understanding of the religion with which the child is associated. It is also inaccurate to ask about *belonging* to a religion: concepts of membership vary according to individual religions, and seeking to collect answers to such questions may lead to inaccurate records, and thus to encroachment on children's rights.

A further paragraph of the DoH Guidance notes:

> The importance of religion as an element of culture should never be overlooked: to some children and families it may be the dominant factor so that the religion of foster parents, for example, may in some cases be more important than their ethnic origins. (DoH 1989a, Section 2.41)

Advice to staff about provision of opportunities for children to practise their own religions recognises that:

The extent to which staff can do this will ... depend upon their own religious persuasion. It may be necessary to help a child make contact with a local church or group of adherents of the child's religion. Great sensitivity may be needed and the child's own family should be asked to assist. If the child is in close contact with his own family it is possible that he could join his family for religious service (DoH 1989a, Section 1.123)

The CRDU adds another perspective, since children in care do not have the right to apply for a Section 8 order to override the imposition of religion against their wishes, although this provision is made in the same Act of Parliament, the Children Act 1989, which governs their presence in care. The CRDU considers that they 'are therefore offered less opportunity to challenge the imposition of religion against their will' than children living at home, potentially contravening the requirement under the same Act to 'ascertain the wishes and feelings of the child'. It recommends that 'Children should be consulted about their wishes on religion and, where they are competent to exercise a choice, their wishes should prevail' (CRDU 1994, p.11).

However, the Department of Health Guidance (DoH 1989a) expands the Children Act requirement that the local authority 'shall not cause the child to be brought up in any religious persuasion other than that in which he would have been brought up if the [care] order had not been made' (Section 33.6(a)), thus:

This does not prevent the child determining his own religious beliefs as he grows older; it simply requires the local authority not to bring about any change by their own action or inaction. They should not, for example, place a child who has been brought up in a particular religion with a foster parent who, deliberately or by omission, would be likely to prevent the child continuing to practice his beliefs for as long as he wished. (p.36)

The reference to 'as he grows older' is unclear, and links with the comments on development and maturity above.

It is also unclear whether the Guidance recognised children's right to respect for denominational differences. As Janet Seden (1995) comments with particular reference to children in foster care:

It is ... important to be aware of differences within affiliations, for example, Roman Catholic, Orthodox and Baptist within Christianity or Sunni and Shi'a within Islam. There are important differences between orthodox and less orthodox groups as in Judaism. These theoretical differences or one based on geographical origins can have very tangible outcomes in dress, food, ritual expressions of beliefs or observances of rules. (p.12)

Janet Seden discusses the implications of 'Religious persuasion and the

Children Act' to foster care, emphasising the importance of partnership with parents. Plans for rehabilitation, for example, are enhanced by:

> enabling the practice of religion through worship, services and meetings; the maintenance of links with faith communities and their activities, such as festivals or holy days; enabling the maintenance of customs concerning food, prayer, dress, hygiene in the home; and providing the opportunity to hear the stories, myths, beliefs, teachings and values of their own religion. Young people also need the opportunity to discuss and exercise their own views regarding their identity, including religious views; and to have their questions answered by someone from the same religious background as themselves. (Seden 1995, p.8)

In other words, they have the right to *freedom of expression* and *of thought, conscious and religion* (Articles 13 and 14).

QUESTIONS

- Do you consider that children known to you are enabled and encouraged to fulfil religious obligations and observe customs and day-to-day practices connected with religious beliefs?
- Do children known to you consider that they are enabled and encouraged so to do?

SUGGESTIONS

With colleagues and children:

- Discuss one another's ideas about the questions above.
- Identify ways in which you can enable and encourage fulfilment of religious obligations, for example through diet and dress, prayer and attendance at a place of worship.
- If there are any difficulties, explore ways in which your agency could improve service to children, for example through learning from local religious communities and children's families.
- Consider the *Looking After Children* questions above.
- Plan ways in which to celebrate festivals and ensure that fasts are observed as appropriate.

Article 16: Protection of privacy

1   **No child shall be subjected to arbitrary or unlawful interference with his or her privacy, family, home or correspondence, nor to unlawful attacks on his or her honour and reputation.**

2   The child has the right to the protection of the law against such interference or attacks.

You have the right to a private life. For instance, you can keep a diary that other people are not allowed to see. (Nurnberg 1995)

Article 19: Protection from abuse and neglect

1   States Parties shall take all appropriate legislative, administrative, social and educational measures to protect the child from all forms of physical or mental violence, injury or abuse, neglect or negligent treatment, maltreatment or exploitation, including sexual abuse, while in the care of parent(s), legal guardian(s) or any other person who has the care of the child.

No one should hurt you in any way. Adults should make sure that you are protected from abuse, violence and neglect. Even your parents have no right to hurt you. (Nurnberg 1995)

Article 34: Sexual exploitation

States Parties undertake to protect the child from all forms of sexual exploitation and sexual abuse. For these purposes, States Parties shall in particular take all appropriate national, bilateral and multilateral measures to prevent:

a   The inducement or coercion of a child to engage in any unlawful sexual activity;
b   The exploitative use of children in prostitution or other unlawful sexual practices;
c   The exploitative use of children in pornographic performances and materials.

You have the right to be protected from sexual abuse. This means that nobody can do anything to your body that you do not want them to do, such as touching you or taking pictures of you or making you say things that you don't want to say. (Nurnberg 1995)

Department of Health Guidance (1989a) recommends that staff in residential establishments should 'allow a child special privacy in order to pray during the course of the day, or to build a small shrine somewhere within the home' (Para 1.124). This appears to suppose that only children who wish to fulfil religious obligations need such privacy; however, protected space and time to pursue private thoughts, or simply time alone, are essential for many children.

Joanna, a 10–year-old interviewed during research into children's spiritual experiences, said: 'sometimes I feel very lonely when I am alone with God because I can't see God and I can't hear God, I just think about God. I feel really lonely, so I like being with people sometimes but sometimes I am pretty glad to be alone, if I've got someone bugging me like my sisters' (quoted in Nye 1996, 2/16). She found spiritual refreshment in an imaginary garden (see also Chapter 3).

The CRDU (1994) notes that:

> The inquiries following a recent series of scandals concerning abuse of children in residential care have demonstrated the fundamental importance of respecting children's civil rights if they are to be able to challenge and prevent recurrences of such episodes. Unless children have access to basic civil rights, including the right to privacy, they will continue to lack the opportunities to take steps to protect themselves. The right to speak and write in confidence and the right to be alone are central to this process. (p.14)

Respecting privacy, both internal and external, includes parents. It includes also choosing which adult(s) shall receive confidences, and the certainty that these confidences will be respected and neither betrayed to other people nor used in any way to harm the child. This is an immense issue in regard to abuse of any kind, and not least if religious matters are involved (see Chapters 11 and 12).

It is not clear why Article 19 refers only to 'physical and mental' assault and neglect; while 'emotional and spiritual' may be implied, it seems strange that 'emotional' is not mentioned at all in the Convention, while 'spiritual' appears in four Articles.

Article 34 is included here not only because it stands on its own, but also because it complements Article 19. All sexual abuse and misuse is intrusive, with implications for all aspects of the person.

QUESTIONS

- Do you consider that privacy of children known to you is respected?
- Do children known to you consider that their privacy is respected?
- Do children known to you have protected time and space for private thought and worship?
- Does your agency respect children's need to choose their own confidants and to communicate in privacy at times of their own choosing?
- Does your agency recognise that abuse may take place in many ways, not necessarily physical, and that children may have difficulty in communicating about this, especially if abuse is associated with adults connected with religious or caring agencies?

SUGGESTIONS

With colleagues and children:

- Discuss one another's ideas about the questions above.
- Identify ways of ensuring privacy and space for everyone: children and adults.
- Explore the problems of confidentiality and privacy in relation to abuse of any kind (emotional, mental, physical, social, spiritual).
- Identify ways of obtaining help if a child complains of abuse connected with religious observances.

Article 23: Disabled children

1 States Parties recognize that a mentally or physically disabled child should enjoy a full and decent life, in conditions which ensure dignity, promote self-reliance, and facilitate the child's active participation in the community.

2 States Parties recognize the right of the disabled child to special care ...

3 ... assistance ... shall be designed to ensure that the disabled child has effective access to and receives education, training, health care services, rehabilitation services, preparation for employment and recreation opportunities in a manner conducive to the child's achieving the fullest possible social integration and individual development, including his or her cultural and spiritual development.

If you are disabled, either mentally or physically, you have the right to special care and education to help you grow up in the same way as other children. (Nurnberg 1995)

It is interesting that *spiritual development* is specified in this precise context, but not in such Articles as 19 (protection from abuse) and 28 (education).

Far from enjoying the rights designated in this Article, disabled children in the UK cannot be confident of fulfilment of Article 2, which requires States Parties to respect all rights within the convention, 'without discrimination of any kind, irrespective of ... disability'.

Margaret Kennedy (1995a) (a consultant/trainer on disability and child protection) finds that 'disabled children are negatively valued'. For example:

a counsellor said to a mother whose disabled child had been abused, 'well, it would have been worse if it had been one of your other (non-disabled) children'. A QC said of a disabled child who had been abused and was applying for criminal injuries compensation, that as the child would obviously (!) not be engaging in sexual relationships in adulthood the harm of the sexual abuse was likely to be less and refused criminal injuries compensation. Such examples of professionals seeing disabled children as 'worthless' are unfortunately not uncommon. (p.128)

Rights under Articles 19 (protection from abuse and neglect) and 34 (sexual exploitation) may also be at risk. Quoting Kennedy and Kelly (1992), Kennedy comments: 'we neglect to consider their child protection requirements. When I asked a senior policy-maker what she was including in her child protection policies for disabled children ... she pondered and then said, "let me sort out the *normal* child *first*"' (Kennedy 1995a, p.128). She emphasises the importance of regarding children with a disability in terms of 'rights, not charity', as distinct from their placement in the Children Act 1989 category of 'children in need' (p.129).

In order that children with a disability may receive full service as implied in Article 23, in Kennedy's view it is necessary to recognise that:

they often have very different needs in relation to communication, mobility, dexterity, physical strength and cognitive abilities. Adapting the current ways of working with non-disabled children seldom works, for it fails to grasp the fact that disabled children's experiences are unique and sufficiently different to necessitate a new approach to service provisions. (p.145)

Among requirements for service she includes:

1   Intimate care policies which promote confidentiality and privacy and safety for disabled children.
2   Disabled children's rights policies which encourage and enable choice and decision-making.
3   Training which will challenge workers' stereotypes, disabilist attitudes and prejudices.
4   Assertion training for disabled children which promotes self-respect, high self-esteem and confidence. (p.145)

Attention to Articles 12 and 13 (children's opinions and freedom of expression) may also be deficient.

Since Article 23 refers specifically to 'spiritual development', failure to fulfil all or any of the duties specified in this Article implies failure to nurture spiritual well-being.

QUESTIONS

- Does your agency/establishment nurture the cultural and spiritual well-being of children with some disability – emotional, mental, physical, social?
- If so, how is this achieved?
- If not, what changes and improvements can be made?
- Do children consider that their spiritual well-being is nurtured?

SUGGESTIONS

With colleagues and children:

- Discuss one another's ideas about the questions above.
- Identify how children with some disability can be enabled and encouraged to live full cultural and spiritual lives, and to contribute to the cultural and spiritual lives of others.

Article 29: 1(a) and (d): Aims of education

1 States Parties agree that the education of the child shall be directed to:

a The development of the child's personality, talents and mental and physical abilities to their fullest potential;

d The preparation of the child for responsible life in a free society, in the spirit of understanding, peace, tolerance, equality of sexes, and friendship among all peoples, ethnic, national and religious groups and persons of indigenous origin.

The purpose of your education is to develop your personality, talents and mental and physical abilities to the fullest. Education should also prepare you to live responsibly and peacefully, in a free society, understanding the rights of other people, and respecting the environment. (Nurnberg 1995)

It is not clear why the aims of education refer only to 'mental and physical abilities' when, for example, Articles relating to disability (23) and labour (32) specify *spiritual*, well-being/development. The complex requirements of Article 29: 1(d), however, refer to *the spirit* of understanding, for example. Children are to be encouraged to develop responsible lives in relation to *all peoples*, including all *religious groups*.

QUESTIONS

- Do you consider that the education of children known to you is based on the aims defined in this Article?
- Do children known to you consider that their education is based on these aims?
- Do you consider that 'spiritual' should be included in Article 29(a)?
- How do you define 'a responsible life' (Article 29: 1(d))?
- How do children known to you define 'a responsible life'?
- Do you consider that an aim of education is to prepare children to live in friendship with all peoples, including those of different religious groups?
- Do children known to you consider that an aim of education should be preparation to live in friendship with all peoples, including those of different religious groups?

SUGGESTIONS

With colleagues and children:

- Discuss one another's ideas about the questions above.
- Define the aims of education.
- Discuss connections between religion and education: for example, should education include teaching about religion?
- Consider whether schools have any responsibility for children's spiritual well-being and development.

Article 32: Child labour

1   **States Parties recognize the right of the child to be protected from economic exploitation and from performing any work that is likely to be hazardous or to interfere with the child's education, or to be harmful to the child's health or physical, mental, spiritual, moral or social development.**

You have the right to be protected from working in places or conditions that are likely to damage your health or get in the way of your education. If somebody is making money out of your work, you should be paid fairly. (Nurnberg 1995)

As discussed above, concepts of development differ, not least in relation to spirituality (see Chapter 2).

Article 17: Access to appropriate information

States Parties recognize the important function performed by the mass media and shall ensure that the child has access to information and material from a diversity of national and international sources, especially those aimed at the promotion of his or her social, spiritual, and moral well-being and physical and mental health. To this end, States Parties shall:

a Encourage the mass media to disseminate information and material of social and cultural benefit to the child ...;
c Encourage the production and dissemination of children's books;
e Encourage the development of appropriate guidelines for the protection of the child from information and material injurious to his or her well-being ...

You have the right to collect information from radios, newspapers, television, books, etc, from all around the world. Adults should make sure that you get information you can understand. (Nurnberg 1995)

With regard to the Convention itself, the CRDU (1994) noted: 'it has been put on sale in government bookshops, circulated to local authorities, and a few hundred leaflets distributed. Nothing has been directed at the UK's 13 million under 18-year-olds' (p.xi).

QUESTIONS

- How can economic exploitation and labour conditions harm children's spiritual development?
- How can the mass media affect and influence children's spiritual well-being?
- Should children be protected from any aspects of the media?

SUGGESTIONS

With colleagues and children:

- Discuss one another's ideas about the questions above.
- Describe how economic exploitation harms children's spiritual well-being with reference to your local working conditions.
- Study television and radio programmes, newspapers and magazines, advertisements and books, and identify how these affect and influence children with reference to spiritual well-being.
- Identify ways in which children can influence policy-makers in different media.

Summary

The concept of 'children's rights' is still controversial, although the first formulation was drafted in 1924. Despite ratification of the UN Convention on the Rights of the Child by the UK Government in 1991, agencies such as the Children's Rights Development Unit (now called the Children's Rights Office – CRO) find that neither the spirit nor the letter of the Convention have been fully, or even largely, implemented in the UK. Children experience lack of opportunity to express their views or to gain adult attention for those views.

When the concept of 'children's rights' is accepted and honoured, it is essential for both children and adults to recognise the definition offered by 9-year-old Alexander Nurnberg:

> Your *rights* are about what you are allowed to do, and what people responsible for you have to do for you to make sure you are happy, healthy and safe. Of course you have responsibilities towards other children and adults, to make sure they get their rights. (Nurnberg 1995)

Perhaps the acceptance and fulfilment of responsibilities is another, and fundamental, right of both children and adults.

References to religious and spiritual rights never occur in the same Article, and they are omitted from some Articles where one or both would seem essential – for example, Articles 19 and 28.

The implications of rights for religious and spiritual nurture and well-being become clearer when discussed in the context of religious observance and concepts of spiritual needs, experience and abuse.

Part 2

Children and spirituality

2 Ideas about spirituality

A common currency of shared understandings

'It's not something you think about over your second cup of tea.' This social worker and his colleague proceeded to think about 'it' – spirituality – over mugs of coffee, with increasing interest and many ideas and insights. Essentially, it became clear that vocabulary associated with spirituality can be an immense obstacle, especially when there are confusions about and/or with religion.

In many conversations enjoyed in preparing this book (and the CCETSW Training Pack – Crompton 1996), I experienced difficulty in explaining what I meant by 'spirit' or 'spiritual' and in asking other people to discuss their own ideas and beliefs. I was greatly aided by the good spirit with which my stumbling attempts at communication were received. The main problem seemed to be diffidence in using vocabulary which might be regarded as strange, even weird, and offputting or intrusive, and I went to convoluted lengths to distinguish between spirituality and religion.

Social workers and others concerned with the care and welfare of children have explored ideas about, and offered definitions of, spirituality but this has not been a major area of interest, and takes little if any place in academic curricula or in-service training. Research in this area has been focused mainly within the broad field of education, where theories about, for example, spiritual development have been formulated.

It is notable that, unlike education legislation and the UN Convention on the Rights of the Child, the Children Act 1989 and the *Looking After Children* questionnaires (DoH 1995) make no reference to spiritual development/ well-being. Yet the children for and with whom social work practitioners are engaged are the same children who attend school and possess those rights ratified by the UK government.

The Education Reform Act (England and Wales) 1988 requires 'that a school must have a balanced and broadly based curriculum which "promotes the spiritual, moral, cultural, mental and physical development of the pupils at the school". Thus the *spiritual* development of children should be an integral part of the educational endeavour in all schools.' McClure (1996) (a principal lecturer – theology and religious education) notes the 'necessary and important distinction ... between spirituality and faith' (p.5).

The OFSTED (1994) discussion paper on *Spiritual, Moral, Social and Cultural Development* comments:

> There will be genuine differences in the approaches taken to the idea of the 'spiritual' by different individuals – for example, by those with religious belief and by non-believers. For those with a strong religious faith, the spiritual is very much at the heart of life: for many religious people, there is no concept of the secular as distinct from the spiritual; for some who make no religious profession, it may be hard to accept the very term ... It is vital to press towards a common currency of shared understandings. (p.8)

The document asks: 'Is it reasonable to define spiritual development in a way acceptable to those with a non-religious perspective and to those with religious beliefs?' (p.10). The present discussion of children and spirituality seeks to stimulate practitioners to explore this and associated questions.

Concepts of spirituality in a different context – that of holistic care, which 'is based on the premise that there should be balance of mind, body and spirit for the maintenance of health in a person' – have been explored for many years within the nursing profession (Narayanasamy 1993, p.196). This concept of holistic care – attention to the whole person – underlies social work practice too. For example, Bradford (1995) (chaplain missioner for The Children's Society) introduces the concept in the title of his book, *Caring for the Whole Child: A Holistic Approach to Spirituality*.

For social work practitioners, as for nurses, there are difficulties in defining 'the whole person': for example, does the whole person include a spiritual element? Narayanasamy (1993) summarises the assumption that mind, body and spirit 'are inseparable and function as an integrated unit within the whole person with each dimension ... affecting and being affected by others'. Therefore, 'nurses need to understand and care for the total person, including the spirit'. The 'spiritual dimension ... is broader than institutionalised religion, although it is not uncommon for spirituality to be expressed and developed through formal religious activities such as prayers and worship services' (p.196).

However, there is 'concern within the nursing profession that the provision for spiritual care of patients is inadequate', largely because of 'inadequate educational preparation ... in this important area of care' (p.196). In 1973, Chadwick wrote of research which demonstrated that 'many nurses were aware of the presence of spiritual needs in at least some of their patients, but said that they would like further education in meeting spiritual needs in patients'. Questions included: 'Do you personally feel that patients have spiritual needs?' (Narayanasamy 1993, pp.197 and 201).

By 1996 it seems that little progress had been achieved. Oldnall (a charge nurse) surveyed literature relating to spirituality and holistic care between 1980 and 1994 in relation to its relevance to nursing. He found, despite 'a growing concern amongst nurses to study aspects of caring and its implications for nursing practice', that 'it may be argued that nurses pay little attention to the concept of spirituality in holistic care because of a lack of personal understanding and guidance from the nurse theorists and educationalists' (Oldnall 1996, p.138).

Social work practitioners also may lack 'personal understanding and guidance from ... theorists and educationalists'. They may not be concerned about concepts of spirituality in relation to their own lives, or they may regard such ideas as profoundly private, deeply embarrassing or, perhaps, distressing. Nonetheless, whatever practitioners' own beliefs, experiences and feelings, it is essential to study implications of spirituality as part of the whole person in the context of the beliefs, experiences and feelings of children, whether or not these are associated with any religion.

The three chapters which comprise this part of the book focus on different aspects of spirituality and development/well-being, offering introductions to ideas and theories about, and experiences of, spirituality with particular reference to children.

Ideas about and definitions of the spirit/spirituality from a wide range of sources are introduced in order to offer practitioners access to the breadth and depth of this concept. No single formulation is presented as definitive, for, as will be seen, such concepts depend on beliefs about religion, the meaning and nature of life, and/or the existence/destiny of the soul, for example. It is hoped that practitioners will use this material to develop awareness of and clarity about their own beliefs and experiences, and those of the children with and for whom they work.

A language of spirituality with which we all feel comfortable

For many people, ideas associated with spirituality are acceptable only if dissociated from religion. Allen (1991), writing during nursing training as a mature student, found: 'spirituality as a topic for discussion has the status of a footnote. Any attempt to expand on its meaning or significance is met with blank stares, dazed expressions. Tutors who allude to God are received with muffled hoots and "Bible basher" taunts.' She identified the problem as lack of 'a language of spirituality with which we all feel comfortable', while noting that 'Even with a common language, it may still be an intensely private matter for us or our clients' (pp.52 and 53).

The focus of this section is the importance of finding, if not a language, at least vocabulary acceptable to people who do and do not hold religious beliefs.

Referring again to OFSTED (1994): 'For those with a strong religious faith, the spiritual is very much at the heart of life: for many religious people, there is no concept of the secular as distinct from the spiritual' (p.8). However, both between and within individual religions, definitions of and beliefs about *the spiritual* vary enormously. For example, many people believe in transmigration of souls after death into new living forms, while others believe that the released spirit progresses to a new environment – purgatory, heaven, hell. Another belief is that the spirit relinquishes individual identity and returns to the world store of energy, just as the body gives its components back to the earth and atmosphere. For many, the spirit merges with the world soul; for others, there is no discrete spirit, the quality of spirituality is integral to the whole person and ends, except in the memory of survivors, at death. Yet people holding any one of these, or other, understandings of 'spirit' or 'spirituality' can find 'a common currency of shared understandings'.

For example, discussion of spirituality often leads to realisation that 'spirit' and associated words occur frequently in everyday descriptions of feelings and behaviour, for example:

You seem to be in good spirits today.

His attitude showed a very poor spirit.

She put up a spirited defence.

I haven't the spirit for it anymore.

He tackled the task with a good spirit.

They're always very high-spirited, a bit too much for me!

She's in tearing spirits.

This'll raise your spirits.

Show a bit more spirit, can't you?

Keep your spirits up, it can't last for ever.

Don't be so mean-spirited.

The spirit is willing but the flesh weak.

The spirit of the age ...

The spirit of the place ...

She's the life and soul of the party.

He's a good soul.

That book was really inspiring.

She always seems, well, rather spiritual.

Colin (a social worker) described a girl whose parents did not love her as 'dis-spirited': she rarely smiled, and spent most of her energy in trying to attract attention from her rejecting family. She 'had no spirit, a shell, no life or verve'. He associated spirituality with 'positive movement, light, involvement, emotional congruence', and 'wanted to pour it in' to the girl. But 'the parents had the lock to the bottle top', and work with the family was constantly blocked (see also Chapter 11).

While holding religious beliefs himself, Colin considered that 'in an a-religious society people would still have a spiritual being'. He suggested that the existence of the word 'dispirited' implied the existence of that which is described as 'spirit'. His colleague Bill firmly separated spirituality from religion, and identified a need for 'a language to articulate what spirituality is', including ideas about growing and developing. He wondered 'where do children get "golden moments" and what happens if they don't?' and offered the phrase 'a spiritual hole', empty, if a child has suffered emotional abuse.

'Beth' (a senior practitioner in a hospital) thought how the phrase 'his spirit was crushed' describes the body language of children, 'dragged down, slumping, their exuberance crushed' (see also Chapter 11).

QUESTIONS

- Look again at the phrases above: what do all or any of them mean?
- What do 'spirit' and 'spiritual' mean to you?
- Are these words exclusively associated with religion?
- Can the words be used without any religious associations?
- If you are comfortable with this kind of vocabulary, can you understand why other people may find it difficult or embarrassing?
- If you are not comfortable with this kind of vocabulary, can you identify the reason?

SUGGESTIONS

With colleagues and children:

- Discuss one another's ideas about the questions above.
- Think of phrases in everyday speech which include the words, 'spirit' or 'spiritual'.
- What do such phrases mean to you? What do they make you think of?
- Notice the vocabulary used by children and their families and be aware of the implications of such words as 'spirit' in conversation.

Spirituality and religion

When commissioning papers on seven religions or the CCETSW Training Pack (Crompton 1996), I asked writers to comment on children's spirituality. Only when I had read the eventual papers and learnt from other material did I begin to realise the implications of this question when children are integral to the worshipping community and spirituality is inseparable from religion.

Dion Hanna (1996) (a lawyer) emphasises the paramount importance of children in the Rastafarian movement:

> Children and young people are precious, raised with love, affection and royal dignity ... to live in accordance with the moral lifestyle of the Rastafarian movement, encouraged to be proud of their Afrikan heritage and to seek the truth through constant study of the Bible and history ... [They] form the nucleus of the movement ... Respect and love for children begins in the womb and abortion is condemned as murder. (3/73)

Adults are enjoined to care for the young Princes and Princesses (young Rastafarians), and warned with the words of Jesus that 'whoever causes one of these little ones who believe in me to sin, it would be better for him to have a great millstone fastened round his neck and to be drowned in the depth of the sea' (Matthew 18:6).

Seth D. Kunin (1996) (a rabbi and lecturer, Nottingham University) stresses the importance of observance: 'Young Jewish children's spirituality is focused on particular times of prayer', including public worship and private prayers 'before and after eating to thank God for providing sustenance … upon going to sleep and waking up … [including] the Shema, which is an affirmation of the Oneness of God and God's connection with the Jewish people' (3/61). By the age of 13, other religious duties in the home are also observed: for example, praying with *tefillin* (leather boxes containing verses from the Bible) and *tallitot* (prayer shawls). Kunin regards it as 'essential that children should be helped to maintain ties with a Jewish community as many elements of religious and cultural life can be practised only with such a connection' (3/67).

For these as for other religions, worship – an expression of spirituality – is centred in both the home and such designated places as the synagogue, mosque or *gurdwara*.

Graham Bird (1996), studying the relationship between the 'secular and individualistic values' of social work and the value bases of 'minority ethnic groups whose … "world view" is informed by a religious tradition that stresses the collectivity and inter-correctedness of people, communities and life in general', identified many aspects of Hinduism, Islam and Sikhism with fundamental relevance to the present discussion. He quotes Younger (1972): 'Indian religious thought does not make the familiar Western distinctions between the divine and the human, or between man and nature' (cited in Bird 1996, p.20). The 'self' is not, as in the West, 'a centre of willed autonomy', but 'a manifestation of consciousness … [shared] with one's fellow creatures … thus in developing self-awareness one is not moving away from one's fellows … one is simply moving into a greater fullness in which we all share' (cited in Bird 1996, p.25).

Nigosian (1994) writes: 'Hindus do not believe that a person is "created in the image of God"; rather, a person is God, or divine … The absolute is not "up there" or "beyond", but within' (cited in Bird 1996, p.22). Bird comments: 'This provides a distinctive contrast to the Western model of separating the divine and the human … The spiritual is so intrinsic to that perspective that it could be at no point removed from any aspect of existence' (p.22).

In Islam, 'The belief in God permeates every walk of a Muslim's life and finds expression in every cultural or social practice, whether it be the etiquette of everyday life or the norms of human inter-relationships' (McDermott and Ahsan 1986, cited in Bird, 1996, p.27).

The duality, or rather tripartiality, of prevailing Western thought underlies much official documentation. Clarke (1993), for example, criticises the theological and philosophical basis of the National Curriculum Council's *Discussion Paper on Spiritual and Moral Development* in terms of the assumption of 'a tripartite view of the human being where body, mind and spirit are separate entities and therefore spirituality and morality are discrete dimensions of humanity' (Clarke 1993).

He introduces Buddhist analysis, which 'perhaps more accurately reflects the reality of the human condition and leads to a harmonious view of education for the whole child' – and not only education, but also care, welfare, all aspects of life. Life comprises 'a temporary, physical or material form (*ketai*, or *ke*), a non-substantial or spiritual form (*kutai*, or *ku*), and a force or energy which binds the two (*chutai*, or *chu*: the Middle Way)'. Clarke emphasises that these 'three aspects are not separate entities, but rather three different, though interrelated, perspectives on the entirety of life'. It is important to recognise that 'there is no fundamental distinction between the physical and the mental, or spiritual. Instead, mind and body, that is spirit and body, are merely two inseparable aspects of individual life.'

Clarke identifies some consequences of 'The Western tradition of regarding them as separate entities', which leads to 'the conception of their being opposing entities', suggesting that: 'The inability to reconcile these two apparently contradictory aspects of human nature, coupled with the desire to maintain our fragile sense of human dignity, has been reflected in history in the tendency to elevate the spirit and deny the flesh', which can lead 'to severe distortions in society and even, paradoxically, to the degradation of human dignity'. In contrast, the contemporary 'tendency has swung the other way, so that the materialist, consumerist values have become dominant at the expense of the spirit. The social confusion which has resulted from this distortion of reality cannot be unravelled without a true understanding of the relationship between the empirical and the spiritual.'

In conclusion, Clarke directs attention to the goal of education (and thus, it is reasonable to argue, of all service to children), which must: 'accord with the goal of life: to be happy'. Happiness is defined as: 'wisdom, compassion and courage', which qualities are to be encouraged by teachers (and others who are engaged with the care and well-being of children). Buddhism teaches that 'unhappiness and suffering are caused by anger, greed and ignorance, particularly ignorance of the true nature of life'.

Children need to understand: 'that there is only an artificial distinction between the body and the spirit, between a human being and his or her environment, between life and death, between spirituality and morality'.

QUESTIONS

- If you hold religious beliefs, what do you understand by 'spirit'?
- Do you believe that there is a relationship between a deity and humans? If so, what is it?
- Does your religion include any teaching about children?
- Does your religion include any teaching about 'the true nature of life'?
- Do you think that the goal of life is to be happy?
- If so, how is the spirit involved in the attainment of happiness?

SUGGESTIONS

With colleagues and children:

- Discuss one another's ideas about the questions above.
- Define 'happiness'.
- Identify causes of unhappiness and suffering.
- Learn about the beliefs and teachings about children associated with religions which are represented in your locality and/or establishment.
- Find out about the ideas about the nature of life which underlie religious and other teaching in local schools.
- Identify ideas about the nature of life which underlie work in your establishment.
- Consider ideas about the nature of life which appear to inform the behaviour and attitudes of children and their families known to you.

Concepts and models of spiritual development

Whether or not spirituality is regarded as inseparable from religion, academic interest has been shown in exploring the concept of *spiritual development*. The idea in itself raises fundamental questions about, for example, the propriety of associating 'development' with 'spirituality'.

Reference to two contrasting quotations from the New Testament illustrates part of the dilemma. In Matthew 18:3–4, Jesus says: '"unless you turn and become like children, you will never enter the kingdom of heaven. Whoever humbles himself like this child, he is the greatest in the kingdom of heaven."'

Paul the missionary demonstrates a different view of both children and spirituality: '"When I was a child, I spoke like a child, I thought like a child, I reasoned like a child; when I became a man, I gave up childish ways."' Paul apparently ignores the advice of his spiritual leader and model to discover and adopt the qualities of children, and suggests an onward and upward programme of spiritual and moral development: '"For now I know in part; then I shall understand fully ..."' (I Corinthians 13:11–12).

For the poet William Wordsworth, development, far from being progressive, is regressive: The newborn baby is nearest the life of the spirit, for:

> Our birth is but a sleep and a forgetting:
> The Soul that rises in us, our life's Star,
> Hath had elsewhere its setting,
> And cometh from afar:
> Not in entire forgetfulness,
> And not in utter nakedness,
> But trailing clouds of glory do we come
> From God, who is our home:
> Heaven lies about us in our infancy!

But soon:

> Shades of the prison-house begin to close
> Upon the growing boy. ('Ode: Intimations of Immortality from Recollections in Early Childhood')

Jungian psychoanalyst James Hillman (1988) pursues this idea, describing the child's soul as: 'A being close to angels, it arrives knowing everything essential ... its collective unconscious is replete with primordial awareness' (p.xiii).

Is the newborn baby a blank sheet, ready to develop spiritually in a manner parallel to physical, cognitive and emotional progress? Or is the child spiritually complete, facing not growth and progress, but diminution and separation from full spiritual life?

Whichever approach is adopted, questions about free will, genetic inheritance and other factors which influence development are raised.

Although study of spiritual development attracts attention among academics, there are reservations. Nye (1996) comments:

> in contrast to the developmental paradigms of researchers looking at children's religious intellectual abilities, few have attempted to construct an account of spiritual development which addresses the particulars of, or stages in, the developmental process by which the vast range of phenomena associated with children's spirituality may evolve together. One reason for this apparent oversight may be a resistance to the concept of 'development' applied to spirituality. (2/12)

Nye identifies two obstacles to pursuing research into spiritual development: 'The concept of development is potentially controversial since it implies moving from a less valued to a more valued state, such as suggested in the terms *underdeveloped, developing, highly developed*. It also implies a consensus about an idea end state, such as agreement about what maturity is.' She refers to the work of Hull (1991b) (Professor of Religious Education, Birmingham University), who suggests that 'as the concept of development usually implies that early forms of the phenomenon will be inferior, impoverished and less valuable, it seems an inappropriate model to capture the richness demonstrated by children's spirituality in its own right' (cited in Nye 1996 2/12).

Crompton (1994) proposes that:

> to the adult ear, the language, the symbols, used by children to express perception and experience of the spiritual aspects of their lives seem immature, 'childish'. Yet the unformed cognitive command forms the base from which springs the ladder of Jacob, busy with angels, the messengers of God, symbols of communication. Without that firm base, the ladder must crash, destroying the communication. (p.146)

Spirituality is not a commodity for measurement or testing; there is no examination which can be passed or failed or one approved language of communication. Neither is it associated with self-consciousness and verbal communication (for example, see the discussion of Edward at the beginning of Chapter 3).

Although there are many reservations about the propriety of constructing hierarchies of spiritual development, such models can be useful as metaphors contributing to understanding children's inner lives (Nye 1996, 2/13).

Most influential in this area, perhaps, is the work of James Fowler in the USA. Fowler's (1981) model of faith development defines faith as: 'our way of discerning and committing ourselves to centres of value and power that exert ordering force in our lives' (pp.24–5). This model, constructed after research with children and adults (mainly from a Christian background), proposes several stages of faith, which includes 'the way people see life and cope with its crises, their values and above all their quest for meaning' (Minney 1993). The three stages from Fowler's model of faith development which relate to children and young people may be summarised as follows:

- **Stage 1 – Intuitive-projective Stage (age 3–7):** Children live in worlds of fantasy, images, mood, story, action and examples. To move out of this, they need to develop rational thinking and fantasy–reality distinction.

- **Stage 2 – Mythic-literal Stage (age 7–adolescence):** Story is of central importance, fairness and justice are central concerns. Children may become convinced of their exceptional goodness/badness.
- **Stage 3 – Synthetic-conventional Faith (adolescence):** To reach this, children need good personal relationships and more awareness of the larger environment (Nye 1996, 2/13).

Although Fowler sees progression as spiralling rather than linear, and 'avoids Piaget's assumption that earlier, less-developed stages are left behind … his basic method is still dependent on Piaget in that he takes a finished or completed stage [stage 6] as being the norm against which all the others are measured' (Minney 1993). He adopts: 'a complex image of mature faith' as the culmination of 'developmentally related prior or preparatory stages' (Fowler 1981, p.199).

Reviewing this model, Nye notes: 'The later stages may not be reached by all people,' and stage 6 may be achieved by only 'such rare individuals as Gandhi, Mother Theresa and Martin Luther King', implying 'that the early stages are rather more easily and naturally passed through than those later'. She suggests that 'the problems of the "development" concept are clear, rather than celebrating each stage as complete in itself, adults categorized at lower levels may feel this suggests that their spirituality is inadequate and childlike'. This returns to the paradox noted above: 'Christians … are taught that they must become like children to enter the kingdom of God and that spiritual growth entails "putting away" childish things' [Matthew 18:3; I Corinthians 13:11], (Nye 1996, 2/14).

Fowler's model has links with Erikson's (1965) 'eight ages of man' pattern, seeing: 'a life crisis or other factor which disturbs previous equilibrium as the necessary stimulus for growth or development of faith' (Minney 1993; Fowler 1981, pp.100–1). Or, as Berryman (1985) suggests: 'we are born into the world unfinished and needing stimulation from the environment to become "finished" for further development' (p.120). (Discussion of Fowler's model can be found in Fowler et al. 1991, and McClure 1996.)

Other definitions of spiritual development also depend on response to stimulation. For example, a summary of points made at workshops organised by the National Council for Voluntary Youth Services (NCVYS) includes:

Spiritual development is the process by which we learn to cope, learn how to discover our place in the world. It occurs as we are introduced to the crisis points in life, e.g. birth death, unemployment, handicap, personal relationships, under the watchfulness of someone who cares.

We all have singular experiences, sometimes tragic, with which we have to grapple. Our spiritual development takes place as we use time and space to reflect on these experiences. (Cattermole 1990, p.ii)

OFSTED (1994) summarises 'the concept of development' as: 'closely related to the ideas of growth and maturing; it does not happen without stimulus and nourishment' (p.6).

Erikson's model forms the basis of a table of spiritual development discussed by Shelley et al. (1984b, p.23). Writing from a nursing perspective, she comments that 'The study of spiritual development is a wide-open field with a great need for solid research', echoing the view of Goodall (1984) that it is 'extraordinary that the areas of conceptual and spiritual understanding have been so neglected' in paediatric training (p.10).

Shelley offers definitions of spiritual development which reflect the models of Erikson and Piaget. For example,

Table 1: Piaget's stages of cognitive development as related to spiritual development

Sensorimotor stage (under age 2) – Understanding of God is vague, associated with parents. Prayer may provide comfort and deepen bond between parents, child and God. Responds to environment of love and warmth. No sense of conscience. Wise use of diversion better than punishment for wrongdoing.

Table 2: Outline of spiritual development as related to Erikson's eight ages of man (1963) Lois J Hopkins, M.S.N.

Prenatal period – Developing child's environment is influenced by love, joy, good health. Preparation of parents for task of childrearing includes their own spiritual well-being, as well as plans for a child's religious upbringing.

Birth to age one – Stage of basic trust vs. basic mistrust. Child needs a dependable environment, security in care, and love from a mother figure. Ability to trust, which develops during this stage, is essential for a growing faith in God ...

Age 12–18 – Stage of identity vs. role confusion. Adolescent rebellion against parents may include rejection of the religious beliefs of their upbringing. Becomes more interested in a personal relationship with God, but may be opposed to institutional religion. Often begins asking deep religious questions, but hesitates to discuss them with peers for fear of ridicule. (Shelley et al. 1984b, pp.24–5)

Although the table containing this material is entitled 'Outline of spiritual development', it appears to focus on the progress of belief in God, particularly in relation to relationships with parents, peers and institutions. Berryman (1985) defines 'spiritual' as 'the relationship children have with God ... The child's spirituality is assumed to be a comprehensive relationship with God that involves the whole person in an ultimate way' (p.20).

Writing as a Baha'i, Maia Pihlainen (1993) offers a definition of spiritual development in the image of a journey:

> Spiritualization is ... a process of growth that occurs as new understandings enlighten our beliefs, values, emotions, attitudes and actions. Thus, for example, a Sufi tradition – as explained in the Baha'i writings – describes this process as a seven-stage journey that begins from the valley of search and proceeds, through the valleys of love, knowledge, unity, contentment and wonderment, to the valley of 'true poverty and absolute nothingness', i.e. to the condition of total detachment from the material self, leading to 'the summit of realities' ...
> It is at this stage that the individual can most fully comprehend and experience the wholeness and connectedness of all existence. (p.3)

For many people, relationships with a deity, family and community do define spirituality. For others, the spirit, whether or not it can be associated with growth and development, cannot be described by the language of religion.

QUESTIONS

- Do you think a new-born baby is 'a being close to angels'?
- Do you think experience of life leads away from spiritual perfection?
- Do you think children are spiritually immature?
- Do you think experience of life leads towards spiritual maturity?
- Do you think spiritual maturity exists?
- If so, can you think of any people, of any age, who are spiritually mature? Can you describe them?
- Do you think it is possible and appropriate to construct models of spiritual development?

SUGGESTIONS

With colleagues and children:

- Discuss one another's ideas about the questions above.
- Think about your own childhood: consider whether the ideas introduced in this section apply to your own experience.
- Discuss one or more of the definitions of 'spiritual development' above.
- If you find 'spiritual development' a useful idea, construct a model which might be helpful in your work.

Some approaches to defining 'spirituality'

A number of people experienced in work with children have formulated definitions of 'spirituality' and 'spiritual development', seeking to use language not primarily or necessarily associated with religion.

Bradford responded to the Children Act 1989 with *Caring for the Whole Child* (Bradford 1995). He regards 'spirituality' as a 'tripartite concept, the three parts of which – human, devotional and practical – fit closely together and complement the whole ... totally multicultural and multifaith in its applicability' (p.1). He defines 'spirituality' as:

> a healthy attitude towards and a positive pattern of engagement
>
> i   with ourselves and our family;
> ii   with our God and our faith community; and
> iii with our day-to-day activities and our involvement with others in the wider world. (p.35)

He defines 'spiritual development' as:

> the ongoing and to some extent cylindrical process by which ... our human spirituality
>
> i   is established and grows in relationships with and concern for others;
> ii   is extended into devotional spirituality, influenced by sound tradition and supported by membership of a faith community; and
> iii becomes integrated within a profile of practical spirituality – or day-to-day positive and interpersonal engagement in life – in a world for which we are both thankful, and also in which we are committed to contributing towards the struggle for the common good. (p.40)

Spirituality is essentially about 'becoming in the sense of being "in process": open to growth, open to response, open to renewal and open to hope. This is applicable to every stage in life' (Bradford 1995, p.39). Growth and development are associated with 'finding – or being found by – God', not necessarily 'the discovery of Divine "power" ... but rather some indication of "presence", "providence" or the sense of the companionship of a "hidden friend"' (p.31).

Bradford (1995) defines 'spiritual needs' thus:

> a child or young person's human-spiritual needs of being valued and nurtured in a rounded way by ... parents and family devotional-spiritual needs of being integrated in a balanced manner within their own faith community, and of being affirmed in their distinctively personal expression of reverence ... practical-

spiritual needs of being prepared for and having the opportunity to engage creatively, caringly and thoughtfully in everyday life. (p.35)

Under the heading 'Human spirituality', Bradford (1995) names the fundamental needs of children as: love, security, new creative experiences, affirmation of others, taking part in and contributing to the social well-being of family and neighbourhood, expressed also as love, peace, wonder, confidence and relatedness (p.4). These are related to 'devotional spirituality'.

Relationship between human and devotional spirituality

Human spirituality		Devotional spirituality
Being loved	*becomes*	Having identity as a member
Feeling secure	*becomes*	Being nurtured in sound tradition
Responding in wonder	*becomes*	Having a framework for worship and a focus for contemplation
Being affirmed	*becomes*	Being empowered to affirm others and to share peace or *shalom*
Sharing together	*becomes*	Participation in community.

Source: Bradford (1995), p.14.

Bradford suggests: 'involvement in a particular religion [may be] functional in giving a distinctive framework, context and language to a child who might otherwise be experiencing sporadic moments of spiritual attunement such as experiences of awe and wonder, or of transcendental love and acceptance' (1995, p.15).

In the search for vocabulary which can aid communication about spirituality, whether or not associated with a religious framework and context, it is useful to note again the key words naming spiritual life and needs: *love, peace, wonder, confidence, relatedness.*

Four small groups of day, foster and residential carers attending a training session on child development were asked to make charts demonstrating their own ideas about children's needs, using any format and set of headings. Two groups listed physical, emotional, cognitive and spiritual needs; the other two chose physical, emotional and cognitive.

Children's needs: the carers' views

Physical	shelter, warmth, food, sleep
Cognitive	to be encouraged and supported
	direct and indirect teaching

Love and understanding

Emotional	freedom and security to try and fail or succeed
	to be heard and understood
	to be special and treated as an individual
	to be accepted by peer groups
Spiritual	to give meaning to life
	to be aware of the mysteries of life
	to develop one's own beliefs and get acceptance for them

Using Bradford's five fundamental needs, it can be seen that most of the needs listed by the care workers could be identified as 'spiritual': for example, encouragement and support in education (confidence), freedom and security, being heard, understood, accepted (confidence, relatedness). Shelter, warmth, food and sleep, listed as 'physical needs', may also be linked with peace, for without peace, physical care and nurture are threatened, and without such care it is difficult to feel peaceful. This group placed love and understanding at the centre of their chart, indicating the centrality of these needs to the whole of life. This is not to impose a concept of spirituality, but to propose that accepted ideas about needs, experiences and qualities may contribute towards development of an acceptable language with which to describe the welfare of the whole person.

The 'spiritual dimension' is defined by the British Humanist Association in terms which echo those of the priest and the practitioners:

[It] comes from our deepest humanity. It finds expression in aspirations, moral sensibility, creativity, love and friendship, response to natural and human beauty, scientific and artistic endeavour, appreciation and wonder at the natural world, intellectual achievement and physical activity, surmounting suffering and persecution, selfless love, the quest for meaning and for values by which to live.

Humanists see these qualities as the highest part of the human personality but yet as part of it, having evolved naturally. (BHA undated b, p.i)

Some humanists define 'spiritual' as the dominance of emotional over intellectual aspects of the personality, positively and based on scientific/reason-based philosophy.

'The quest for meaning and for values by which we live' is a basic aim of spirituality as described by the Department of Education and Science in guidelines for the curriculum for 11–16-year-olds (DES 1977):

> The spiritual area is concerned with the awareness a person has of those elements in existence and experience which may be defined in terms of inner feelings and beliefs; they affect the way people see themselves and throw light on the purpose and meaning of life itself. (p.10)

The number and vagueness of the concepts compacted into this brief statement reduce its impact. In summary, spirituality is awareness of feelings and beliefs which in turn stimulate self-awareness and answers to 'why' questions about life.

This definition was included in a religious education syllabus with the comment:

> For some people this awareness relates to God, but for others to some kind of ultimate reality or truth. It can be evidenced by human aspirations such as love, hope, compassion, forgiveness, faith, self-giving, altruism etc. Sensitivity to this dimension can be present long before intellectual understanding is possible. (Suffolk Education Department 1991)

Here again are *awareness, aspiration, love, hope,* but also *compassion, forgiveness, faith, self-giving, altruism,* qualities involved in Bradford's 'engaging creatively, caringly and thoughtfully in everyday life' (1995, p.35). While some people will dispute the idea of 'ultimate reality or truth', the identified human aspirations are widely accepted as desirable attributes.

QUESTIONS

- Do you think that 'spirituality' can be defined?
- Do you find one or more of the definitions given in this section useful?
- Do you think children have spiritual needs?
- If so, what are they?
- If not, how would you describe those needs which are described in the definitions in this section as 'spiritual'?
- How are the spiritual needs of children known to you met?

SUGGESTIONS

With colleagues and children:

- Discuss one another's ideas about the questions above.
- Study one or more of the definitions above.
- Devise your own definition(s).
- Draw up a chart indicating how spirituality relates to other aspects of life.
- List ideas about children's needs.
- Draw up a chart indicating how spiritual needs relate to others.
- Identify how children's needs, including those which can be described as 'spiritual', are met in your setting.
- Identify how meeting these needs could be improved.

Summary

While I was writing this chapter, a senior practitioner in a home-finding project for children with severe learning disabilities telephoned to express her concern at the lack of attention to their spiritual needs, resulting from the multiple problems involved in making and maintaining placements. Our conversation increased my conviction that spirituality is neither an 'optional extra' nor a fashionable adjunct.

One difficulty for practitioners lies in finding vocabulary with which to express and discuss experiences and attributes which can be recognised as essential to the whole life of the whole child.

Quotations from writers on some religions illustrate ways in which the inseparability between religion and spirituality, self and community may be expressed.

Models of spiritual development explore the concept of maturity as applied to spirituality and introduce taxonomic approaches.

'Spirit' and 'spiritual' and associated words are commonly used in everyday speech; consideration of such usage and meaning may offer a foundation for communication.

Many other words appear in endeavours to define 'spirituality', sometimes without reference to religious belief. Study of such vocabulary and definitions can help to clarify individual concepts and contribute towards development of generally acceptable language with which to discuss children and spirituality.

3 Experience of spirituality in childhood

Oozing spirituality

'Edward is oozing spirituality.' Edward is 2, and exhibits: 'all the capacities and predispositions of an individual who has an awareness of the spiritual dimension of ... life – and who also might come to faith'. Edward's spirituality (which may or may not lead to religious faith) is defined by McClure (1996) (a principal lecturer in theology and religious education) in terms of his capacity for silence and reflection, concentration and delight in play: 'He is happy with his own company ... [and] has the capacity to become totally absorbed in what he attends to – a picture, some music, a puzzle' (p.9).

McClure writes of her observations of Edward's growth since birth, 'physically, cognitively and spiritually', recognising the essential integration of all three aspects of life: 'He is delightful quite simply because he has a highly developed capacity for delight', and rejoices 'in each new possibility, whether it is the unexpected brightness of colour, any representation of the sun, moon and stars or the rhythm of music which instinctively makes him dance'. He can experience 'ecstasy, totally absorbed in and drawn towards realities outside himself' (1996, p.9).

Edward demonstrates wonder and mystery, delight, awareness and meaningfulness – concepts which recur throughout this chapter as descriptive of spiritual experience. He responds to visual and aural stimuli, enacting through silent contemplation expressions of wonder and joyful movement (dance) the core activities of worship.

The vivid evocation of the real boy illustrates McClure's exploration of Fowler's stages of faith (see Chapter 2) in the context of spiritual development (Education Reform Act 1988). McClure bases her proposals for

47

practice on observation of the child's experience, rather than theoretical taxonomies.

Endeavours to define spirituality or construct models of spiritual development are intended to clarify ideas, to offer means of communication through language and metaphor, and to express the inner world of children by means of essentially cerebral activity (research, writing academic papers and books) (see Chapter 2). Some research, like that of McClure, seeks to learn from and about their spiritual experience by direct communication with children (for example, the contributions of Rebecca Nye, David Hay and Robert Coles are introduced in this chapter). Attention is also given to some of the many influences, including physical environment, which may aid or inhibit opportunities for reflection and insight.

The phrase 'spiritual well-being' reflects the usage in the UN Convention on the Rights of the Child.

Core qualities of spiritual experience

When David Hay and Rebecca Nye of Nottingham University undertook 'a study of the spirituality of randomly selected groups of primary school children in Nottingham and Birmingham', Hay (1995) noted:

> We have yet to come across a child who does not have at least an implicit spirituality. Even in the most resolutely secular boy (it is usually a boy), evidences of spiritual sensitivity emerge, sometimes through self-contradiction, or allusive metaphor, or through Freudian slips of the tongue. Our task is not to detect the presence of spirituality, but to understand how it becomes suppressed or repressed during the process of growing up.
>
> The data suggest that the common secularist interpretation of spirituality is the reverse of the truth. Far from being created by social pressure and having no basis in reality, children's spiritual awareness is artificially blotted out by secularised society. (p.1, 271)

The Nottingham study was based on a list of 'four core qualities' which are 'often associated with spiritual experience by adults, which at the same time seemed within the ordinary range of children': these are defined in terms of sensing a changed quality in *awareness*, *value*, *mystery* and *meaningfulness* or *insight* (Nye 1996, 2/8).

Awareness

Nye and Hay (1996) comment: 'The *awareness* associated with spirituality typically refers to a reflexive ... process, that of being attentive towards one's attention' (p.146). Nye (1996) refers to 'a sense of raised or altered awareness [which] might be experienced in moments of stillness or concentration' (2/8).

Four sub-categories are proposed. *Tuning* (described in Schutz 1964) suggests 'the kind of awareness which arises in heightened aesthetic experience, for example when listening to music' or 'feeling at one with nature' (Nye and Hay 1996, p.147).

Flow (identified in Csikszentmihalyi and Csikszentmihalyi 1988) 'refers to the experience of concentrated attention, giving way to a liberating sense of one's own activity managing itself, or being managed by some outside influence'. Examples are taken from 'subjective reports of skiers, rock-climbers and chess players. The factors essential to flow seem to be ... the preceding challenging nature of the activity contrasted with the release of the flow' (Nye and Hay 1996, pp.147–8).

Focusing (Gendlin 1963) 'implies a recovery of respect for the body as a source of spiritual knowledge' and refers to 'the natural knowing of young children before they become inducted into the Cartesian intellectualism that is our cultural heritage'. Nye and Hay note that 'this is an area of experience that children of primary age are more easily in touch with than adults', and refer to Tamminen (1991), who finds that 'spiritual experience is more common among children than older people' (Nye and Hay 1996, p.148).

Here and now experience is identified by Donaldson (1992) as 'the most basic mode of the mind's operation and as such undeniably available to children', suggesting that it is through this that 'entry is gained to the spiritual dimension of adult experience' (cited in Nye and Hay 1996, p.148). Children reported this kind of heightened awareness:

> sensing moments in contexts ranging from the bustle of the playground at the end of the school day to the stillness of a maths test. In each case, children went on to reflect on the special quality and value they recalled such moments as having, and frequently made associations between these feelings and traditional religious themes. (Nye 1996, 2/8)

Developing these ideas in a paper for teachers, Hay (1995) explains:

> children are very familiar with intense bodily awareness when they become immersed in a task, or feel in tune with a situation. They are in touch with the here-and-now of our experience. On the other hand they are often, so to speak, unaware of their awareness. It is this awareness that is the central component of profound prayer. (p.1,271)

Nye and Hay (1996) hope: 'that identifying these four kinds of awareness will serve to direct attention when listening to children's accounts of general experience such that potentially spiritual aspects of that experience are recognised, affirmed and perhaps explored further'. (p.148)

Value

Sensing value is derived from Donaldson (1992), associating the intensity of emotional response to experiences with 'a measure of value, reflecting a stance towards what is felt to matter' (Nye and Hay 1996, p.149). Expressions of delight and despair in particular were studied, 'since these extremes of emotion are likely to reflect feelings towards issues of ultimate, though possibly subjective, importance' (Nye 1996, 2/8). Despair was found, 'often associated with the child's personal experiences of being taken for granted or used', linked with environmental concerns (Nye and Hay 1996, p.15). Concepts of ultimate goodness and evil are also associated with value sensing, and develop from earliest childhood through day-to-day experience of parental comfort and security, or the reverse. Hay (1995) comments:

> we know from our studies how important community, the family and interdependence are to children. Yet the individualism of modern life draws us emphatically into teaching children to be self-sufficient. This emphasis quickly leads to ruthlessness and injustice in society, whilst being associated with a loss of spiritual awareness that leads us to combat such structural evil. (p.1, 271)

Mystery

Sensing mystery, which implies both wonder and awe, may be expressed about any subject or object, including: 'the incomprehensibility of technology ... and the awesome transcendent "beauty" of a large shopping centre' (Nye 1996, 2/8). Mystery is not simply a sense of not-understanding, for example, how something works. Imagination is essential in order:

> to conceive what is beyond the known and what is 'obvious'. Studies of children's ability to enter into fantasy show that they have a powerful capacity for (and enjoyment of) letting go of material reality, or using it in a new way to discover meanings and values in response to their experience, especially experience for which their language is inadequate. Imagination is central to religious activity through the metaphors, symbols, stories and liturgies which respond to otherwise unrepresentable experience of the sacred. In children's imagination, seen in their play, stories, art work and perhaps also their fears and hopes, we may at times be encountering a window on this aspect of their spirituality, which is perhaps more than simply a response to what 'adult' religion has defined as sacred. (Nye and Hay 1996, p.149)

Hay (1995) notes that:

> scientific explanation in the classroom very often blots out mystery. Young children find the simplest phenomenon mysterious, for example the flame that appears when a match is struck. They need to understand that scientific explanation is never more than a humanly constructed account of the fundamentally enigmatic nature of physical reality. (p.1, 271)

Meaningfulness or insight

The fourth core quality, sensing meaningfulness or insight, may be regarded as:

> the means by which the other aspects are drawn together and reflected on. The ability to make one's own connections is essential to the creation of meaning, and children's *imaginations* are therefore likely to serve them well in the elaboration of experience and their spiritual characteristics. (Nye 1996, 2/8–9)

Hay (1995) explains:

> all children are interested in the fundamental questions of meaning: 'Who am I?' 'Where have I come from?' 'Where am I going?' 'What am I meant to do?' So far in our research we have not come across a single exception. It is when these questions begin to be pushed out of consciousness, usually at about the age of 10 or 11, that spiritual awareness is edged out. (p.1,271)

These core qualities recognise the experience and needs of the whole child, referring to perception and imagination, emotion and intellect, physicality and fantasy, security and discovery. Concepts familiar from models introduced in Chapter 2 appear: for example, wonder, relatedness, awareness, meaning. It is interesting to note the categories of spiritual needs identified by Bradford (1995) alongside the four core qualities discussed here.

- needs:
  - love
  - peace
  - wonder
  - confidence
  - relatedness

- qualities of experience:
  - awareness
  - mystery
  - value
  - meaningfulness and insight

Nye and Hay are concerned not with models of development or guidelines for behaviour (as with altruism, forgiveness); rather they present the here and now of the children they studied. Nye (1996, 2/9) notes the difficulty of their approach, for 'it is the nature of spirituality to spill over into every other domain: emotional, physical, moral, intellectual'.

The research method comprised informal interviews which 'involved asking children about themselves and their life experiences to investigate whether these categories did emerge and suggest potential sources oralternative languages of spirituality'. Identification of 'a spiritual quality in children's talk' was based on three basic principles.

First was 'an apparent shift in *style of manner of expression*, away from conversation which was characterised by an emphasis on knowledge and facts and towards a more emotional, discursive style'. This could be accompanied by 'a change of tone and fluency of expression'. A fluent, extrovert speaker might become more reflective, while 'a rather hesitant, even reticent child suddenly opened up on finding a theme for which they had heart felt inspiration'.

Second, the potential categories of spirituality (the four core qualities) 'served as pointers towards the *broad kinds of content* in which to begin a search for children's spirituality'.

Finally:

> as we become more familiar with the texts of the conversations with the children, it became possible to suggest connections between the meanings expressed by the children and 'traditional' spiritual content. For example, recognising an analogy between a child's favourite story, *Snow White*, and the Christian resurrection myth was a key to understanding why the story could be so personally significant – it was in fact a profoundly spiritual metaphor about the child's response to his Uncle's death and his realisation of his own desire to make a fresh start and relinquish his bullying.
>
> In making sensitive use of cues which indicate profundity and intensity on children's talk, and looking at the talk in these three ways, it was possible to discover numerous themes and areas of life associated with our four core qualities. (Nye 1996, 2/9)

This approach recognises the subjectivity and range of what may be regarded as spirituality and spiritual experience. It emphasises the importance of attending fully to the whole child if the adult is to be aware of and learn from and about that child's life and view of this, and any other, world. It also demonstrates how children and adults may communicate about 'spiritual' matters using 'ordinary' language and vocabulary and focusing on everyday, every-minute matters.

I have become convinced that the search for meaning and direction is of critical concern for children. This is more so when their image of themselves is cloudy of flawed, as is often true for children in care. Such questions may not be answered but must be addressed. (p.27)

Children may find it difficult to ask such questions, and practitioners may find it hard to enable them to do so. Yet one of the terrible experiences of abused children is the loss of innocence and sense of worth. The question 'What sort of person am I?' may attract, in the child's mind, a destructive answer, and the search for meaning may lead to guilt, shame and despair (see Chapter 11).

QUESTIONS

- Thinking of the example of Ruby Bridges, have any children you know been helped to face and survive problems by religious faith and/or spiritual qualities?
- Can you remember what you thought about 'the world and what it's all about' when you were a child and adolescent?
- Do you know what children think about such questions?
- How can you show respect for children's private thoughts while learning what they think?

SUGGESTIONS

With colleagues and children:

- Discuss one another's ideas about the questions above.
- Make opportunities for children to tell you their thoughts and stories and share their 'private sense of things'.
- Notice drawings which may express some aspect of religious belief and/or spiritual experience.
- Give attention to expressions of spiritual experiences when reviewing progress and making plans with and for children.

The spiritual environment

Many children are profoundly influenced by experience of what is sometimes termed 'nature mysticism', feeling in some transforming manner a new awareness of themselves in relation to the environment. A 63-year-old man recalled his first spiritual experience aged about 5:

> It was a calm, limpid summer morning and the early mist still lay in wispy wreaths among the valleys. The dew on the grass seemed to sparkle like iridescent jewels in the sunlight, and the shadows of the houses and trees seemed friendly and protective. In the heart of the child that I was there suddenly seemed to well up in a deep and overwhelming sense of gratitude, a sense of unending peace and security which seemed to be part of the beauty of the morning, the love and protective and living presence which included all that I had ever loved and yet was something much more. (Robinson 1977, p.33)

It is common for people to experience spiritual awakening in a beautiful natural setting, sometimes really seeing, for the first time Wordsworth's 'splendour in the grass' and 'glory in the flower', or being overawed by the immensity of the sea or grandeur or a mountain. These experiences illustrate the senses of awareness, mystery and meaningfulness discussed by Nye (1996), and of wonder and relatedness noted by Bradford (1995).

Goudge (1974) believed that 'most children have an awareness of God in very early childhood', attributing her own 'clearness' partly to loneliness in childhood, partly to the beauty of her home. She asks: 'How can a child in a slum experience God? Can it have a theophany with nothing to look at but dustbins and brick walls and never a moment of silence and loneliness?' (pp.73 and 74).

It can be very difficult to find, and even harder to tolerate, silence in the late 1990s, when external noise is apparently so important that the Walkman has become an almost permanent prosthesis. It is hard for young people to be still and to listen into silence. Loneliness, in the sense of feeling alone however much surrounded by people, is all too familiar, but Goudge means the 'aloneness' sought by Joanna (aged 10), for whom:

> spiritual refreshment was found in an imaginary garden, where it was always sunny and peaceful, in contrast to the gloominess of home life and endless chatter of her noisy sisters. Preference for quietness made her ambivalent about desire for solitude and the company of others. Without the knowledge of her secular family she had developed her own spasmodic prayer life. (Nye 1996, pp.2–16)

Whatever Joanna had to look at with her physical eye – even if only 'dustbins and brick walls' – her inner eye provides richly for nurture of and by the imagination, for spiritual well-being, for the theophany, the revelation of God and of 'greater good':

> sometimes I feel very lonely when I am alone with God because I can't see God and I can't hear God. I just think about God … if *everyone* stopped and thought about what they were doing, you might actually have a better life – because people might understand you a little better – So I think if life is a little brighter you see brighter things. (Nye 1996, 2/16 and 17)

However sterile and stunted the outer environment, children can be encouraged to develop inner resources which may themselves help to recognise and transform ugliness and squalor.

Nevertheless, spiritual damage and handicap may be associated with children's surroundings, as suggested by Bradford (1989):

> It is possible for a child or young person to suffer spiritual damage for example by cruelty or violence, from the atmosphere of extreme ugliness or squalor and acute deprivation, or through the influence of the impact of damaging ideas (not excluding the possibility of these being through the mass media) which decry the principle of humanity and respect for the inherent dignity of the human person. Such experiences may result in what might be called 'spiritual handicap'. (p.11)

In a packed paragraph, he suggests an appalling scene, using strong, vivid words – 'cruelty', 'ugliness', 'squalor' – which lead the mind immediately to foreign battle zones and refugee camps, and then, reluctantly, to local living conditions which every practitioner can recognise. Bradford identifies inner as well as outer violence and deprivation, fed by ideas and images which militate against the UN Convention's 'respect for the inherent dignity of the human person'. Spiritual well-being requires nurture and appropriate environment as much as physical, mental and emotional well-being do.

Nye (1996) addresses the connection between the whole environment and spiritual well-being or deprivation:

> A materialistic, mechanistic and emotionally sterile environment will fail to nurture the idea that there is anything 'more' to life than more of the same; no mystery, no greater 'good', no sense of purpose that transcends the mundane. Without such an 'inoculation' of spiritual values from the social and moral environment, the prognosis for fully enjoying or surviving the inevitable ups and downs of life may be poor. The protective functions a sense of spirituality can contribute are only partially understood, however research suggests that individuals who possess such a sense are more resilient in the face of traumas including childhood sexual abuse. (2/15)

She suggests the exposure to an emotionally – and spiritually – sterile environment has direct relevance for practitioners: 'A logical consequence may be that some children and young people experience problems which cannot be traced to physical or emotional neglect and abuse but subtly suggest difficulties arising from responses to the spiritual environment' (Nye 1996, 2/15).

It would be fruitful to identify and explore emotional and spiritual richness and stimulus in the worlds in which children live, both in their own homes and in residential and other establishments including hospitals. It may be that hospices rate high for spiritual richness; but if death stimulates ease with matters of the spirit, and space for staff to engage with such concerns, surely care for young people embarking on what may be long lives demands the same.

The greatest abuse of children's rights to 'a standard of living adequate to ... physical, mental, spiritual and social development' (Article 27) is war, whether or not children take up arms themselves or are deprived of home, family, education and food. Physical, cognitive, emotional, spiritual and social well-being and progress are disrupted, and children are assaulted by appalling experiences of loss and terror. Reactions include hallucinations, nightmares, illness, constant crying, lethargy; some children are too frightened to get out of bed. Children in Uganda saw whole villages massacred:

> When they reached the safety of orphanages, they were very disturbed and had terrifying nightmares, when they dreamed of the dreadful things they had seen. But these eventually stopped and, instead, they began to dream of their dead parents telling them to carry on with life. These children went on to try to help others in need. (Daly and Vaughan 1988, p.26)

Fergal Keane (1995), a journalist, described a 14-year-old boy beating bound neighbours to death in Rwanda. The boy had become both victim and oppressor, every aspect of his life perverted; could pride in manly strength and fidelity to his colleagues be accounted as virtuous? (See also p.72.)

In 1975, poems and paintings by Arab and Jewish children were published in *My Shalom, My Peace* (Zim et al. 1975). They included the following poem by Amit Tal (aged 11):

Father and son

He has always wept and suffered without end.
He wanted just this once
To live again with his Dad
Through those pleasant childhood days
When they would walk together hand in hand.
When a warm hand used to take him to school
And he not wanting to part.
Then came the war, and the hand was cut off
Forever and ever.

The Arab boy also feels suffering.
He wanted just this once, again he wanted –
To pass with his father through the same village
The chickens clucking, the cattle lowing
And the two of them happy and singing a lively tune.

But the war silenced the song,
A love song of a father and his son.

O why the immense hate?
Why shouldn't there be
Peace? (p.50).

Children do not have to live in a distant war zone to suffer such assaults on the peaceful conditions in which to develop in security and health. Inter-religious and/or racial hatred and violence are well known within the UK.

QUESTIONS

- Do any aspects of your living/working environment nurture respect for people and the idea that there is 'more' to life – mystery, a greater good, a sense of purpose?
- If not, do you think this environment is sterile and poor?
- If so, what are the positive aspects of the environment?
- Do children known to you live in emotionally and spiritually sterile environments?
- If so, what aspects of their environments inhibit spiritual well-being?
- If not, what aspects of their environments nurture spiritual well-being?
- Can spiritual experience be gained only amidst natural beauty, or can it be found in any environment, however brutal and ugly?
- How can you recognise and encourage children's need for spiritual experience, including silence and aloneness?

SUGGESTIONS

With colleagues and children:

- Discuss one another's ideas about the questions above.
- Describe the ideal environment for children's well-being and development in all areas of life.
- Explore ways in which children can be alone in their own place.
- Encourage children to write poems and draw pictures expressing their visions of a better life, which may be included in their life-story books.

Summary

Direct observation of children's spiritual experience has been carried out by Nye and Hay (1996), who identified and explored four core qualities concerned with *awareness, value, mystery* and *meaningfulness/insight*. These can be linked with Bradford's (1995) identification of spiritual needs as *love, peace, wonder, confidence, relatedness*.

Robert Coles studied children's attitudes towards and experience of religion and spirituality in many countries, learning from extensive conversations and numerous drawings and paintings.

Children often respond to stimulus from the environment which may take the form of 'nature mysticism', when the experience may be full of wonder and new awareness. However, the environment may also be sterile and squalid, inhibiting development of respect for human dignity, for example. Children can escape from external difficulties into their imaginations, finding peacefulness and privacy. Some environments are so appalling that children's development and well-being are inevitably distorted: for example, war zones.

4 Spiritual distress

Distressing aspects of spiritual experience

Although spirituality and religion have associations with many desirable attributes such as mystery and awareness, love and security, identity and community, attention must also be given to difficult and dangerous aspects.

Spiritual and/or religious experiences may themselves be directly distressing and lead to fear, even terror, perhaps despair, sometimes because of misunderstandings or communication difficulties.

It is not unusual for children to experience spiritual crises, although these may not be recognised or offered attention by adults. Learning about the universality of death may cause fear. Such crises can lead to desolation, despair, even suicide, especially if children have no one with whom to share anxieties.

Misunderstanding religious teachings and symbols can stimulate harmful responses, sometimes in attempts to attain spiritual perfection. Similarly distressing is the recognition of sinfulness and failure. The quality of awareness is associated with penalties for too much knowledge, especially if a religion forbids, for example, seeing the deity; examples are found in traditional and contemporary stories.

This chapter links these ideas with definitions of spiritual and religious rights, qualities, needs and values discussed in the earlier chapters.

Spiritual crisis

'The years from 8 to 11 I remember as pretty agonising. I was afraid of death and of life for that matter, and subject to severe panic attacks which nobody seemed to notice. I couldn't explain them at that age of course, but looking back I don't really

61

think they were caused by any mental instability but simply by my having reached a religious crisis at a ridiculously early age and being quite unable to cope with it.' (quoted in Robinson 1977, p.111)

The anonymous writer was 21 when she recalled so vividly the feelings of half her lifetime ago. This simple account is full of distress and is itself distressing, illustrating several aspects of disturbing spiritual experience.

The writer is still – not surprisingly – unable to trust her own perceptions or the responses of people with whom she tries to communicate. The attempt at communication cited above was made to a remote and unknown recipient in response to a questionnaire contributed to the Religious Experience Research Unit, answering the question: 'Can you recall any particular moment, or period, when you had a feeling of emerging into self-consciousness, that is of feeling yourself to be an individual person, with some degree of freedom and responsibility? And was this associated with any religious feelings or ideas?' (Robinson 1977, p.159). Far from emergence into self-consciousness as an individual being a high and holy moment, the writer knows despair. Her *freedom* is to feel fear, her *responsibility* is to mask her panic.

The young woman remembers as agonising three of four years of childhood which are commonly regarded as characterised by increasing mastery in all areas of activity and development. She was full of fear which must have been exacerbated by the failure of any adults to notice her *severe* panic attacks; (she risks a strong adjective). Not only were her demeanour and behaviour unnoticed, but her inability to find words to explain her experiences suggests that no adult gave enough attention to enable expression of feelings.

Her vocabulary is chosen mainly to minimise the actual impact of her terrible times. *Pretty* attempts to reduce the force of *agonising*. The failure of adults to attend to her agony is turned into her own failure to explain, attached to the concept of age-related communication ability and dismissed with the sad comment *of course*. For, of course, there is no reason why, with an attentive audience, she could not have explained.

Fears of death and life are augmented by fear that she was mentally unstable, still not completely lost by the time when at 21 she looks back. She protests that she doesn't *really* think that she was mentally unstable but when people don't *really* think something they usually *really* do. It is not clear from the statement whether the writer feared mental instability as a child or imposes the ambivalent assessment from the perceptions of young adulthood.

However, as an adult she uses more minimising vocabulary to control, maybe dismiss, experience which had been so overwhelming. Far from indicating mental instability, she proposes that her experiences were caused *simply* by a religious crisis and that at a *ridiculously early age*. How can any age be too early or too late for a crisis of any kind, let alone one associated with the great and fundamental issues of existence, death and life?

She adds that she was *quite unable to cope with* the religious crisis, as if she might have been expected so to do. Even with attentive adults, the agonising experiences, fears and panic attacks would have been hard to bear and manage. Alone and, in this respect at least, neglected, no child and few adults could cope.

The girl remembered by her older selves, and still and forever part of them, suffered. Her confidence and self-esteem were reduced. In terms of the four core qualities (Nye 1996; see Chapter 2) awareness, mystery and insight seem all to have been associated with fear of both death and life, preventing experiences of joy and wonder and the ability to attribute value and meaning. Lack of trust in the inattentive adults surely inhibited development of relationships with them and others in the surrounding world. For this child, privacy, so precious to many children beset by demands, implied lack of care and communication, and loneliness in which to face in fear and panic her increasing agony.

Discussing implementation of the UN Convention on the Rights of the Child, Hamilton (1996) notes that children and young people 'felt that adults did not listen to them, respect them, take them seriously, or value what they had to say'. Moreover, they felt that 'childhood is characterised by low status, little power and almost no control over the outcomes of their lives' (p.1). Andrew West (1996) reports that 'Children are not heard even when they speak, and have no impact' (p.8).

The anonymous writer's account of her spiritual distress powerfully demonstrates the effects of ignoring children's endeavours to be heard, respected and taken seriously. Article 19 of the UN Convention requires that children should be protected from 'all forms of physical and mental ... neglect and negligent treatment'. Although spiritual and emotional neglect and abuse are not specified, such inattention to a child's distress as that described above illustrates violation of the right to protection.

QUESTIONS

- Does the idea of 'spiritual distress' mean anything to you?
- Have you ever experienced anything like the distress described by the girl quoted above?
- If so, what do you think caused it?
- Did you receive attention and understanding from any adult(s)?
- Have any children known to you experienced distress of this kind? If not, can you think of any children whose distress you might not have noticed?

SUGGESTIONS

With colleagues and children:

- Discuss one another's ideas about the questions above.
- Consider how adults could recognise and attend to such a crisis as the girl describes.
- Discuss the question posed in Robinson's questionnaire: 'Can you recall any particular moment, or period, when you had a feeling of emerging into self-consciousness, that is of feeling yourself to be an individual person, with some degree of freedom and responsibility? And was this associated with any religious feelings or ideas?'
- Think about the words children use to describe ideas and experience, and discuss how they communicate strength of feeling.
- Describe how adults could show more respect and value for children's experiences.

Consciousness of death

Spiritual distress and fear are not confined to such all-embracing and undefined experiences as that described above. For many children, the idea of death can stimulate anxiety and terror. A 51-year-old woman vividly remembered herself aged nearly 5, 47 years earlier:

> I would often cry bitterly at night ... at the realization that some day my parents would die, and indeed the overwhelming knowledge that everything in the world would die some day. I found it an absolutely terrifying thought. I can still remember the feeling of utter desolation. Although I knew then that there was a life after death I was always so afraid that there would be a journey, a long, dark journey and people would perhaps get lost or too tired before they found Jesus. (quoted in Robinson 1977, pp.124–5)

This little girl became aware of both physical and spiritual reality in the context of the whole world. Her personal insight within the framework of religious belief led to terror and desolation, an expression of the despair noted by Nye (1996) in her study of value-sensing, which:

> incorporates attitudes and feelings towards issues of exceptional importance [and] refers to a stance about what really matters, and hence a kind of personal philosophy, often a kind of theology. In our research we have sought children's intimations of delight and despair in particular, since these extremes of emotions are likely to reflect feelings towards issues of ultimate, though possibly subjective, importance. (2/8)

For some children, associations with concepts of ultimate goodness and evil are linked with 'explicitly religious awareness' (Nye 1996, 2/8).

For this child, the desolation stimulated by awareness of death is not alleviated by religious belief in an after-life. On the contrary, that belief leads to further anxiety as she visualises a long, dark journey which may prevent attainment of the goal: Jesus. The concept of the ordeal-journey may have been derived from misunderstanding Christian hymns and stories which liken life on earth to a pilgrimage, for example:

Lead us, heavenly Father, lead us
O'er the world's tempestuous sea;
Guard us, guide, us, keep us, feed us,
For we have no help but thee.

Thou didst tread this earth before us,
Thou didst feel its keenest woe;
Lone and dreary, faint and weary,
Through the desert thou didst go. (hymn: 'Lead us, heavenly Father, lead us')

Through the night of doubt and sorrow
Onward goes the pilgrim band. (hymn: 'Through the night of doubt and sorrow')

The image may have come from Psalm 23: 'Even though I walk through the valley of the shadow of death ...' or the writer may (like the present author) have been given a copy of Bunyan's allegory (first published 1678), *The Pilgrim's Progress* as a Sunday School prize. In the book, Christian's danger-filled journey includes imprisonment by Giant Despair in Doubting Castle before encounter with the valley of the Shadow of Death, 'which is as dark as pitch; ... and over that valley hangs the discouraging clouds of Confusion; Death also doth always spread his wings over it. In a word it is every whit dreadful, being utterly without Order' (Bunyan 1954, p.63). Such stories can be very frightening.

Her first encounter with the idea of death led Alison Uttley (1974) to awareness, insight and value-sensing, bringing despair rather than delight. As a young child, she noticed some white hairs in her father's hair and whiskers. Although far from aged, he told her that they were 'a sign of old age', and when she asked, 'Can't you stop them getting white?' he answered 'Nay. It's Nature. It's the way we must all go.' The little girl:

was desolated. Did it mean that when all his hair was white he would die? I wondered sadly, but I couldn't say the words. A terror shot through me, wounding me to the heart, for this was my first realization of the mortality of those whom I had thought to be immortal. I turned away and hid my apprehensions. In my new knowledge I felt wiser and older than my father. For a long time the figure of

Death coming up the hill, climbing the steps by the orchard wall, walking by the edge of the lawn, then turning in at the wicket-gate to the door, haunted me. He would knock and my father would go away with him.

When I lay down at night I composed myself in fateful readiness, with feet together, and hands folded together, so that death would find me ready, too, when he came. Over our best bed hung a statuette of an Italian angel and I copied his posture. (p.151)

The child is 'desolated', 'terrified' and 'wounded', but she cannot convey her feelings to her parents, least of all to the father whose thoughtless failure to anticipate or understand the impact of his generalisation has stimulated her spiritual distress. The experience leads to knowledge as well as fear, and a strikingly practical and loving solution to the unbearable prospect of separation from her loved father. However, this glimpse into a child's world leads to the question: how many children bear such desolation, knowledge and fear in silence and alone?

QUESTIONS

- Can you remember when you first learned that everyone must die?
- Was this associated with any religious beliefs?
- How did you feel?
- Did any adult recognise what you were feeling and offer attention?
- What knowledge, belief about and understanding of death have children who are known to you?
- If you don't know, how could you find out?
- Would you be aware if children were distressed by their beliefs about death?
- If not, how could you become aware?

SUGGESTIONS

With colleagues and children:

- Discuss one another's ideas about the questions above.
- Consider the experience of despair in the lives of children.
- Discuss the impact on spiritual well-being of different and individual beliefs about death and images of it.
- Discover how adults can learn about children's responses to death and fears about it.
- Study Part 5 of this book, 'Children and death', and Chapter 16, 'Communicating about death and loss'.

Sensing sin and failure

Misunderstanding the apparent teachings of a religion can lead to danger as well as distress. Yvonne Stevenson (1976) (a scientist and daughter of a Christian Anglican vicar) identified closely with the suffering of Jesus as he was crucified. During the three-hour service on Good Friday when this is remembered, she determined to emulate the saints and martyrs and suffer for God by driving a rusty nail through her right hand:

> The service became sublime. My feelings were ecstasy and anticipation. As we studied the sayings on the Cross I felt that I could look Christ in the face and say: 'In a little while I shall really suffer with Thee. Not just in theory, but with real pain through my hand.' (p.43)

At home, she prepared for the deed, but, just as she raised the hammer, she was called for tea. This reprieve she saw as 'a message from God, telling me to stop – Just as He had told Abraham to stop before he slew Isaac' (in the Bible story, God orders Abraham to demonstrate his faithfulness by sacrificing his son, but provides a ram as substitute at the last minute: Genesis 22:1–14; see also Chapter 15). The positive result of this spiritual and emotional suffering was a sense of 'my mother's love all about me, as if she were bending down with her arms around me saying, "No, child, that isn't the way at all"' (p.43). It led also to a new awareness and understanding of the meaning of such stories as that of Abraham and Isaac being: 'examples, sometimes actual, sometimes mythical, of the *growth of human thought*, *understanding*, and *conscience*, from primitive to the most civilized way of thinking yet known. We do *not* add to the suffering of this world. We dedicate ourselves to alleviate it' (pp.43–4).

Although the girl has been led into dangerous error by her emotional response to spiritual experience, she is enabled to transmute what she herself describes as 'fancying and imagining and ruminating along false lines' into insight and awareness, at least in part, by the sense of her mother's love and new understanding of her father's teaching. She endures the ordeal alone, and makes the leap of awareness while eating tea, never telling or discussing it with her parents, but confronting the spiritual problem in silence (see Chapter 15).

For other children, the silent spiritual ordeal concerns the recognition of failure to live up to the standards set by religion, 'a sense of sin'. Goudge (1974) wrote in old age about a crucial moment in childhood:

> I know the exact spot on a field path where I first knew the vileness of sin in myself; and can recapture the misery I felt because it has been repeated so many times since. What had caused this first conviction? Was it because Christ had come

alive? Or because I had come to know and love my father [an Anglican clergyman] better and perhaps subconsciously compared myself to him? Partly perhaps the shock of joy caused by my mother's homecoming [after illness], because it was to her I ran when I got home and to her that I poured out the tale of my wickedness ... she stood up to it well and was able to assure me of God's forgiveness. (p.74)

The little girl's life had been lonely, with a remote father and an often ill mother. At the time of her 'conviction of sin', both her mother and her beloved Nanny were away and she spent more time with her hard-to-know father. They learnt to play together, and he gave religious instruction. The visual images of Christianity in the house were somewhat dour, including 'a very large framed engraving of the Last Judgement. The companion picture ... showed Christians being thrown to the lions' (p.70), which 'mercifully' could not be seen clearly. Books about Christianity could also give worrying messages: 'At the pictures of the passion of Christ I refused to look. I had caught a glimpse of one and that was enough.' Her father did not insist on her looking at the frightening image of a bleeding man and turned the pages straight from Palm Sunday to Easter Day, 'ignoring the crux of the matter altogether' (p.73).

Sharing spiritual experience with adults helped the child to confront and learn from distress. With her mother, Elizabeth Goudge could confess to sin and learn about forgiveness.

For other children, however, awareness of sin, of failure, linked with guilt and shame, may not be shared with and alleviated by a caring adult. The child may feel not only failing, but a failure. Whether or not children are brought up within a religious code, adults define standards of behaviour and performance from which it is all too easy to fall short. The sense of being sinful, a failure, leads to distress, depression, even despair, the opposite of the senses of value and insight described by Nye (1996). It also inhibits the ability to develop relationships and connections with other people and the world of nature, for a feeling of un-worth and lack of self-esteem suggests the impossibility of attracting affection and trust, of being acceptable and effective. In the extreme, this may lead to suicide.

For other examples of extreme spiritual distress stimulated by misunderstanding, see the references to *Michel, Michel* (Lewis 1967) in Chapters 12 and 15.

QUESTIONS

- Have you ever experienced suffering because of misunderstanding some religious story or other teaching?
- Has religious teaching ever led you to harm or danger?
- Have you ever experienced a sense of yourself as sinful or failing?

- If you have felt distress of this kind, did any adult(s) recognise how you felt and offer understanding and comfort?
- Do any children known to you have experiences of this kind? If not, how could you become more aware of children's feelings and experiences?

SUGGESTIONS

With colleagues and children:

- Discuss one another's ideas about the questions above.
- Consider how adults can become more aware of the anxieties and fears which can arise from misunderstanding religious stories and teachings.
- Consider how adults can become more aware of children's distress and fears when they feel themselves to be sinful and or failing to attain the standards set by religious communities and parents.
- Identify how children can describe feelings and responses which are concerned with spiritual crisis and distress.

Penalties of awareness

The experience of awareness can have other penalties. In some religions it is forbidden, even impossible, to look at the supreme being. Christianity supplies intermediaries between humans and God in the persons of Jesus and, for some worshippers, Mary. Jewish prophets received direct communications from Jahweh through such visual and aural representations as a burning bush or a still, small voice. Allah gives instructions through the Qur'an, revealed to Mohammed. 'Allah is always there but you can't see Him' (cited in Ipgrave 1995, p.9). Angels convey divine messages to Christians, Jews and Muslims. The One God of Hinduism, Brahman, the Spirit of the Whole World, is also unseeable: 'Brahman is in everything, everywhere and always. But we cannot see, hear or touch Brahman' (Aylett 1992, p.8). Brahman is represented on earth by numerous incarnations. El Onkar (the Sikh name for the One God) is also without tangible form for humans.

Attempts to see the supreme being can lead to disaster, or at least dramatic results. Some Muslim children spoke about Musa, who:

> went up to the tree and said, 'God, please let me see you, let me see you!' God goes that, 'You just won't be able to see me.' He goes, 'Let me see you, please.' So God goes, 'OK, look at that mountain and if it stays then I'll let you see myself.' He just showed a glimpse of His light and the mountain turned into ashes.' (Ipgrave 1995, pp.9 and 10)

Some younger Muslim children expect that 'In Jannah [Paradise] you'll meet God, but when you look at Him you'll think it'll be about five minutes, but it'll be 40, 50, 500 years' (pp.9 and 10).

Once in Jannah, a few hundred years devoted to looking on the face of Allah will not be missed, but the Hindu god Krishna (incarnation of Vishnu) recognised the danger to his foster mother, Yasoda, when, on looking into his mouth, she saw everything:

> the whole eternal universe, and heaven, and the regions of the sky, and the orb of the earth with its mountains, islands and oceans; she saw the wind, and lightning, and the moon and stars, and the zodiac; and water and fire and air and space itself; she saw the vacillating senses, the mind, the elements and the three strands of matter. She saw within the body of her son, in his gaping mouth, the whole universe in all its variety, with all the forms of life and time and nature and action and hopes, and her own village, and herself.
>
> Then she became afraid and confused, thinking, 'Is this a dream or an illusion wrought by a god? Or is it a delusion of my own perception? Or is it some portent of the natural powers of this little boy, my son?' (O'Flaherty 1975, pp.220–1)

Then Yasoda bowed down before 'the god, whose nature cannot be imagined or grasped by mind, heart, acts, or speech; he in whom all this universe is inherent, impossible to fathom'. Krishna rescued his foster mother from awareness of 'the true essence', which would be too overwhelming to bear in everyday life, destroying their parent–child relationship. He 'spread his magic illusion in the form of maternal affection. Instantly the cow-herd's wife lost her memory of what had occurred and took her son on her lap. She was as she had been before, her heart flooded with even greater love ... she considered him to be her son' (O'Flaherty 1975, pp.220–1). The god, in the form of a human boy, retained his divine nature and power, but protected a beloved human from knowledge, awareness which would destroy both the woman and their relationship. Yet the experience of that awareness, although lost to her conscious memory, enhances her spiritual quality as 'her heart flooded with even greater love', and she regards the boy as no longer a foster child but her son.

Sudden awareness and astounding knowledge may be permitted but accompanied by injunctions to secrecy, as in the Christian story of the transfiguration of Jesus. Taking only three close companions, he leads them up a high mountain where they can be alone; there his clothes become 'dazzling white, with a whiteness no bleacher on earth could equal'. The transfigured Jesus is joined by the Hebrew prophets Elijah and Moses, 'conversing together'. Peter proposes to erect shelters, 'For he did not know what to say; they were so terrified.' At this moment a cloud suddenly overshadows them, and a voice says, '"This is my Son, my Beloved; listen to him,"' and they are once again alone with Jesus. Returning down the mountain, Jesus instructs his companions to keep their experience a secret (Matthew 17:1–9; Mark 9:2–9).

Peter and his friends are terrified, filled with awe at the revelation of their familiar friend and leader as divine, in shining clothes and conversing with the long dead prophets. Peter endeavours to deal with his fear by practical action, proposing to build an unnecessary shelter. A moment later a cloud has appeared from nowhere and the voice of God is speaking directly to the three men. They are privileged to witness something wonderful, but the price is terror. Even the shepherds informed by an angel of the birth of Jesus, a wonderful and joyful experience during which 'the splendour of the Lord shone round them', are 'terror-struck' (Luke 2:8–10).

These experiences are awe-ful: 'awe' is a word which has lost its force through overuse. One dictionary definition is: 'reverential fear or wonder'. Experiences of wonder and mystery are regarded as essential to spiritual well-being, but wonder must not be separated from awe, nor mystery from fear. The spiritual importance is, in part at least, recognition of power, of the unknown and unknowable, of that which is worthy of reverence.

The transfiguration story echoes the meeting of Moses with the deity on Mount Sinai to receive the Ten Commandments. Although Jahweh descends to the mountain, he may not be seen, and orders Moses to: '"Go down and warn the people, lest they break through to the Lord to gaze and many of them perish."' Death would be at the hands of other humans as the penalty for desecrating the mountain, not directly from the deity. The search for personal awareness, direct experience of the deity is to be prevented (Exodus 19).

Even when a deity makes direct contact with a human, rules about identification may be strict, and penalties severe. The Greek/Roman myth of Eros/Cupid (son of Aphrodite/Venus) and Psyche tells how the human is loved by the young god, who visits her only at night and on condition that she never seeks to see him. Tempted by her sisters, Psyche gazes at the exquisite male by lamplight, but drops hot wax on his shoulder. He instantly returns to his mother, while the pregnant girl endures many ordeals before reunion with her divine husband. Semele is destroyed by her lover, the disguised god Zeus, when she asks to see him in his true form.

In a popular twentieth-century form of the myth, the true identity of the godlike Superman is hidden from Lois Lane, who loves both him and his alter ego, Clark Kent. Only his foster parents know the truth. In one story, a woman who learns the secret immediately dies in his arms, following rescue from a car bomb explosion. In another, Lois Lane unravels the mystery and expresses anger, but like Yasoda, is reprieved from the penalty for awareness, and the memory is erased.

While such momentous events are not common, these stories illustrate the powerful effects of spiritual experience and the possible penalties of exposure to too much knowledge.

On a more homely level, Goudge (1974) reflects on fellow writer Laurie Lee's memory of an experience at the age of 3:

> The June grass, amongst which I stood, was taller than I was and I wept. I had never been so close to grass before. It towered over me and all around me, each blade tattooed with tiger skins of sunlight. It was knife-edged dark and a wicked green,'thick as a forest and alive with grasshoppers that chirped and chattered and leapt through the air like monkeys. High overhead ran frenzied larks, screaming, as though the sky were tearing apart. (Lee 1959 cited in Goudge 1974)

Goudge comments: 'He felt fear as well as awe and he was right. In our weakness it can seem a terrible as well as a beautiful world' (p.75).

A little boy who had become 'aware' of God through attending Sunday School was found by his mother in bed, completely covered by sheets. He explained: '"If God is everywhere, can he see me here?"' His sense of awe expressed not reverence for the omnipresent deity but terror of an almighty spy (Crompton 1990, p.54). Other examples of auditory, visual and other experiences of enhanced or changed perception can be found in *A Sense of Presence* (Beardsworth 1977).

Fears may be stimulated by contact with unfamiliar religious beliefs and observances. For example, some Muslim children feared 'demons' in Christian churches and graveyards, although they had no fear of Muslim cemeteries: 'some had been told that churches were full of ghosts', and when visiting a church, expressed relief 'that there's nothing nasty there' (Ipgrave 1995, p.67).

Unfamiliar pictures, statues and stories may raise anxiety. For example, children unfamiliar with Christian Roman Catholic symbols might be confused by pictures of bleeding hearts and statues of dying men displayed in an apparently peaceful and affectionate foster home. Similarly, the beheading of Ganesha by his mother's husband could raise fears in a child unfamiliar with Hindu stories (see Chapter 15).

Confrontation with horror can lead to spiritual despair about the future of oneself or of the whole world. Fergal Keane (journalist) (1995) listened to a 14-year-old Rwandan boy 'describe how he took a club and beat his elderly neighbour's head to a pulp and then, cheered on by soldiers, moved through a field meting out the same death to other neighbours lying tied up on the ground' (p.4). Until then he had 'managed to retain a faith in a world where the triumph of evil was prevented by an ultimate force for good. That belief has disappeared' (p.4). In a world constantly going mad, the penalty for awareness is loss of faith, of hope, of trust.

QUESTIONS

- Have you had any terrifying experiences connected with religious belief?
- Have you experienced fear when becoming aware of the world around you?
- What do you feel when you consider atrocities committed against and by children?
- Have children known to you had any terrifying spiritual/religious experiences?
- If you don't know, how could you learn about children's terrors?

SUGGESTIONS

With colleagues and children:

- Discuss one another's ideas about the questions above.
- Tell and listen to stories from different religions which include reference to awe, fear and terror.
- Explore how children manage feelings of awe, fear and terror, and how adults might be of help if these feelings are overwhelming.

Summary

Distressing and disturbing aspects of spiritual experience, whether or not associated with religious belief and tradition, may easily be overlooked in discussions of spirituality, especially in connection with children. Yet children experience spiritual crises whose effects may be lifelong. If children are unable to reveal feelings and fears to adults, anxiety and distress are increased.

Subjects which particularly stimulate such distress are the discovery of death and the sense of sin and failure.

The desirable spiritual quality of awareness can lead to distress if the experience is too great or shocking.

An ultimate penalty for too much awareness is loss of faith, hope and trust.

Part 3

Children and religion

5 Religion in everyday life

Religion and social work with children

The UN Convention on the Rights of the Child refers to religion four times. All rights ratified in the Convention are to be respected and ensured by participating states 'without discrimination of any kind, irrespective of … religion' (Article 2). Children have the right to freedom of thought, conscience and religion (Article 14). Religious background must be taken into account when accommodating children apart from their families (Article 20). A major aim of education is preparation for 'responsible life in a free society, in the spirit of … friendship among all peoples', including 'religious groups' (Article 29).

The discussion of these and other Articles in Chapter 1 links the convention with provisions of the Children Act 1989, Department of Health Guidance on that Act, and the *Looking After Children* (LAC) questionnaires (DoH 1995). All who are responsible for the care and well-being of children, in whatever context, are responsible for ensuring that religious beliefs are respected and obligations fulfilled as appropriate.

Practitioners involved in direct work with and planning for children need to know about and understand relevant religious traditions, beliefs and experiences. This is essential not only to ensure that children receive appropriate care (including nurture of the spirit), but also in assisting development of a sense of identity and in understanding and helping with problems and anxieties. Apart from improved knowledge about and understanding of individual children, information can contribute to life-story books and enrich daily life within foster and adoptive families, residential and day care, medical and penal establishments, for example.

In the UK, children and practitioners embrace a wide diversity of religious beliefs, or none. It would be impossible for all practitioners to be familiar with the religion of every child with whom they might come into contact. Even if practitioners have some knowledge of a number of religions, it is neither possible nor necessary to know details of every denomination (subgroup) of every religion. However, it is essential that practitioners should have access to information and advice on any religion (and denomination) with which children with whom they currently work are associated.

The LAC questionnaire headed 'Essential Information Record: Part 1' (DoH 1995) asks: 'Does the child/young person have a religion?' While omitting to explain the intention and implication of the verb 'to have' in this context, the next question asks: 'If yes, please give details and indicate whether nominal/practising?' These apparently straightforward questions require practitioners to have information about and understanding of religion(s). The accompanying note explains the reasons for these questions:

> When placing children outside their families of origin, it is important to think beyond the obvious racial issues. Children of the same race do not necessarily belong to the same culture; an Asian Christian child may, for instance, find it hard to relate to a Hindu family. It is important to know a child's cultural identity as well as his/her racial identity and to be aware that it is possible to identify with more than one culture. (DoH 1995)

Where children are accommodated with families of their own race, questions of religion are of equal importance. For example, what are the implications of placing a child from a non-religious background with a family professing strong devotion, or vice versa?

The questionnaire entitled 'Care Plan' requires comments on 'What *long term* needs does the child have which the placement *must* meet?', including separate points on ethnic/racial origin, religion and culture. The accompanying note refers to the appointment by many childcare agencies of 'special advisers on racial and cultural issues … Local community groups and religious organisations can also give advice and information.'

Religious belief and practices may not seem important to children residing with their birth families. Everyday observances and annual festivals may be taken for granted; indeed, weekly attendance at a place of worship or fulfilling daily obligations may be regarded as boring interruptions of more fascinating occupations. However, if children are separated from families and local religious congregations, patterns of daily, weekly and annual observance may be lost, contributing to disorientation and perhaps confusion about identity. Maintaining such patterns can help develop confidence.

Under 'Identity', for example, an LAC questionnaire about children aged

1–9 asks: 'Is the child provided with positive role models of the same racial/ethnic origin(s) as him/herself?', although this does not specify religion. Carers are expected to make 'efforts to ensure that toys, pictures, books and music in the placement positively reflect the racial/ethnic background(s) and culture(s) of the child's birth family'.

Regarding children aged 5–9 only, a question under 'Identity' asks: 'Do the carer(s) share the same religion as the child's birth family? If not, what efforts are being made to help the child to follow the religion of his/her family of origin?' What follows if the answer to the second question is 'None'?

Children aged 10–18 are asked directly, 'Do you belong to a particular religion?' This question raises several problems, including the inappropriate use of 'belong' in relation to religion, and the ambiguity of 'particular'. Responses are offered as: 'No, I am not interested'; 'No, but I would like to'; 'Yes.' If the answer is 'Yes,' the child is invited to respond to: 'If so, do you have enough opportunities to attend religious services?' But by what criteria is 'enough' to be assessed? The child is also invited to comment on: 'Do you have enough opportunities to follow the customs of your religion (for example, festivals, prayers, clothing, diet)?'

Although these questions are directed to and about children accommodated by local authority social services departments, attention to religious aspects of children's lives is important in every setting. Noorjahan Kharbach (1996) (of Barnardos), for example, studied service needs of families with children under 11 in an area of Oldham with a high Bangladeshi population. She found that while 'Identity, or rather problems with identity, was not an issue cited by professionals', ethnic and religious identity were regarded as a priority by both parents and children: 76.7% of the children 'wanted to learn about their religion, 65% wanted to read Arabic – ie to read the Qur'an, 63.3% wanted to learn how to perform salat and 95% said they thought it was a good idea to have Islamic discussion groups. (Some ... could already perform salat and could read Arabic)' (p.18).

It is important also to be aware of the impact on children accustomed to the patterns, visual images and observances of one religion (or of none) who are accommodated in establishments or households where different, or no, such patterns and images are in evidence. For example, a child brought up in a household professing no religious belief might be confused, even disturbed, in a house where the symbols of Christianity (crucifixes, pictures, statues) were displayed.

Discussion so far may seem to suggest that the importance of religion in children's lives is entirely functional, a social device. However, that devotional activity which is broadly described as 'worship' essentially implies the engagement of the spirit, whether or not the child professes any religious belief. Most religions do not differentiate between the spiritual and other aspects of life. For those who do profess religious faith, attention to spiritual well-being through the fulfilment of religious obligations, individual and corporate, is fundamental to whole and healthy development (see Part 2).

Not all experience associated with religion is conducive to spiritual well-being. Children may respond to stories, pictures and teachings with fear, anxiety and distress. They may also suffer neglect and abuse (see Part 4). Practitioners in every setting can themselves contribute to distress, even neglect and abuse, perhaps innocently.

Some aspects of some religions are concerned with control. For example, codes of ethics and morality based on religious teachings may be strict, including expectations not about only fulfilment of devotional obligations but also dress and sexual behaviour. Transgressions may be punished both by human intervention and fear of divine retribution. Most religions seek to define and control belief, formulating doctrines with which worshippers must conform. Some Christian services, for example, include the corporate recitation of the Crede, which begins: 'I believe in ...'. Failure to accept and conform to doctrines may also attract retribution.

Children may experience oppression in the form of bullying by other children, stimulated by dietary or clothing observances, for example. Understanding and respecting their religious beliefs and observances by adults is an essential protection for children, and can help to relieve much anxiety and to contribute to developing strength.

It is hoped that the introductory information in the following chapters will aid practitioners engaged with these and other matters of care and well-being of the whole child in every context and aspect of life.

It may be difficult for practitioners to encourage religious observances with which they do not themselves agree and which they may consider to be in conflict with their own beliefs (including having no belief). For example, sacred objects may be associated with idolatry and false beliefs, or may be regarded as ridiculous. However, showing respect for and tolerance of children's religious beliefs and observances demonstrates that respect for children themselves which is fundamental to all practice.

Difficulty may also be associated with the LAC questionnaires in the context of practitioners' views about religion. For example, a practitioner who is indifferent or hostile to any or all religions may not pursue matters concerning religious nurture, whereas one with an open attitude or active interest in religious well-being may regard the implications of the LAC questions and other matters relating to religion with positive concern.

Similarly, since neither religion nor spirituality are mentioned in the Dartington Social Research Unit (1996) guidance on assessing needs and planning provision of services, it is possible that these may be overlooked by practitioners who themselves have no interest in the subjects.

The purpose of this part of the book is to introduce brief examples of beliefs and observances of particular relevance to the everyday life, care and well-being of children, associated with aspects of the traditions of several religions.

It is impossible to offer detailed or comprehensive information or provide an equal number of examples from each religion in a book of this size. This material is intended to alert practitioners to the range of beliefs and observances with which children may be associated, and to indicate some reasons why familiarity with the child's religious background is of importance in daily care.

Although reference is made to only seven religions, and examples are necessarily limited in number and detail, it is hoped that this material will encourage practitioners to learn more about these and other religions as appropriate.

Detailed information is best obtained from the children themselves, their families and local religious congregations; any material and ideas acquired from other sources (including this book) should always be augmented by referring to people who practise the religion.

Many excellent texts on a number of religions represented in the UK are available at low cost. Particularly recommended are series designed for children, beautifully illustrated with clear descriptive text, often introducing religious observances, items of sacred dress and food, places of worship and prayers (see 'Bibliography' and 'Further reading').

6 Rites of passage

Children and rites of passage

Celebrations of rites of passage are often associated with religious beliefs and ceremonies. Whether the focus is welcoming a new member of the community or parting with one who has died, the ceremony usually involves all members of the family and religious congregation, although some observances in some traditions are exclusively male. From birth to death, children are essentially concerned in rituals of celebration and commemoration which help to define identity with, and of, the religious congregation.

Although in the UK rites of passage are not always associated with religious beliefs and observances, just as a secular wedding includes ceremony and tradition, so it is possible to celebrate or commemorate movement into other stages of life without reference to a deity. There is a universal desire to mark important events, and the development of non-religious ceremonies is undertaken by the British Humanist Association, for example.

Celebration of transition between stages of life may be of particular importance to children separated from their birth families and communities. Events which are taken for granted when daily life within the family goes smoothly assume new significance if that life is disrupted, especially if children are separated from their home and family, perhaps in residential or foster care, hospital or a penal establishment.

The purpose of this chapter is to introduce some aspects of rites of passage, illustrating both the range and variety of such beliefs and observances, and their importance to children, families and communities.

Anthropological background

The concept of 'rites of passage' was introduced by Belgian anthropologist Charles-Arnold van Gennep (1960, first published 1908). Through studying rituals from pre-literate societies and Christian, Hindu and Jewish sacred writings, he developed a theory for interpreting changes of status in human society. Rites of passage, often associated with religious ceremonies, enable communities to celebrate or commemorate with and on behalf of the individual(s) directly involved in the change.

Using the model of a house, he proposed that moving through the stages of ordinary life is analogous to moving from room to room: every move entails crossing a threshold between two rooms or states of being. Many moves also entail a period, brief or extended, in the neutral territory of a corridor or passage. Van Gennep described three phases in the process of change in social status: leaving the old room, being in no room at all (a passage or corridor), and entering the new room. The ritual process acknowledges separation from the original status, a period apart from the usual status, and the conferring of new status. Referring to the Latin *limen* ('threshold', 'doorstep') he named these stages pre-liminal, liminal, post-liminal.

At these times, individual people experience an unusually intense sense of community, named by Turner 'communitas' (1969/82; cited in Davies 1994b, pp.1–9). Involvement in rites of passage can heighten emotions and focus attention on relationships between individuals. Ancient grudges and smouldering jealousies may take new life. The whole period of the rite of passage, from invitation to 'thank you' letter, is an opportunity for the sense of communitas: emotion can be expressed, truth told and reconciliation achieved at these times when family members are particularly aware of one another and of events which have still, for many people, religious significance.

Birth and naming

Ceremonies associated with birth express welcome to the child and gratitude for the safety of the mother, while indicating the attitudes and expectations of the family and religious congregation.

For example, Sikhs regard the birth of a child as *waheguru di dat* ('gift of God'). A boy is greeted with much rejoicing and exchange of gifts, since his birth ensures not only inheritance of paternal property but also eventual fulfilment of funeral rites for his parents. A male birth is celebrated at the January festival of *Lohrdi*.

Five weeks after birth of a son, the ceremony of *chhati* is held, a feast for relations and members of the *biradari* (members of the same *jat* – 'caste' – in the neighbourhood). These celebrations reinforce the patriarchal nature of Sikh society.

The birth of a girl attracts less attention, for her membership of the family is essentially transitory: her destiny is to marry into another family, costing her father both dowry and a wedding.

A naming ceremony is held at the *gurdwara* ('place of worship'), where the first letter of a section of holy scripture becomes the initial of the baby's personal name. The *granthi* (who officiates at services) dissolves sugar in water with a *khanda* (a small, double-edged sword) while reciting a prayer, and then, with the tip of a *kirpan* (a miniature ceremonial sword) places a few drops of this *amrit* ('nectar') on the baby's tongue and head; the mother drinks the remaining *amrit*.

Sikhs in the UK also receive the traditional title of 'Singh' ('lion') or 'Kaur' ('princess').

Thus the Sikh baby is formally introduced to the essential elements of religious and community belief and practice, including the discrepancy between the founder Guru Nanak's doctrine of social and sexual equality and the actual practice of caste and gender discrimination. The celebrations and ceremonies associated with birth and naming confirm for parents, family and community, social and religious, the already designated role and expectations of the new Sikh.

The many ceremonies which mark transitions between stages of existence for Hindus are called *samskaras*. *Simanta*, the first, is performed during the sixth or seventh month of pregnancy to ensure the well-being of the mother (who receives presents) and her unborn baby. Presents are later given to the newborn child. The birth of a son is regarded as especially auspicious. The birth ceremony *jatakarman* includes careful washing, and then the shape of the sacred word 'Aum' or 'Om' is made on the baby's tongue with honey.

Eleven or twelve days after birth, when purification obligations have been fulfilled, the baby is named in the *samskara namakarana*, attended by friends and relations, who bestow blessings and gifts. A priest prepares a horoscope and proposes names from which the parents choose, perhaps a deity such as Sita or Rama, or a desirable characteristic such as *prema* ('love'). While the baby sits on the mother's knee, the father whispers the name into its ear. The next *samskara* follows immediately, as the baby is taken to the door to see the sun, the power necessary for life.

Before or shortly after the first birthday, the heads of babies (usually only boys) are shaved during the important *samskara chudakarana*, cleansing the new child of any impurities and bad influences remaining from former existences. Through these ceremonies the child is welcomed into and identified with the individual family, local community and religious congregation, representing the spiritual and physical worlds.

In some Christian denominations, too (for example, the Church of England / Anglican Church), the sacrament of naming, 'baptism' or 'christening', involves renunciation of any evil influences already present in the child. Parents are joined by two or three godparents, who take special responsibility to oversee spiritual welfare. On behalf of the baby, they renounce evil and promise to follow Jesus. A priest makes the sign of the cross (on which Jesus was executed) on the baby's head using water which has been blessed. This water represents cleansing from, and forgiveness of, sin, and passing from death to life. Some Christians believe that the water itself washes away sin. Roman Catholic priests also anoint the baby's head with 'chrism' (consecrated oil).

Russian Orthodox baptism involves dipping the baby three times in consecrated water, remembering the baptism of Jesus in the River Jordan by his cousin, John the Baptist, and symbolising cleansing of sin, and new life as a Christian. Immediately after baptism, the baby is dressed in white and then confirmed as the priest makes the sign of the cross ('chrismation') on forehead, eyelids, nostrils, ears, lips, chest, hands and feet with chrism, blessing all senses and activities.

Methodists involve the whole congregation in a commitment to nurture children in their faith. Some denominations (for example, Baptist, Pentecostalist) welcome babies in a service of dedication, postponing baptism or other acknowledgement of Church membership until the individual can make a personal commitment (see 'Commitment' below). In other denominations, baptism is an option for older children and adults.

A certificate of baptism is issued, and the newly christened person's name is entered in the baptismal role.

Names of saints or Bible personalities are popular with some denominations: for example, Mary and Joseph (the parents of Jesus), Saints Catherine and John, and Old Testament names such as Sarah and Adam. In the UK it is not usual to name children after Jesus. Some Christians celebrate their 'name day', the annual commemoration of their patron saint. First names traditional within the family may also be used.

Some baptisms are followed by a meal or small party at the baby's home for close family and friends. The baby is formally welcomed into the family, and there may be observance of traditions such as wearing a christening robe worn by earlier generations of the family. Gifts may include a silver cup, a prayer book or a Bible. Other children in the family may also receive presents.

Baptism into a Christian denomination may not mean much to children who do not attend church. However, solemn promises have been made on their behalf, and they have become members of not only the Christian Church in general, but also a special group with particular beliefs and practices. Children who do maintain association with a church have entered membership of a religious congregation through the first great sacrament of life.

Rastafarians often favour names from the Bible; they also choose names of African origin. Birth brings great joy to both family and congregation, and is often celebrated with ceremonial Nyabinghi drumming, libations and prayers to Jah Rastafari, the living God of creation. Names are often bestowed in the presence of the local Rastafarian community. Rastafarian children are referred to as Princes and Princesses. Through choice of names, Rastafarians demonstrate devotion to the laws of Moses and African ideals, including their longing to return to Africa.

Names from the first books of the Bible (the Torah) are also popular in Jewish families: for example, Abraham (a prophet), David (a king) or the heroines Esther and Ruth. According to origin and tradition of individual families, names of relations, living or dead, are also given. A Hebrew name is used in the synagogue and on such religious documents as wedding certificates.

The first religious ceremony for a Jewish boy is *brit milah*, the covenant of circumcision, eight days after birth (if the child is in good health). A *mohel* surgically removes the foreskin from the penis, signifying continuation of the covenant between God and Abraham that the Jews would be God's chosen people. A room at home or in hospital is prepared with a table bearing two candles and wine. A chair is set aside for the prophet Elijah (sometimes referred to as 'the protector of children' because he saved the life of a boy). At least ten men must be present; the mother is in attendance, but takes no part. Prayers and invocations are made, and the baby is placed briefly on Elijah's chair before being held on the knee of a family friend, the *sandek* ('godfather'), where the circumcision is performed. After more prayers, the baby is named.

A girl is named during synagogue service on the first sabbath after birth, when her father is 'called up to the Torah' to announce her Hebrew name.

Pidyan haben is celebrated on the 31st day after the birth of a boy who is the firstborn child of a woman who has had no miscarriages. The ceremony commemorates the ancient tradition of dedicating all firstborn sons to the service of God in the Temple. The father presents the boy to a *cohen* (a priest descended from the priestly families) with five special coins. The money symbolically redeems the child from priestly service.

Jewish ceremonies emphasise the importance of boys in religious life, and thus in the life of those families and communities for which religious observance is essential and integral. The baby boy is physically marked as a member of a people dedicated to and chosen by its God, and through prayers and rituals spiritually dedicated to that God. He is identified as a member of a family and congregation whose consciousness of history is constantly reinforced through such ceremonies.

Muslim children are also linked at once with their religious and cultural history. Children are gifts from God. Immediately after birth, the *immam* (leader of the local Muslim congregation) conducts a simple ceremony. He whispers the *adhan* in the baby's right ear, and the *iqamat* in the left (prayers in Arabic). These should be the first words heard by the child. A few days later, dates and honey placed in the baby's mouth represent the hope for a sweet, untroubled life.

Seven days after birth comes the ceremony of *aqiqah* or *isma*, when the child is named. The father shaves the baby's hair, which is weighed; money of equivalent (or greater) weight is given to charity. Then the *immam* speaks the child's name, which may be one of the 99 names of God, for example Raschid ('guide'), or have other religious and cultural significance, such a Mohammed or Khedjidja (the prophet and his wife). Prayers are said. Choice of name is made carefully to avoid causing embarrassment in later life.

At this ceremony *khitana* (male circumcision) is usually performed, although it may be postponed to any time until the 13th birthday; Ishmael (oldest son of Abraham) was said to have been circumcised at 13. This commemorates the total obedience of Abraham to God's will, and the covenant made between God and Abraham, and also has implications for health and hygiene. After the ceremony, a meal is given, in the UK usually at the mosque. Some food is given to poor people.

From an early age, children hear the Qur'an and learn to repeat it, word for word.

Children are born into *fitrah* ('the pure nature of Islam'). These first ceremonies celebrate the gift of life and the entrance of a new Muslim into the congregation. Historical and religious traditions are marked, both through the names, and for boys, the physical signing. The baby's spiritual life is established and celebrated from the first few minutes after birth, while the social responsibilities of Islam are fulfilled by the parents.

Buddhist parents often visit the temple for blessing during pregnancy, returning soon after birth with the baby. A monk may be consulted about suitable names, which usually begin with an auspicious sound. The baby may be welcomed with an especially prepared candle and gifts. At about four weeks the baby's head may be shaved and sacred threads tied round the wrists. Attendant monks chant blessings.

QUESTIONS

- Have children known to you been welcomed and/or named in any religious (or secular) ceremony?
- What are the beliefs and expectations of that religion about children?
- Have children known to you any tangible souvenirs of birth and/or naming ceremonies?

- Do records show not only religion but denomination accurately?
- Do names of children known to you have religious and/or family significance?

SUGGESTIONS

With colleagues and children:

- Discuss one another's ideas about the questions above.
- If no naming ceremony has taken place, arrange one, either with members of the appropriate local religious congregation or by creating a personal secular celebration.
- Tell traditional stories about famous people (saints, gurus, gods, prophets, etc.) after whom children have been named, at bedtime, or during group story sessions, for example.
- Discover stories of family members after whom children have been named.
- Include these stories in life-story books.
- Include pictures and descriptions of naming ceremonies in life-story books.
- Provide published books and videos about famous people after whom children have been named.
- Encourage children to create books/pictures about famous people and family members whose names they share.
- Celebrate days on which famous people are commemorated.
- Enable and encourage children to attend celebrations for relations and friends, ensuring that appropriate gifts are taken or sent, and including welcoming and naming ceremonies.

Commitment

Once children are deemed capable of responsibility for their own decisions, they may be required to undertake in their own right the commitments made for them at birth. These rites of passage represent development from infantile dependence to the position of a young adult who can be expected to play a more responsible role in the life of the religious congregation.

In many religions, ceremonies take place in chronological and legal childhood, while the young person is still not credited with the ability to make such solemn commitments in other areas of life (for example, marriage, voting).

Islam includes no such 'coming of age'. Since babies are regarded as fully admitted to *fitrah* from birth, no declarations of commitment are required.

Every day should be lived according to Islamic beliefs as a celebration of commitment to Allah. However, the growing child is gradually admitted to full practice of the observances as age and strength permit. For example, the first fulfilment of *sawm* (fasting from dawn to dusk during the month of *Ramadan*) is usually delayed until puberty. Another important moment is the first attendance at *juma* (Friday prayers in the mosque).

Buddhism, too, includes no special ceremony to mark attainment of adulthood. In some traditions (for example, in Burma and Thailand), boys may take temporary ordination as monks and live in a *vihara* ('temple') for a while.

In contrast, transition to adulthood is the most significant rite of passage for Rastafarians, whose training from earliest childhood is towards mastery of doctrine, observances and oratorical skills, with the will and ability to live a pure and upright life. Young men begin to wear their hair in dreadlocks and exchange the designation 'Prince' for 'Kingman', while 'Princesses' become 'Empresses'.

Some religions provide important ceremonies to mark the young person's passage from infancy to full involvement in observances. Some include an item of dress. A Hindu boy aged between 8 and, usually, 12 undertakes *upanayana* ('initiation'), the tenth *samskara* (he must be a member of the upper castes – priest, warrior, merchant). A sacred thread comprising two separate links is hung over the left shoulder and tied below the waist on the right. Each link contains three cotton threads, each made of three strands. These threads may be seen as symbolising aspects of Brataman personified as Brahma, Vishnu and Shiva, united three in one. They can also signify both the constant, surrounding presence of God, and the need to control body, mind and speech. The sacred thread must never be removed, except for annual renewal or because it is dirty, when the old thread remains until replaced by the new thread.

A priest or religious teacher officiates at the boy's own home, and speaks sacred verses. The initiate undertakes to be celebate during this period, and to follow a period of religious study with a *guru*. He is a 'twice-born' Hindu, this second birth signifying passage from childhood to new responsibility and discipline. Not all Hindu boys of eligible caste undertake *upanayana*, choosing not to fulfil such requirements as vegetarian diet or religious study. In the UK, boys may delay *upanayana* until they have left school.

Upanayana involves wearing the thread, which may not be understood by people who have no knowledge of Hinduism. A sign of pride and commitment to the Hindu may stimulate embarrassment, even attract bullying. The outward sign demonstrates to the boy himself and to other Hindus that he has accepted commitment to the beliefs and observances of his faith; it confirms also his membership of a high caste.

For a Sikh boy, the garment which signifies his passage from childhood to adult status is the *pagri* ('turban'). When the boy can tie the turban himself, at about 11, his family organises the ceremony of *pagri bananan* at the *gurdwara* or at home. After readings from the holy book, the *Guru Granth Sahib*, a senior member of the congregation ties the *pagri* onto the boy's head. The congregation chants holy words in approval and joy. The family presents money and food to the *gurdwara*, and the boy receives gifts from parents and relations. He is now addressed as '*gabroo*' ('of marriageable age'), although by UK law he may be several years too young for marriage.

Young people over 16 may choose initiation into the *Khalsa* through the ceremony *Amrit Pahul*. *Khalsa* Sikhs of both sexes undertake to live according to Sikh teachings, to pray to only one God, and to serve the whole community. They must not smoke or take drugs, eat meat that has been prepared for religious purposes or commit adultery, and they should set a high standard of behaviour. They carry symbols of commitment known as the 'five Ks': *kesh* (uncut hair), *kara* (steel bracelet), *kanga* (comb), *kirpan* (small sword), *kaachs* (undershorts).

Initiates are baptised with *amrit* ('holy water') prepared from sugar and water, which has powerful connotations of spiritual transformation. They drink five times from *amrit* poured into their cupped hands. *Amrit* is then sprinkled onto their eyes and heads, five times each. Prayers of dedication are offered.

Young Jews attain religious adult status at puberty, usually 12 for girls and 13 for boys, and formally indicated by the appearance of two pubic hairs. Details of ceremonies differ; for example, while most Orthodox congregations permit only boys to become *bar mitzvah* ('son of the law or commandment'), Progressive, Reformed congregations celebrate the attainment of girls to *bat mitzvah* ('daughter of the law or commandment'). At this ceremony, young people publicly accept responsibility for their own observance of Jewish beliefs and practices.

The ceremony is held in the synagogue, and follows preparation with the *rabbi* and attendance at Hebrew classes. Boys wear the *tallith* (a fringed prayer shawl), *yarmulka* (a skull cap, which men must always wear in the synagogue) and *tefillin* (little boxes containing prayers). For the first time they read aloud from the Torah to the congregation and recite the *bar mitzvah* prayer. Girls also attend classes. At the ceremony, they recite together from Hebrew liturgy, then individually read from the scriptures about such great Jewish women as Deborah and Sarah. At home, relations and friends bring presents and share a meal.

For young Christians, the age of initiation depends on denomination. Roman Catholic children may take first communion from the age of 7. 'Communion' or 'eucharist' is the central feature of worship in most Christian denominations. Consecrated bread and wine are served to communicants; to some, these become the actual body and blood of Jesus, to others they are symbols. Permission to take communion indicates that the young person has been admitted to full membership of the Church.

Roman Catholics take first communion before being confirmed, but other denominations (for example, the Church of England) require confirmation first. Only people who have been baptised may be confirmed or take communion. The candidate for confirmation attends classes in preparation for accepting responsibility for the maintenance of religious and spiritual life undertaken by godparents at baptism. In denominations which have bishops, candidates from several churches within the diocese meet to make their public commitment and receive the bishop's blessing (signified by laying his hands on the head). Children wear new clothes for these ceremonies. Girls may wear white dresses, which in some denominations (for example, Roman Catholic) can be elaborate, making them resemble small brides.

Members of some denominations which do not christen infants practise adult baptism as the ceremony of commitment. Adult baptism is possible in any baptising denomination, and may, as in the Russian Orthodox tradition, be followed immediately by confirmation. Baptists and Pentecostalists practise total immersion in a special pool within the church. Adults of any age from the teens upwards may choose to be baptised when they feel ready to make such a commitment to God.

QUESTIONS

- Have children known to you been undertaken ceremonies through which they are acknowledged to be capable of fulfilling religious obligations?
- What are the implications to these ceremonies for life, both within the religious congregation and in secular society?
- Are children known to you enabled and encouraged to fulfil their religious obligations by attendance at a place of worship?
- Are children enabled and encouraged to fulfil religious obligations in their place of residence (for example, dietary, dress, worship requirements)?

SUGGESTIONS

With colleagues and children:

- Discuss one another's ideas about the questions above.
- Enable and encourage children who are interested to prepare for and undertake ceremonies when they reach appropriate age.
- Enable and encourage children to attend commitment celebrations for relations and friends, ensuring that appropriate gifts are taken.

- Include descriptions and pictures of ceremonies in life story books.
- Be aware that children may be teased or bullied because of behaviour/clothing associated with fulfilment of obligations following attainment of adulthood within a religious congregation.

Marriage

Since the legal age of marriage in the UK is 16 (with parental consent), it is possible for young people known to social work agencies to be (or have been) a bride or groom. More likely, their involvement in the rite of passage known as 'a wedding' is as bridal attendant or guest.

Weddings are important rites of passage which attract the attention and attendance of many members of the two principal families involved, together with friends and members of neighbourhood and work communities and religious congregations. Whatever its private and intimate importance to bride and groom, a wedding has significance for and impact on many other people. Not only the marrying pair change status: all their relations gain new 'in-laws'.

Although for many people weddings have deep religious as well as social significance, many others who do not profess any religious beliefs choose to marry at a place of worship using the ceremony associated with the religious tradition in which they were born.

In terms of Van Gennep's formulation, the whole wedding is itself a 'passage', an event out of the ordinary bringing together people who do not ordinarily meet, in best (often new) clothes, to take part in a ceremony and eat special food. For many it is an event designed to be remembered with photographs and videos, anniversaries, presents and commemorative blessings. Crossing the threshold into marriage is a rite whose significance is reinforced frequently and in many ways.

The pre-liminal state for bride and groom is the period of engagement and preparation. Even when they are already living together, the time before the wedding, when the intention publicly to declare commitment has been made, has a special significance. It is possible that the decision to change status so disturbs the partnership that the relationship ends. For even the quietest wedding, plans and decisions must be made, and the couple becomes the centre of attention. The liminal state is the wedding itself: in the course of a ceremony prescribed by secular and/or religious authorities, the couple and their relations change status. The post-liminal state is the entry into married life, including sexual and domestic as well as relationship implications.

The central ceremony – to be planned, looked forward to, attended and remembered – is important for all participants, not least children, who may be closely related to bride and groom and may play important roles – for example, as bridesmaids.

Novelist Carson McCullers (1962) explores the impact of a wedding on 12-year-old Frankie, who feels 'unjoined' from the rest of the world, a member of no club, and conscious of disturbing changes in herself. Longing for some place and purpose, she attaches her hope for identity to her brother's wedding:

> ... when the old question came to her – the who she was and what she would be in the world, and why she was standing there that minute – when the old question came to her, she did not feel hurt and unanswered. At last she knew just who she was and understood where she was going. She loved her brother and the bride and she was a member of the wedding. (p.7)

This particular wedding is to be in a Christian church in the USA, but the girl's feelings have universal resonance, reflected in the experience of young people of many religious traditions, and none. For Frankie, full engagement in the wedding has deep significance. Unfortunately, she really wants to be a member of the marriage rather than the wedding, but whatever her understanding of and investment in the event, it is for her, as well as her brother, a rite of passage. She returns home changed.

Although the religious aspect of the ceremony is not overtly important to her, she is involved spiritually and emotionally, and the events of the wedding before, during and after affect her whole life and self-concept.

Attendance at a wedding may be a child's first conscious experience of people making a solemn commitment. It also offers reinforcement of the customs and values of the family, social and religious group. The ceremony may be invested with deep religious significance, but it may be only the opportunity for dressing up and fulfilling certain ritual actions. The wedding may be seen as desirable in itself, not so much a rite of passage as an event at which (mainly) girls can star.

QUESTIONS

- Have any children known to you been married in religious and/or secular ceremonies?
- Are any children known to you expected to marry while under 18 according to the convention of their religion?
- What do children known to you expect of marriage?
- What do children known to you expect of weddings?
- What part do children (other than bride and groom) play in weddings

associated with religious traditions know to you, and secular ceremonies?
- What do children learn about their own lives and the values and traditions of their families and religious groups by attending weddings?

SUGGESTIONS

With colleagues and children:

- Discuss one another's ideas about the questions above.
- Enable and encourage children to attend weddings of relations and friends, ensuring that appropriate gifts are taken/sent.
- Enable and encourage children to take part in wedding ceremonies as, for example, bridesmaids.
- Include descriptions and pictures of family weddings in life-story books and personal photograph collections.
- Provide published books showing pictures of and information about weddings in a number of traditions.
- Use public and private weddings to stimulate discussion of marriage customs and beliefs.

Death

All religions have important ceremonies at the time of death to help both the dying person and relations. Children may themselves die or be bereaved, and full engagement in the rites of their religions can offer consolation through connection with co-religionists.

Beliefs about the destination of the soul underlie the whole approach to life and death, including correct disposal of the body. For some children, beliefs and observances may be mystifying and/or terrifying, especially if anxieties cannot be discussed. For others, religious traditions may bring reassurance and consolation.

In some traditions, sons have particular responsibilities in the death rituals of their parents. Many believe that correct performance of death and funeral obligations influences the future welfare of the soul. Roman Catholics, for example, believe that prayer can reduce the period spent by a soul in Purgatory.

The eldest son of a Hindu washes his father's body, rubbing in sandalwood and whispering the name of God in his ear, preparing the soul for its next journey. He is also required to light the funeral pyre or press the button to start cremation in the crematorium. Hindu adults are always cremated, but young children and infants are usually buried. An oil lamp is kept burning in the room with the dead person. White is the colour associated with mourning. Children are involved in cremation and mourning ceremonies and anniversary ceremonies for dead parents, grandparents and great-grandparents. Hindus believe that the soul moves to a new body (not necessarily human or even animal), to be born again and complete a new life cycle.

Jewish families (including children) remain at home for seven days after a death (sitting *shivah*); every evening a service is held, concluding with mourners' *kaddish*, recited by the eldest son, and a *yahrzeit* ('remembrance') candle is kept burning. Other commemorative observances follow, including at anniversaries of the death, when a *yahrzeit* candle is lit and mourners' *kaddish* recited. Cremation may be practised in some progressive communities, but burial is prescribed in traditional communities. Rabbinic literature describes life in this world as preparation in a corridor before entering the hall to which death is the door. The soul spends a period in the purgatory of *gehinnom* before rising to heaven, helped by the recital of *kaddish*.

For Sikhs, death is the ultimate reality, a gradual transition to the next state of being, depending on the life just ending, as the soul moves to rebirth in a new body or progresses to heaven. Funeral rituals are fulfilled by sons, who are responsible for lighting the funeral pyre. During the funeral feast, the oldest son performs *pagri* ('turban'): in the presence of the *Guru Granth Sahib*, he receives a new turban from his maternal uncle, symbolising his new status as head of the household. Sikhs are cremated. White is the colour associated with mourning. A ceremony (*bhaug*) is held ten days after death.

Rastafarians have no ceremony, believing that death is a sign that the individual has strayed from the path of righteousness. They avoid contact with death, and may avoid funerals even of loved relations.

For Buddhists, a funeral is not sad or sombre; rather, it is an opportunity to remember the dead person's good qualities with love and warmth as the life energies pass from the physical body to a new form of life which may be repeated many times before attainment of *nirvana* (union with the Eternal Buddha). Buddhists are usually cremated.

Many Christians believe in the continuing existence of the soul in heaven or hell with, for Roman Catholics, an interim in Purgatory. Those who believe in physical resurrection at the second coming of Jesus, 'the Last Judgement', refuse cremation, but most regard this doctrine as of symbolic rather than literal significance. Russian Orthodox worshippers bring the open coffin into the church, demonstrating that the dead person is still a member of the congregation. Funerals are conducted around the open coffin, and attenders, including children, kiss the body. For many Christians, the funeral or later memorial service is an opportunity to celebrate the life of the dead person.

Like some Christians, Muslims believe in the resurrection of the body at the Day of Judgement, when the good will go to heaven while those who have not obeyed divine guidance are condemned to hell. Dying Muslims should be able to sit up or lie facing Mecca. Following the fulfilment of certain traditions, Muslims are buried facing Mecca. Mourning lasts for about a month.

QUESTIONS

- Have any children known to you experienced death of relations or friends?
- Are any children known to you dying or seriously ill?
- Have any children known to you attended ceremonies associated with dying, funerals and/or mourning?
- What are your beliefs and observations regarding death and future existence?
- What are the beliefs and observances regarding death and future existence of religions with which children are associated?
- How are these understood by children?
- What parts are children known to you expected to play in parents' funeral rites?

SUGGESTIONS

With colleagues and children:

- Discuss one another's ideas about the questions above.
- Enable and encourage children to attend funerals and fulfil other obligations as appropriate and according to their clearly expressed preferences.
- Become familiar with some of the excellent introductory texts available.
- It is often difficult for children to understand beliefs about death and future existence. Ensure that information is available when children show interest and/or display anxiety.
- Children may be frightened by ideas about death and future existence particularly when misunderstood. Be aware that children may be suffering anxiety and fear which are difficult to express.
- Include descriptions of death ceremonies of relations/friends in life-story books.
- Make a chart/calendar of monthly/annual memorial obligations.
- Read Part 5 and Chapter 16 of this book.

Summary

Ways in which families and communities celebrate and commemorate great transitions of life and death demonstrate and reinforce their beliefs. Events which are taken for granted when daily life within the family goes smoothly assume new significance if that life is disrupted, especially if children are separated from their home and family, perhaps because they are in care, hospital or penal establishment.

Practitioners need access to information about beliefs and observances of religious groups with which children with whom they work are associated.

Information about and understanding of significance and customs associated with rites of passage enriches both day-to-day care and long-term planning. It also enables recognition of anxieties and fears, and increases opportunities for effective communication and helping.

Respect for children's family and religious backgrounds reinforces respect for children themselves, and helps to strengthen a sense of identity.

Aspects of ceremonies, celebrations and commemorations associated with the great life transitions of birth and naming, commitment, marriage and death can be incorporated in social work activities, including life-story books.

7 Fasts and festivals

Children, fasts and festivals

The religious or liturgical year is characterised by annual commemorations and celebrations of the beliefs of individual religions, often based on events in the lives and deaths of deities, *gurus* or saints. Some fasts and festivals dominate not only the sacred but also the secular calendar, and have significance for people who are not members of the particular (or any) religious congregation – for example, in the UK Christmas and Easter are celebrated by many people who are not practising Christians.

Associated with religious beliefs are references to the rhythm of the natural year: for example, people who are not Christians but who celebrate Christmas may be seen as continuing the tradition of those who enjoy a midwinter feast of light and mark the birth of a new year. In December, Jews celebrate *Chanucah*, when special lights are lit, and Sikhs celebrate the birthday of the 10th guru, Gobind Singh. Hindus and Sikhs celebrate other festivals of light in November.

Secular celebrations separate the enjoyment and indulgence of festivals from such religiously observed periods of preparation as the Christian fasts of Advent and Lent which precede Christmas and Easter. However, liturgical festivals cannot be regarded as independent of periods of fasting: the annual pattern includes both. For Muslims, for example, both fasting during the month of *Ramadan* and celebrating *Eid ul Fitr* (the festival of fast-breaking) are essential.

Children brought up in any religion learn the pattern of fasts and festivals, looking forward to those which involve gifts and parties, and taking part in rituals within the family and at the place of worship. These annual events offer information about traditions and beliefs, reinforcing (through repetition of not only the event itself, but also customs, songs, gifts, cards, meals, ritual dialogues) the form, framework and history of the religion, and a sense of connection between present worshippers and those of the past.

When children live with their birth families, observance of and participation in fasts and festivals may be taken for granted. The importance and meaning of these events is demonstrated within the routine of everyday life. However, if children are separated from their homes and communities, the pattern may be lost.

Children living apart from their families may find festival times difficult, for example being unable to express reactions to missing a family celebration or feeling disorientated and isolated as the religious/spiritual texture of everyday life disappears. A Jewish boy in a gentile foster home was described by a social worker as 'indifferent' when asked if he wished to celebrate *Pesach* (Passover) (DoH 1992, p.134). Perhaps his family was non-observant, but equally, the practitioner may not have understood the significance of this festival, essentially a family-centred celebration. Apparent indifference may mask reluctance to reveal true feelings or respond truthfully to questions about sensitive matters.

Participation in fasts and festivals has personal, individual significance as children gain both spiritual and social experience, learning and becoming part of the inner and outer expressions of belief of their religious congregations. Consequently, preventing them joining fully and easily in celebrations may injure the development of their sense of identity, of connection with the culture of their birth. While they should never be forced to take part in religious ceremonies or any other forms of observance, children should receive opportunity and encouragement.

Practitioners need access to information about patterns of fasts and festivals associated with the religious beliefs and observances of the children with whom they work. This can both increase understanding of individual children and their religions, and enrich the life of foster and adoptive families, and residential, day and hospital units as new celebrations are introduced.

It may be appropriate to invite parents, siblings and other relations to join special meals and exchange gifts, or for children to visit home or friends to join in family celebrations. Practitioners associated with different (or no) religions may accompany children to places of worship, demonstrating respect for and interest in this aspect of their lives. Cards and other mementoes may be collected and stored carefully, and descriptions and pictures of festivals included in life-story books.

The purpose of this chapter is to introduce brief summaries of some commemorations and celebrations which have particular significance for children.

Special birthdays

Guru Nanak's birthday

The most important festival in the Sikh calendar celebrates the birthday (in 1496) of Guru Nanak, who founded the Sikh religion. Such festivals are called *gurpurbs*, and begin with continuous reading from the holy book, the *Guru Granth Sahib*, at the *gurdwara*. On the last day of the festival, Sikhs of all ages join in the usual worship, which may be augmented by speakers and visiting musicians. The regular free meal served in the *langar* is eaten by all who attend in a festive mood, and celebrations may last all day. In India, the *Guru Granth Sahib* is carried in procession through the streets, but this is not always possible in the UK. The birthday of the 10th guru, Gobind Singh (in Patna in 1666) is celebrated on 22 December.

Christmas

The most popular festival in the Christian year in the UK is Christmas, whereas for many Christians the most important festival is Easter. The festival is preceded by the month-long fast of Advent, during which Christians prepare to celebrate the birth of Jesus as the son of God on 25 December, near the winter solstice. Members of Orthodox Churches celebrate it in January. Rastafarians follow the custom of the Ethiopian Church and celebrate on 7 January, although they focus on the life and work of Jesus, not his birth.

Because this festival is associated with birth, children are often the centre of attention, giving and receiving presents and cards. Choirboys and girls often take a special part in carol services in which hymns welcome the birth of Jesus. Some churches hold Christingle services, at which children carry oranges decorated with candles, nuts, raisins and red ribbons, symbolising the world, light, food and the blood of Jesus who was crucified. At school and/or church, children may take part in Nativity plays which tell stories about the birth of Jesus. Cribs (models representing these stories) may be displayed in churches. Christmas cards often show scenes from the Nativity, with the baby Jesus as the central figure.

Vesak or Buddha Day

Buddhists of the Theravada tradition celebrate this festival on the day of the full moon in May, commemorating the birth, Enlightenment and passing of Gautama Siddhartha (Buddha). A full day's programme at the *vihara* (temple) includes a service, teaching, meditation, *dana* (almsgiving to the monks) and a communal meal. In Japan, the birth is celebrated in April, at *Hana Matsuri*, when images of the baby are washed in an infusion of hydrangea leaves.

The birthday of His Imperial Majesty Haile Selassie I

Rastafarians celebrate this birthday on 23 July and, as on the anniversary of his coronation (2 November), all generations join a day of Nyabinghi drumming, hymns and prayers. The birthday of Marcus Garvey, a Jamaican who taught that all black people should return to Africa and predicted the coronation of Emperor Haile Selassie I as king and saviour of all black people, is celebrated on 17 August.

Janashmati

The birthday of Lord Krishna is celebrated by Hindus on the night of the new moon in August–September. Everyone, including children, fasts all day until midnight, the time of Krishna's birth. In the *mandir* (temple) a special shrine is made. Celebrations begin when a little model of baby Krishna crawling is bathed in a mixture of curd, milk, dried fruit and tulsi leaves called *charnamrita*. A decorated cradle is rocked by worshippers. *Arati* is performed by moving a lamp in circles and throwing flower petals, and the fast is broken by sharing *prasada* (symbolic food). Hymns celebrate the love of Yasoda for her foster son, Krishna, whom she protected from the threat of murder by his uncle.

Eid-Milad ul-Nabi

The twelfth day of the Muslim month Rabee-ul-Awwal marks both the birth and death of Mohammed, the last prophet through whom Allah revealed himself. A Muslim community in the UK may process through the streets to the mosque, where worship includes an address celebrating the life and teachings of the prophet. This may be followed by a feast, and Muslims should give to charity. At home, all members of the family join in telling stories about Mohammed.

Periods of fasting, reflection and preparation

Ramadan and Eid-ul-fitr

During the lunar ninth of *Ramadan* (ninth month of the Muslim lunar calendar) healthy Muslims over 12 may not eat or drink during the hours of daylight. *Sawm* (fasting) is one of the Five Pillars of Islam. The period begins and ends with the first appearance of the new moon. During *Ramadan*, the prophet Mohammed, while fasting and praying, was told by the angel Jibrail that he was to be the messenger of Allah. The messages of this and later visions were recorded in the Holy Qur'an, and the night of Mohammed's first visions is celebrated during *Ramadan* on *Lailat-ul-Quadr* (the Night of Power). Many Muslims spend the whole night in the mosque. The end of the month of fasting is celebrated on Eid-ul-Fitr, the first day of the month Shawwal.

Rosh Hashanah and *Yom Kippur*

The Jewish New Year begins on the first day of the month Tishri (September/October) and is marked by ten days known as the High Holy Days, the Days of Awe or the ten Days of Repentance. The first two days constitute *Rosh Hashanah*, when Jews repent of anything wrong in their lives. Children do not attend school. The preceding month of Elul is a preparation for *Rosh Hashanah*, with special customs in the synagogue, such as blowing the *shofar* (ram's horn). On the two nights of *Rosh Hashanah* itself, special family meals include a loaf baked in the shape of a ladder, symbolising the desire that prayers may rise to God, and recalling Jacob's ladder from earth to heaven. Other symbols decorating the loaf are a bird or crown. Honey is customarily served. On the first afternoon of *Rosh Hashanah*, Jews perform *Taslich*. On the bank of a river or stream they recite a prayer for forgiveness, then shake dust and fluff from their pockets, or some breadcrumbs, into the water, symbolising throwing away old sins and beginning a new life in the New Year.

    Yom Kippur (the Day of Atonement) is the tenth day of the month, and is set aside especially for asking God's forgiveness for sin. Jews fast for 24 hours from sunset on the preceding day. Children under 13 may fast for shorter periods. Observances during this period include services at the synagogue which end with a loud blast on the *shofar*.

Advent and Lent

Christians observe two periods of preparation, although nowadays most do not fast. Some may voluntarily abstain from meat or some luxury. Advent prepares for the coming of Jesus, and comprises the four weeks before Christmas. Special hymns may be sung, and children may enjoy opening little doors or windows on Advent calendars, one a day.

Lent is the period of 40 days preceding the festival of Easter. Christians reflect on the life and death of Jesus. In some churches, statues are shrouded. Events in the last days of Jesus's life are commemorated: for example, the fourth Sunday in Lent is called Palm Sunday, remembering his entry into Jerusalem. The last day before Lent is Shrove Tuesday (or Mardi Gras), which is well known as a day for carnivals; traditional food in the UK is the pancake. On Ash Wednesday, the first day of Lent, many Christians go to church to ask forgiveness for sins and to receive the sign of the cross traced in ashes on the forehead.

The fourth week is Holy Week. Maundy Thursday remembers the Last Supper of Jesus and his close friends, which is commemorated in the Eucharist or Holy Communion. As Jesus was a Jew, the Last Supper was a *seder*, the ritual meal at *Pesach*. Good Friday is the most solemn day in the Christian year, commemorating the crucifixion of Jesus. In some churches a model tomb is guarded by young boys. Three-hour-long services are often held, marking the time it took Jesus to die. Christians continue to mourn throughout Saturday while Jesus remained in the tomb. Many Churches hold services of vigil from Saturday evening into Sunday, which is Easter Day. The dates of Lent and Easter vary every year; Orthodox Churches observe these ceremonies later than Churches of the Roman tradition. On Good Friday it is traditional to eat hot cross buns (sweet buns made with dried fruit and marked with a cross).

Great events in the history of the religion

Holi

The Hindu festival of *Holi* is a celebration of spring at the full moon in the month of Phalguna (February/March). One story tells of the victory of Krishna over the demon Putana, who had been sent by his wicked uncle to kill the baby god. Putana took the form of a wetnurse, but Krishna recognised her evil nature and sucked away the life from her breast; her body was cremated. Through this story, Hindus celebrate the destruction of the enemies of all children, and the victory of good over evil. At *Holi*, families visit the temple, where statues of Krishna and his wife, Radha, have been washed in scented water, dressed and decorated. Worshippers clap their hands, sing hymns to Lord Krishna and perform *arati*. Then *prashad* (blessed food) is served before a huge bonfire is lit.

Purim

This boisterous March festival celebrates the deliverance of Jews from persecution by Haman during exile in Persia, through the agency of Esther, consort of King Ahasuerus and niece of the wise Jew Mordecai. Children often act plays (perhaps at school), and both children and adults may attend parties at which fancy dress representing the characters in the story is worn.

Easter

After crucifixion and entombment, Jesus rose from death and was seen by many of his friends. This is a day of great rejoicing, and is celebrated with special services in Christian churches which have been decorated with flowers. For many this is the most important day in the year. The name 'Easter' comes from a pre-Christian goddess of spring, and the symbols and customs celebrate new life – for example, Easter eggs and cards showing birds and flowers. Traditional foods include simnel cakes decorated with marzipan and sugar eggs.

Pesach

The Jewish festival of *Pesach* (Passover) extends for eight days during the month of Nisan, and is a family celebration with many symbols and customs. It commemorates the escape of the Israelites from oppression in Egypt in the time of Moses. Throughout *Pesach*, no yeast is eaten, and bread is replaced by *matzoth* (plain biscuits). On the first two evenings the *seder* (a special meal) includes a dish containing symbolic foods. Children play a special part. The youngest child asks four questions, which are answered by the father reading the story of the escape from Egypt. Later, children seek a hidden piece of *matzah*; the finder is rewarded, and all share the found morsel.

Raksha Bandan

This festival, celebrated in the month of Sravana (July–August), has special significance for Hindu brothers and sisters. *Raksha* means 'protection', and the festival reinforces the duty of brothers to protect their sisters. One story remembers how the god Vishnu gave the wife of the god Indra a thread to put on his wrist to protect Indra against attack. Another story tells how Padding, a Hindu queen, gained protection from a Muslim emperor to whom she had sent a *rakhi* (decorated thread). At *Raksha Bandan*, sisters tie *rakhi* around their brothers' wrists and give sweets. In return, brothers give money and promise protection.

Diwali

Both Hindus and Sikhs celebrate *Diwali*, a festival of light, in October–November. For Hindus, this marks the new religious year and commemorates the victory of Rama and Sita over evil. Lakshmi (goddess of wealth) is also worshipped.

Sikhs celebrate an event which took place during the Hindu festival. Hargobind became the sixth *guru* in 1606, but was soon imprisoned, together with 52 Hindu princes. Eventually, the Muslim emperor ordered the release of Hargobind, but he would leave only with the princes. The emperor instructed that only those princes who could pass through a narrow gate while holding onto the *guru*'s clothing might leave. Hargobind's cloak was fringed with long tassels, one for every prince. Thus everyone could leave the prison while obeying the emperor. This occurred during *Diwali*. Every room is illuminated with *diwas* (little lamps). For two days before the festival, Sikhs read the *Guru Granth Sahib* in the *gurdwara*, then *prashad* is shared. More special food is eaten at home, and children receive gifts. In the evening, bonfires and fireworks are lit.

QUESTIONS

- Do children known to you know the stories and customs of fasts and festivals of their own religions?
- Are children known to you enabled and encouraged to fulfil special roles in religious fasts and festivals?
- Some religious fasts and festivals focus on children with, for example, gifts, food, celebration of childhood; how can children who are separated from their families and religious congregations be enabled to enjoy these?

SUGGESTIONS

With colleagues and children:

- Discuss one another's ideas about the questions above.
- Enable and encourage children to attend religious services associated with fasts and festivals.
- Explore ways for children living apart from their own families to take part in family based celebrations.
- Ensure that children are enabled to observe fasting traditions, as appropriate to age and state of health.
- If children are unable to join family celebrations, provide gifts, cards and food as appropriate.

- If children are unable to visit home, invite relations/friends to special meals.
- Obtain a calendar of religious and other fasts/festivals.
- With children, make a calendar of their own/other religious and other festivals.
- Be aware of and show interest in celebrations of religious festivals in schools.
- Provide story books and pictures about festivals, and ensure that appropriate stories are told at festival times.
- Include stories and pictures in life-story books, especially of any festivals on or near children's birthdays.
- Help children to keep cards and other mementoes of festivals, and store them carefully, in a scrap book, for example.

Summary

Fasts and festivals provide a regular and recurring structure to the year, whether sacred or secular. Both preparation and celebration are important to members of religious congregations, focusing attention on fundamental aspects of belief and observances. Through participation in great annual events, children can develop identity both with local religious congregations and the historical context of their religion.

While children are living within their birth families, observance of fasts and festivals can be taken for granted. For children separated from their families, for whatever reason, the texture of annual events, including religious observance and family custom, may be interrupted. Celebrations which belong within the family and in which children have a particular role may not be transferable into another context, especially if the residential establishment or foster family does not practise the same religion.

Respect for children's family and religious background reinforces respect for children themselves, and helps to strengthen a sense of identity.

Summaries of some fasts and festivals in which children are especially involved offer a model for gaining further information (see also Chapter 15).

8 Worship

Children and worship

The basis of most religious observance is worship of a deity (or deities). Form, expression and location of worship vary between religions, denominations and individual worshippers.

Within Christianity, for example, Roman Catholics usually decorate churches with statues of Jesus, the Virgin Mary and saints, and services are based on a set form of prayers and Bible readings. At points during the service, worshippers make the sign of the cross (touching themselves on forehead, breast and shoulders) and stand or kneel. The most solemn moment is when a priest administers communion, placing a small wafer or piece of bread on the communicant's tongue, and distributing sips of sacramental wine. When praying alone, they may count repetitions of prayers on a rosary, pushing a small bead along a looped thread at every repetition (such strings of beads are also used by Buddhists and Muslims). Roman Catholics often wear pendants in the form of a cross, and in their homes display model crucifixes (crosses) bearing figures of the dying Jesus, and pictures with religious significance (see Chapter 9).

Members of the Religious Society of Friends (Quakers) hold Meetings for Worship in a simple room without any statues, pictures or other symbols of faith, sometimes in a private house or hired hall. They sit in silence for an hour, during which some people may 'give ministry' (speak according to leading by the Spirit of God). There is no priest and liturgy or order of service. When Quakers pray at home, they do so in silence.

Although their practices are so different, the worship of both Roman Catholics and Quakers is within the Christian tradition. Worship is natural for humans, even when they do not believe in a deity. For example, people may experience strong feelings of awe or reverence on mountains and in forests, and a great sense of joy and praise on a beautiful spring morning or at the birth of a baby. Worship need not be confined to organised religious observance.

When forms of worship are integral to a religion, adherents (including children) fulfil their obligations corporately (at the place of worship), within the family, and individually. When no form of worship is desired or required, it is important that children should be encouraged to experience and express 'natural worship'.

Worship may be said to describe: 'patterns of human behaviour, expressing what people believe to be the most important aspects of life. In worship the meaning of life, death and the universe crystallises out in prayers and other devotional activity' (Davies 1994d, p.3).

Worship comprises such components as thanksgiving, praise and repentance. Formal and informal expression may be through prayer, physical position and movement (including dance), reading and reciting sacred scriptures, and silence. Music holds a central position in most religious traditions. For example:

> In Hinduism the very idea of the sound of a *mantra* or sacred verse is of fundamental importance, in the belief that it reflects something of the sound which lies at the centre of all reality. The *mantra* is, in a sense, a meaning in sound. To repeat it is to engage in an activity that brings benefit to the devotee. In a similar way the use of chanting in Buddhism, as a means of meditating on sacred scriptures, achieves a similar end. It is through chanting or rhythmic recitation that many sacred scriptures are learned, and become an immeasurably important resource for the worship both of communities and individuals. This is also true in Judaism, in Islam and in Sikhism. Within the Christian tradition, worship very largely takes place through the medium of music. Liturgies are sung or chanted and the hymns of Christendom have become one of its major developments over the last two hundred years. (Davies 1994d, p.5)

Worship in evangelical Christian Churches is particularly characterised by powerful, often lively singing.

In some religious traditions, observances are associated with such disciplines as praying at certain hours and in prescribed positions. Failure to fulfil obligations may lead to internal guilt and/or external censure, including threat/fear of divine displeasure.

Concepts of worship differ radically and subtly, both between and within religions, depending on and identifying 'the central concern of a religion, pinpointing its meaning and focusing the significance of people's religious life' (Davies 1994d, p.3).

Davies (1994c, p.1) notes that 'Among the most visible aspects of religions are those sacred places either built as ritual arenas or else selected from nature through association with the history and myths of a religion ... even when a religion wishes all life-contexts to be sacred' (for example, Hinduism, Islam, Sikhism). He instances as sacred places 'a small domestic shrine, as in Hindu households, or a single crucifix in a Roman Catholic family home'. Most religions either require or encourage fulfilment of devotional activities, both within the home and at a place of worship, sometimes purpose-built, sometimes a secular hall or private house. Both settings are illustrated in this chapter.

In addition, most religions identify 'a framework of sites of special historical significance, especially those where some crucial revelation was obtained by a religion's founder' (Davies 1994c, p.1). Such sacred places may comprise whole cities, such as Mecca and Medina (Islam), Amritsar (Sikhism) and Jerusalem, with its multi-religious associations and shrines. For example, shrines commemorating miraculous events and appearances of deities or saints, like holy cities, form the destination of pilgrimages during which devotees seek merit or miracles. Muslims, for example, aim at least once in a lifetime to complete the *hajj* (pilgrimage to Mecca, birthplace of Mohammed), one of the Five Pillars of Islam. This chapter does not discuss such sacred places (see Davies 1994c).

Children separated from their families and communities may find difficulty in fulfilling the obligation and/or desire to worship. Even short absences may inhibit praying, washing/eating customs or attendance at the place of worship. Even children living within their birth families may experience reluctance to fulfil all the observances required by parents and religious leaders. Encouragement is needed, and the sense that what is done is natural and important to the family.

Practitioners who do not share the beliefs of children need information about the particular practices of individual families within the context of the religion. For example, some (but not all) Christian families say grace (pray before meals): some repeat a preferred form of words, some pause in silence before eating, some give thanks afterwards.

It may be difficult for those who are caring for children to introduce and encourage religious observances with which they do not themselves agree. However, maintenance of regular repetition of prayer and attendance at place of worship may be invaluable in helping children to retain and develop the sense of identity so often damaged at times of strain and separation. Spiritual strength and well-being may also be nurtured.

Worship within the home

Daily worship usually includes prayer, formal and/or informal, and often associated with a regular, repeated pattern. Particular observances within any religion differ between denominations, sects, castes and other groups; the following examples are broad illustrations only, offering guidance for practitioners to learn details about the religious obligations of individual children.

For some children, prayer at home is essentially private, and may be silent. For others, praying is a corporate activity associated with other members of the family and led by a parent. For some, the day is marked by regular, designated periods of prayer. For others, praying is linked with such ordinary events as meals and bedtime. Prayers may be repetitions of prescribed forms or spontaneous conversations with a deity.

Many children are associated with no religion but have a strong sense of worship and a need to practise it. This might be expressed in celebrating (perhaps boisterously) the first snow, or really seeing, for the first time, the details of a flower or the colours in a gas jet.

Christian children often say grace before and/or after meals, giving thanks for food and other blessings for family, friends, and sometimes pets. Older children may pray privately and in silence, perhaps asking for help with difficult relationships and anxieties. The conventional position for praying is kneeling with hands together and eyes closed, but many Christians sit, and grace is usually said standing or sitting at table. Books of prayers are available, but families often make up their own. Roman Catholic children repeat the 'Hail Mary' (addressed to the mother of Jesus), and children of many denominations may say the 'Lord's Prayer':

Hail Mary

Hail Mary, full of grace,
The Lord is with thee,
Blessed art thou among women and blessed is the fruit of thy womb Jesus,
Holy Mary, Mother of God, pray for us sinners now and at the hour of our death.

The Lord's Prayer

Our Father in heaven, hallowed by your name,
Your kingdom come, your will be done, on earth as in heaven,
Give us today our daily bread,
Forgive us our sins, as we forgive those who sin against us,
Lead us not into temptation but deliver us from evil,
For the kingdom, the power and the glory are yours now and forever, Amen.

Repetition of such a prayer may offer the security of contact with something familiar associated with home, even if children do not have a sense of connection with God.

Jewish children may also pray before and after eating, thanking God for providing sustenance. Prayers on waking and before sleeping include the *Shema*:

Shema

Hear, O Israel: the Lord our God is one Lord; and you shall love the Lord your God with all your heart, and with all your soul, and with all your might (Deuteronomy 6:4–5).

This is usually the first Hebrew a child learns, and Jews are instructed to 'teach [these words] diligently to your children, and … talk of them when you sit in your house' (Deuteronomy 6:6–9); they should be the last words spoken before death.

By the age of 13, boys pray with *tefillin* (leather boxes containing biblical verses tied onto their forehead and arm to symbolise mind and heart). They also wear *tallitot* or *tallisim* (prayer shawls) and cover their heads, often with *yarmulkas* (skull caps).

The most important day of the week is the Sabbath ('rest'), from sunset on Friday until sunset on Saturday. It commemorates the day on which God rested after creating the universe, and Jews observe the fourth commandment of the prophet Moses: 'Remember the Sabbath day, to keep it holy. Six days you shall labour and do all your work; but the seventh day is a sabbath to the Lord your God' (Exodus 20:8–11). The house must be prepared for the beginning of Sabbath, clean and tidy, the table laid with flowers, best crockery and glasses and polished candlesticks. Candles are lit, and the *kiddush* (a blessing) is said over the wine by the father. He blesses God, the Sabbath, his children and the *hallot* (special loaves), and thanks his wife for all her work. After the meal everyone gives thanks to God.

At times of fast and festival, children are fully involved in family worship and traditions (see Chapter 7).

For Muslim children, prayer is one of the foundations of life, the Five Pillars of Islam. Muslims over the age of 10 are required to say *salat*, praying five times a day. These prayers express the intention to follow the purity and eternal nature of Allah and to control temptation. *Salat* must be performed facing Mecca, the city now in Saudi Arabia where the prophet Mohammed was born. For Muslims in the UK this is in a south-easterly direction. *Salat* is performed on a prayer mat.

Before praying, Muslims perform *wudu* (ablution). The importance of cleanliness is emphasised in the Qur'an: 'Surely Allah loves those who repent and keep clean' (2:222).

Wudu and *salat*

'In the name of Allah the most merciful, the most kind.'

Wash hands to the wrist; rinse mouth three times; wash nostrils and tip of nose three times; wash face three times from right to left and forehead to throat; wash each arm three times; pass wet hands from forehead to neck; clean ears and behind ears; clean nape of neck; wash feet and ankles.

'I bear witness that there is no God but Allah and I bear witness that Mohammed is his servant and messenger.'

The call to prayer; turn to face Mecca. *Salat* is said in a prescribed sequence of positions (slightly different for women).

1   *'Allahu akbar.'* ('Allah is great') [Recite while standing with arms raised.]
2   'O Allah, glory and praise are for you and blessed is your name and exalted is your majesty; there is no God but you. I seek shelter in Allah from the rejected Satan. In the name of Allah, the most merciful, the most kind.'

[Standing with hands together;' recite chapter of Qur'an.]

3   *'Allahu akbar*, Glory to my Lord, the great.' [Repeat three times, bowing from waist.]
4   'Allah hears those who praise him. Our Lord, praise be to you.' [Recite while standing, head bent.]
5   *'Allahu akbar*. Glory to my Lord, the highest.' [Repeat three times, kneeling, head to floor.]
6   *'Allahu akbar.'* [Rest, then prostrate yourself on the floor, repeating 5 above.]
7   *'Allah akbar.'* [Recite while rising to feet.]

(adapted from Aylett 1991, pp.14–15)

Du'ah (other prayers) may be made at any time. Special prayers are said on Friday when Muslims attend the mosque.

Hindus also wash thoroughly before *puja* (worship), which is centred in the home, sometimes in a special room, sometimes a shrine in a corner of the kitchen or on a shelf. Pictures and images of deities include those of the *kula devata* (family deity) and *ishta devata* (personal deity), for example Krishna or Ganesha, which are all personifications of One Reality.

Puja is usually performed in the morning and evening by the mother on behalf of her family: she lights lamps and offers incense, flowers and foods to the deities. Finally, she performs *arati*, moving a lighted oil lamp in circles before the shrine. Prayers, hymns and passages of scriptures are chosen. Then *prasada* (blessed food) is shared.

Hindus seek to pray and/or meditate at least daily, and sometimes three times a day. Prayers first praise and thank God, then ask help. Morning *puja* often ends with a *mantra* from a scripture, for example:

> Peace be in the heavens; peace be on earth.
> May the waters flow peacefully.
> May all the divine powers bring us peace.
> And may that peace come to us.
> Aum. Peace. Peace. Peace. (from Aylett 1992, p.33)

Sikhs perform *puja* as a family group at home in the morning and last thing at night, saying the *nit-nem* (set prayers which form the 'daily rule'). In the morning there is also a *hukum* (a reading from the *Guru Granth Sahib* or a smaller collection of hymns). Sikhs also pray individually in silence, sometimes meditating on the scriptures and aspects of their beliefs and teachings.

Buddhists meditate too. They do not worship a deity, but worship is none the less essential, in the form of meditation and reflection on the life of Gautama Buddha and the *Dhamma* (his teachings). Buddhists identify Four Noble Truths from these teachings, and strive to observe the Noble Eightfold path:

Four Noble Truths

All life includes suffering.
The origin of suffering is craving (or greed).
If craving ceases, suffering will also cease.
The way to achieve this is to follow the Noble Eightfold Path. (based on Thompson 1993, p.9)

Noble Eightfold Path

Right understanding.
Right thoughts.
Right speech.
Right actions.
Right livelihood.
Right effort.
Right mindfulness
Right concentration. (from Goonewardene 1994, p.21)

This is a guide to the Middle Way between luxury and hardship. Meditation helps Buddhists towards right mindfulness, and to gain calmness, insight and compassion. Buddhists perform *puja* at home, making a shrine with an image of the Buddha which represents enlightenment. *Puja* includes chanting *mantras* and meditation.

For Rastafarians, daily worship of Jah is highly personal and concentrated at home. The whole Bible (in the Christian form, including the Apocrypha, and especially the Old Testament) is studied. Worship also includes prayer, meditation and reasoning sessions between Brethren and Sistren. Ritually smoking herbs, including marijuana, as a medium for worship is based on Biblical authority.

QUESTIONS

- What are the worship obligations/customs of children known to you?
- How do children regard worship?
- Are children enabled and encouraged to worship daily, within the family home and/or when separated from families?
- How could you develop opportunities for children to pray and fulfil other daily worship obligations when separated from their families?
- Do children who are not associated with any religion have opportunities to express 'natural worship'?

SUGGESTIONS

With colleagues and children:

- Discuss one another's ideas about the above questions.
- Learn about the customs and obligations of daily worship from children, families and local religious congregations.
- Become familiar with some appropriate texts.
- Encourage children to fulfil everyday obligations such as saying grace, meditating, saying *salat*, performing *puja*.
- Respect children's need for privacy and peace when praying.
- Respect and protect sacred pictures, books and artefacts.
- Notice and encourage any behaviour which might be regarded as worship.

Worship in a particular place

Worship has communal as well as individual and familial significance. Fasts and festivals mark the liturgical calendar, commemorating and celebrating the beliefs and events of the religion, and usually including attendance at a special place of worship – maybe a church or *gurdwara*, *mandir*, synagogue, temple or *vihara*. Attendance is customary (and sometimes required) for weekly worship throughout the year. Maintaining attendance has social as well as religious importance, especially for children and young people who are not living with their own families or other co-religionists. Even if belief in a deity or commitment to religious practices is not strong, regular meeting with people of all ages who share a background, including customs and stories, heroes and ceremonies, can help to hold and develop a sense of identity and connectedness.

For Sikhs, for example, regular weekly attendance at the community-based *gurdwara* demonstrates and reinforces teachings of Guru Nanak (the founder of Sikhism) in several ways. Communal *diwan* (worship) may take place on any day, but in the UK is usually on Sunday, when most people are free.

The word for 'assembly' or 'congregation' is *sangat*. Children take a full part in all activities, learning religious and cultural values; they attend Punjabi classes in order to read the *Guru Granth Sahib*. Worship in the *gurdwara* includes reading from the *Guru Granth Sahib*, singing, praying and speaking about personal religious experience. Worshippers of both sexes and all ages cover their heads, remove their shoes, sit together on a carpet and take part in all activities, representing Guru Nanak's teaching about equality. Offerings of food and money are made. At the end of the service *karah prashad* (blessed food which has been prepared by the *granthi*, custodian of the gurdwara and official reader of the *Guru Granth Sahib*) is shared by everyone, symbolising the blessings of God.

Following this, Sikhs and any visitors move into the *langar* (communal kitchen) where a meal (usually vegetarian) is served free to everyone by volunteers, demonstrating teaching about *seva* (voluntary service) and equality.

Sunday is the regular day of communal worship for Christians, who attend services in special buildings which have different names according to denomination (for example, church, chapel, meeting house). For members of some denominations, the most important aspect of worship is communion (also known as eucharist or mass, according to denomination), when tiny portions of blessed bread and wine are served. Some Christians believe that the bread and wine are transubstantiated into the actual body and blood of Jesus; for others, the food simply represents him, and eating and drinking is an aid to remembering his life and death. Christians may receive communion only when they are deemed to be ready, usually in mid-childhood or early adolescence, when a ceremony marks their acceptance into membership of their Church (see Chapter 6). Communion is one of the sacraments of the Christian Church. Other aspects of worship include singing, praying, readings from the Bible, and a sermon or address.

Children and young people may perform such particular roles as singing in a choir. The ritual of the Roman Catholic mass includes boys who attend the priest at the altar. Many churches provide children's services or Sunday Schools, and family services are also popular.

The weekly holy day for Rastafarians is the Sabbath, from sundown on Friday to sundown on Saturday. Strictly observant Rastafarians do no work at this time, and may fast. Communal worship centres on Nyabinghi drumming and its offshoot, reggae, with chanting and singing psalms and Rastafarian hymns. When praying, the hands are held with thumbs extended horizontally and touching, and forefingers extended downwards and also touching; this form represents both a heart and a spear, peace and war. Some Rastafarians attend services of the Ethiopian Orthodox Church. Children take a full part in Nyabinghi sessions and other communal worship.

The Sabbath is the weekly holy day for Jews too, when, for strictly observant people, no work must be done. Services are held in the synagogue on Friday evening and Saturday morning, following the order of service in the Jewish prayer book. This includes psalms and readings from the Torah, which is written in scrolls kept in a cupboard called the Ark. Some at least of the service is in Hebrew. At the end, the *kiddush* (blessing) is said and wine and cake are shared. Jewish males over 13 should pray every morning, afternoon and evening, ideally in a group of at least ten in the synagogue; when this is not possible, prayer at home is acceptable.

The weekly holy day for Muslims is Friday, when prayers from the Qur'an are said, and attendance at the mosque to pray and hear a sermon is customary, at least for men and boys. There are no seats, and the usual position for prayer is standing in rows or kneeling on mats; shoes are not permitted within the mosque. Cleanliness is essential, and *wudu* is performed before praying. At home, it is customary to entertain or visit relations and friends, and to welcome people who are lonely or on low incomes.

For Hindus, the home is the centre of worship and there is no obligation to attend organised worship in the *mandir* (temple). In the UK, families usually go at the weekend and at festivals. Every *mandir* is dedicated to a particular deity and regarded as her/his home. On arrival, Hindus remove their shoes and ring a bell to inform the deity. They stand or sit on the floor to pray, sometimes with hands together. Prayer may be silent, spoken or sung and accompanied by musical instruments. After praying, an offering of money, food or flowers is placed in front of an image of the deity. The *brahmin* (priest) marks worshippers' foreheads with powder or paste, and returns most of the offering, which may then be given to people in need. The *brahmin* performs *arati* daily, moving an oil lamp in front of the image. In the UK, the *mandir* may also be a centre for social and educational activities.

For Buddhists, too, the home is the centre of worship, but attendance at a *vihara* to perform *puja*, meditate and hear a talk is customary. *Puja* takes place at a shrine which holds an image of the Buddha. Gautama Siddhartha is not worshipped as a deity, but *puja* expresses respect and gratitude for his inspiration and teaching, and is a way of sharing and celebrating with co-religionists. *Puja* comprises chanting, making offerings, listening to readings from holy scriptures and reciting short passages together.

QUESTIONS

- Is there a weekly holy day for children known to you?
- What religious and social obligations and customs are associated with this day?
- Are children known to you enabled and encouraged to attend services with co-religionists?
- Are there problems if services coincide with other commitments and and routines?

SUGGESTIONS

With colleagues and children:

- Discuss one another's ideas about the questions above.
- Enable and encourage children to attend religious centres, perhaps arranging for regular accompaniment by family or co-religionists.
- Enable and encourage children to take part in social and educational activities, including membership of choirs.
- Ensure that money, food and other offerings are available as appropriate.
- Include pictures, descriptions of places and ways of worship in life-story books.
- Value pictures and other items made, for example, at Sunday School.

Summary

Worship, expressed in many ways, is the core of all religions, whether or not belief centres on a deity. Worship is not necessarily connected with any organised form of religion, and many children need opportunities for 'natural worship'.

In some religions, attendance at a centre and joining in prescribed forms of worship is a strict requirement. In others, worshippers are encouraged to attend, but there is no obligation. Sharing worship with co-religionists can offer a sense of identity and cohesion as traditions are observed and beliefs reinforced and explored.

For all religions, worship at home is fundamental, with patterns of prayer both shared within the family and individual. Some religions prescribe set prayers at certain hours. Others encourage silent prayer and meditation.

Failure to fulfil obligations to worship may lead to anxiety and distress derived from fear of censure, even punishment (perhaps by a deity) and guilt.

It may be difficult for children separated from their families and religious congregations to fulfil such obligations, whether within the place of residence or by attendance at a place of worship. Children's own beliefs and wishes to maintain religious routines may not be strong, and there may be relief, even pleasure, at release from what they may see as tedious practices. However, association with a religious congregation may be an essential aspect of developing and maintaining a sense of identity, not only as an individual but also as a member of a family and community.

Respect for children's family and religious background, demonstrated through encouragement to fulfil religious obligations, demonstrates respect for children themselves, and can help to strengthen relationships with practitioners.

9 Symbols and sacred objects

The importance of symbols and sacred objects

Every individual, every family, every community can identify objects, whether natural or artificial, to which some special significance is attached. These may represent status or achievement (such as badges or sporting trophies), or can be used as good luck charms or mascots. But objects may also be invested with and represent such other abstract attributes as divine power.

Such objects or symbols may be represented in pictures or models which themselves may be regarded with respect or awe, even invested with independent power. For example, a statue of a god or saint may be associated with the power to work miracles, perhaps healing sick people who pray to the subject or even touch the image. The miracle is credited to the god or saint, but the power is perceived as being channelled through the particular image at the particular site.

Natural objects and phenomena may also be invested with symbolic significance – for example, a thunderstorm demonstrating divine anger, or severe drought or flood representing punishment. In many cultures, mountains and groves have for centuries been regarded as the homes of deities and attendant beings.

Natural phenomena are imbued with symbolic significance, both in everyday speech and religious language. Light and darkness are powerful examples with many resonances. *Guru*, a word of particular significance for Sikhs (although weakened in secular speech by overusage and incorrect application), means 'a teacher', 'enlightener' or 'religious guide', deriving from *gu* ('darkness') and *ru* ('light'): thus, a spiritual teacher who leads from the darkness of ignorance to enlightenment.

The source of light in this universe, the sun, is a common symbol of life, truth, progress, and was for a long time itself worshipped. Many festivals recognise the importance of the 'rebirth' of the sun in midwinter, representing continuation of life on earth in all its forms, and the miracle of human birth.

The moon and stars also have deep and universal symbolic significance. The crescent moon, symbol of Islam, for example, appears with stars on the flags of several Muslim countries, representing light in the desert, where it is cooler to travel by night, and thus progress and enlightenment for those who follow the teaching of the Qur'an and worship Allah.

Symbolic objects may be large and generally displayed, like flags or sacred buildings, or they may be small and private, such as a Christian silver crucifix pinned in a lapel or pendant from a modest necklace, or the Hindu sacred thread worn under clothing.

Everyday clothing itself may express meaning through form and colour. Some religions require worshippers to don such special garments as prayer shawls, skull caps and turbans.

Children living with their own families and near co-religionists can take such symbols for granted, recognising the form of the symbol without necessarily understanding its significance. However, if children are separated from their parents and home, absent objects may acquire new significance and enhance the sense of loss and depersonalisation attendant on such moves.

Moreover, the new environment will contain new and possibly bewildering symbolic objects and pictures, especially if the caring adults themselves are associated with a religion. For example, children unfamiliar with Christianity may find statues of dying men on crosses or pictures of bleeding hearts frightening, while those who know nothing of the Hindu pantheon may be bewildered by images with elephant heads and multiple arms and legs.

Just as children should be encouraged to bring such loved objects as teddy bears and family photographs from home, so their luggage should include such symbols of their religious environment as pictures, statues, books and clothing. Department of Health Guidance (DoH 1989a) recommends that staff in residential establishments should enable children, as appropriate, 'to build a small shrine somewhere within the home' (DoH 1989a, Section 1.124).

Children should see that their sacred artefacts are respected by carers and other practitioners, whether in hospital, residential or other care. Practitioners visiting families can also show respect or give offence by the attitudes they display towards such objects: offence would be given by handling a statue without permission, while respect might be shown by asking the significance of a picture or flag.

For some practitioners, objects which are sacred to adherents of religions other than their own may be associated with idolatry and false beliefs. For others, whether or not they hold any religious beliefs, such objects may seem ridiculous. If the symbols of other religions have only negative associations, it is difficult to regard and treat objects sacred to children with respect.

Demonstrating interest in symbols and sacred objects aids development of respect for, self-respect by and communication with children, and is invaluable if children themselves experience difficulty with aspects of religion. For example, some who have suffered abuse (in any form) associate that abuse with religious language and symbols: sexual abuse by a father may stimulate confusing responses to the concept of 'God the Father', while ideas of a 'loving Heavenly Father' may be impossible to reconcile with an ever-present image of his son eternally bleeding to death on a cross. Talking about the images may help to reach into such painful, even terrifying confusions (see Chapter 4).

Statues and pictures

Worship in many religions is aided by representations of deities, leaders and holy people. Statues and pictures may be used decoratively or as integral parts of personal or corporate worship. Such images help many worshippers to focus on the messages of their religion through the lives and teachings of the people thus represented. When worshippers cannot read sacred scriptures for themselves, statues and pictures present the stories of the religion, portraying profound ideas through easily recognisable symbols.

Buddhism, Christianity, Hinduism, Judaism and Sikhism are some of the religions which employ such vivid representations. Islam and Judaism forbid the creation or use of any images of the deity. Islam also forbids making images of human or any other animal forms.

Buddhists do not worship a deity; however, they do have images of gods and goddesses who represent such aspects of the Buddha as Tara (compassion). Tibetan Buddhists, for example, focus concentration on pictures called *tankas* and *mandalas*. The image best known to people who are not Buddhists is of Gautama Siddhartha, the first Buddha. Statues show him at different stages of this life, including dying. Some are enormous, and may be painted or gilded. Others are small and personal, easily transported by a child and kept on a shelf. The Buddha is usually shown lightly clothed or nearly naked, in keeping with the custom of the countries of his birth and ministry.

Sculptures and paintings depict such symbols of belief and teaching as the lotus flower and the wheel of the law or the wheel of life. The lotus represents the human search for knowledge, as its lovely flower, turning to the sun, is rooted in mud. The wheel of the law represents the cycle of birth, death and rebirth from which humans can escape by following the teachings of the Four Noble Truths and the Noble Eightfold Path (see Chapter 8). Other human forms are depicted to represent *bhodisattvas* (wise beings whose generosity, loving kindness, self-sacrifice and compassion enable them to live many lives in this world, helping and saving other beings of all kinds).

Most Christians worship one God in three aspects: Father, Son and Holy Spirit. Although Christianity originated as a sect of Judaism, there is no embargo on portraying God in any form. The most common visual image is of Jesus (believed by many to be the incarnation of God) as a human male, usually portrayed as strong and handsome, and in the UK, often with fair skin and flowing brown hair, wearing long robes. Jesus is also popularly represented as a baby (usually with his mother, Mary) or dying on the cross; at both points he is dressed in a white loincloth.

God the Father is less commonly depicted in the UK. In stories about the life, death and resurrection of Jesus and the development of what would become Christianity, the focus is on the human form and on representation of the third aspect, the Holy Spirit. In stories taken from the Old Testament (the early history of the Jews), God is not usually depicted visually.

The Holy Spirit, essentially invisible and intangible, is usually represented by a dove (also associated with peace) and by symbols of fire and light.

Besides Jesus, the most popular visual image in the UK is of Mary, usually in scenes from the story of Jesus's conception and birth, portrayed as a beautiful, slim, young, fair-skinned woman with light hair, clothed in long robes and a veil of blue and white. Tall, white madonna lilies are especially associated with her. Mary is particularly revered by Roman Catholics.

For Orthodox worshippers, a picture is a holy object known as an icon; this is not worshipped in itself, but is an object of respect and veneration.

Not all Christian Churches encourage visual representations of God or saints and other holy people, and it is important to learn the preferences of individual children. Roman Catholic churches, for example, usually contain many statues and pictures, both painted and in the form of stained-glass windows; depictions of Jesus on the cross are prominent. A Roman Catholic home might contain small statues (especially of Mary), crucifixes and pictures. In contrast, Quaker Meeting Houses and homes contain no images of God, holy people or sacred objects. Roman Catholics and Quakers both worship God, but the former find stimulus in visual forms, whereas the latter focus on spiritual communication with as little visual distraction as possible.

Rastafarians, who have close links with the Ethiopian Church, value posters and paintings of, for example, His Imperial Majesty the Emperor Haile Selassie and Marcus Garvey. The colours of the Ethiopian flag – red, green, yellow and black – are often used.

For Hindus, images of the many gods and goddesses who represent the multiple aspects of the Brahman, the One, the eternal, formless World Soul, are integral to everyday life and worship. Both family worship at home and corporate worship in a temple focus on shrines with statues and pictures of deities which are treated with great respect and to which offerings are made, especially at festivals.

Many Hindus follow one or two great manifestations of the Brahman, Shiva and Vishnu. A potent image of Shiva, both creator and destroyer, is the Lord of the Dance, symbolising the eternal energy flowing through the world, birth and death, destruction and recreation. One foot treads on the demon of ignorance, and his four hands hold symbolic objects or make gestures. Shiva is surrounded by a ring of flame representing the circle of time. Such an explanation of this form is simplistic and represents only the superficial layer of meaning in the images of religion. Shiva is also represented by *linga* (cylindrical columns with rounded tips rising from horizontal bases). Vishnu is usually worshipped in the form of one of his ten avatars (incarnations), the most popular being Rama and Krishna.

The *devi* ('goddess') is sometimes regarded as the central deity, the *shakti*, the strength and power behind all things, including the gods themselves. She is worshipped as the special protector of mothers and children. Her forms are multiple, from the beautiful Parvati, wife of Shiva, to the terrifying Kali, decorated with human skulls, who brings disease and war.

Two popular deities are Ganesha and Hanuman. Ganesha has a pot belly, four arms and the head of an elephant with only one tusk; he is accompanied by a mouse. Among his many attributes are those of both setter and remover of obstacles. Hanuman is a monkey, son of the wind god, friend of Rama and saviour of Sita from the demon Ravana (see Chapter 15).

Children living away from their families might be glad to have a statue or picture of more than one deity, maybe Shiva and Ganesha or Vishnu and Hanuman.

Since Moses recorded the commandment, 'You shall not make for yourself a graven image, or any likeness of anything that is in heaven above, or that is in the earth beneath, or that is in the water under the earth; you shall not bow down to them or serve them' (Exodus 20:4–5), Jews have obeyed the prohibition on trying to portray God (Jahweh) visually. The symbols of religion valued by Jewish children would not be statues or pictures (although some editions of the books of the Tenach may be illustrated with scenes of people and angels).

Sikhs also refrain from portraying God, represented by the symbol El Onkar ('One God'), but depict scenes from the lives of the ten human *gurus*. Portraits of the founder of Sikhism, Guru Nanak, are valued possessions, especially at such festivals as Guru Nanak's birthday or Sikh *Diwali*, celebrating the liberation of Guru Hargobind, both celebrated in November (see Chapter 7).

Other symbolic objects in the home

Children may be familiar with other symbols of religion kept within their own homes, or they may be unfamiliar with those in households to which they are moved.

Many Christian households display model crucifixes, maybe free-standing or mounted on a wall. Roman Catholics show the dying figure of Jesus, but Protestants usually restrict the image to a simple cross. Roman Catholics use rosaries (long chains of beads) to aid prayer. The fish is a common Christian symbol: when Christians were persecuted in Rome, the Greek letters *ICTHUS* ('fish') stood for the Greek words for Jesus (I) Christ (C) God (T) Son (U) Saviour (S).

For Buddhists, an important figure is the wheel, representing the wheel of law or the wheel of life.

Judaism is often associated with the six-pointed star of David. A Jewish household usually contains a *menorah* or *hannukiah* (eight-branched candlestick) used at Sabbath and other festival meals. A *mezzuzah* is fixed to the doorposts – a parchment scroll within a tiny, tubular box, inscribed with the first words of the *Shema* (see Chapter 8).

QUESTIONS

- What do you know about symbolic objects associated with religious beliefs and observances of children known to you?
- Do children known to you have personal images or other objects associated with religion?
- Do they understand the significance of such objects?
- Are these objects treated with respect by adults and other children?
- Are there any images or other objects in your household which might stimulate confusion or distress?
- Do any images or other objects in possession of children cause you confusion or distress? If so, what can you do?
- Do any objects associated with religion and in the possession of children cause them anxiety or distress? If so, what can you do?

SUGGESTIONS

With colleagues and children:

- Discuss one another's ideas about the questions above.
- Learn about the images and other objects associated with religious beliefs and practices of children known to you.

- Ensure that all such objects are protected and respected.
- Encourage children to tell stories associated with such objects and relate them to worship and everyday life.
- Be alert to ridicule or bullying by other children.
- Be alert to indications of anxiety or distress apparently stimulated by images or other objects, whether belonging to children themselves or present within your own premises.

Symbolic items of dress

It is common for objects associated with religion to be worn, whether at particular times, as everyday dress, or constantly. This section is concerned with the requirements of children, and does not mention special clothing associated with monks, nuns and priests, for example.

Some objects which have sacred significance for worshippers are worn as casual jewellery by others. For Christians, a small crucifix worn as a pendant or lapel pin is a badge of identification, of belief in Jesus, but every child who wears a silver cross is not a church attender. Christian children do not usually wear special clothing unless they have particular roles within services, such as membership of a choir or assisting a priest. However, Roman Catholic girls wear white dresses, sometimes like small brides, and boys wear suits for first communion, and members of other denominations may also have special clothes for these important occasions (see Chapter 6).

For Rastafarians, the garment of identity is the *tam* (a knitted hat), which usually incorporates all or some of the colours of the Ethiopian flag – green, yellow, red and black. The arrangement of these colours indicates to which of the two main branches of Rasta the individual belongs, Nyabinghi or Boboshanti, and it is important to get this right. Rastafarians usually cover their heads, and it is especially important to ensure that girls attending religious meetings have a *tam* or scarf. Modesty in dress is valued, and African styles and fabrics are often popular.

Headgear and modesty in dress are also important to Sikhs. A male traditionally wears a turban, a long strip of cloth wound around the head. This is worn partly to indicate identification with Guru Nanak and his successors. Boys usually begin to wear turbans when they can tie them themselves, usually at about 11; this is celebrated at *pagri bananan*, a religious ceremony symbolising the attainment of adulthood (see Chapter 3). Wearing a turban can cause conflict with civil authorities, for example when the law requires motorcyclists to wear crash helmets which do not fit over bulky headdresses.

Members of the *Khalsa* brotherhood traditionally wear five signs (the five

Ks), although in the UK adaptations may be acceptable. These are *kesh* (uncut hair), *kanga* (comb), *kara* (steel bracelet), *kirpan* (short sword), *kachha* (roomy underpants). The *kara*, for example, symbolises the continuity of God, without beginning or end; the *kirpan* indicates the duty to defend Sikh beliefs and to protect weak and helpless people. (In the UK the *kirpan* may be represented by a small imitation, perhaps set into the *kanga*.)

Modesty in dress is expected, and women should cover legs, breasts and upper arms, for Sikhs as for Hindus; this may have implications for sports kit.

Upper-caste Hindu men and boys wear a sacred thread, first given at the ceremony of *upanayana*, usually between the ages of 8 and 12, signifying attainment of adulthood. The thread must be removed only when changed at the Hindu New Year or if dirty, and must be cremated with the wearer. It indicates that the wearer has accepted the tenets of Hinduism: for example not eating meat. The sacred thread may be regarded as representing many aspects of Hindu belief, such religious beliefs as the three aspects of the Brahman, Brahma, Shiva and Vishnu, or the wearer's duties to god, parents and religious teachers. Some Hindus wear jewellery with religious significance: for example, a medallion picturing a personal god or *guru*, protective gemstones or amulets.

Muslims are discouraged from wearing jewellery or other forms of apparel which might attract attention or be provocative. Modesty in dress is of the greatest importance, and girls should keep their arms and legs covered (this again may have implications for wearing sports kit). Muslim women usually cover their heads. When praying, it is customary, although not compulsory, for men and boys to wear hats and to kneel on prayer mats which they carry with them.

Jewish males over 13 who are *bar mitzvah* cover their heads for worship, including Sabbath and other festival meals, often with a *kippa* (skull cap). A *tallit* (fringed shawl) is draped across the shoulders in obedience to a commandment recorded in the Book of Numbers (15:38–9). *Tefillin* are bound to the arms and forehead.

QUESTIONS

- Should children known to you wear any special clothing associated with religious belief and observances?
- If so, are they enabled and encouraged to do so?
- Do the children understand the significance of such garments?
- Do you understand the significance of such garments?
- Do you ensure respect for and proper care of them?
- Do any children known to you suffer ridicule or bullying because of such religious observance as wearing special garments?

SUGGESTIONS

With colleagues and children:

- Discuss one another's ideas about the questions above.
- Learn about garments associated with religious belief and observance.
- Ensure that all children known to you learn to respect one another's garments.
- Include pictures and descriptions of such garments in life-story books.

Summary

Symbols of many kinds are inextricably associated with religious belief and observance. For children parted from their own families and co-religionists, such symbolic objects as statues and pictures may gain in importance, particularly in circumstances where the everyday routine of family worship is interrupted. Comfort and continuity can be gained from the possession of an image of a favourite deity or saint.

However, care is needed to discern signs of anxiety or distress apparently stimulated by objects and/or language which may have been associated with abuse (see Chapter 12).

Anxiety, confusion and distress may also be stimulated by images associated with religious belief and observance with which children are not familiar – for example, in a foster home or residential establishment.

Practitioners may themselves find images and objects brought by children to be disturbing, and they may possibly be condemned by the practitioner's own religious teachings.

10 Daily care

Religious associations of daily care

For many people, religious observance is expressed through everyday attention to care of the body, such as cleanliness, hair style, modest dress, and diet. These may be integral to prayer and worship and/or invested with symbolic significance.

Within their own families, children should be assured of appropriate care and attention to such matters. However, practitioners who are not familiar with the customs of a particular religion may not understand certain details of everyday care.

It is not always possible to identify practices which have a religious significance. Since this book is concerned with religion and spirituality, examples in this chapter illustrate practices which can be linked directly to religious belief and observance. However, this does not ignore the equal importance of learning about and being sensitive to apparently secular customs (see Ahmed et al. 1986).

When children are apart from their birth families, even for a few hours a day, deviation from usual care routines can be worrying. Practitioners who attend to such details help children to feel respected and confident. It can be very difficult for children of any age to ask for such attention, especially when in groups in day or residential care or in hospital. They are likely to be strongly motivated to comply with the conventions of the foster home or establishment, and reluctant to ask for special treatment which might identify then as 'odd' or 'different'. Parents are not always encouraged to give information on diet and other care when children are placed.

Children may feel caught between obedience to parental instructions and religious obligations, and conformity with the everyday régime of day or

131

full-time care. Ahmed et al. (1986) note:

> It is important for carers to establish how children really feel about breaking parental instructions and family taboos. For example, Roksana, a nine-year-old Muslim girl in care ate meat contrary to parental injunction. She did not wish to be different and this suited staff greatly. Yet, when she had confidence in our relationship, she expressed anxiety and feelings of guilt, she worried about betraying her mother and wondered about punishment from God. (p.59)

Young children find it difficult, if not impossible, to articulate such anxieties and conflicts. Older children, especially those whose separation from home is due to their own behaviour or to parental abuse or neglect, may be reluctant to expose themselves to complaints of 'being difficult' or 'making trouble'. The example of Roksana demonstrates the possible depths of conflict and anxiety, and the importance of sensitive and informed care.

Messages transmitted involuntarily in the course of everyday care have great impact, and may conflict with communications intended by adults. For example, a practitioner who agreed to encourage attendance at a place of worship and fulfilment of daily prayer obligations might overlook dietary requirements, perhaps regarding them as fads.

Some practitioners may consider that a vegetarian diet (associated with several religions) is unhealthy, and that children cannot thrive without meat. For some, it may be difficult to see any connection between diet and religious belief. There may be temptations to offer children prohibited foods as treats. Such concerns can be helped by advice from practising (and healthy) vegetarians, and if necessary, general practitioners.

When young Muslims are required to fast between dawn and dusk, practitioners may be reluctant to adapt routines so that food and drink are available at appropriate times. They may also fear damage to the young people. It may be necessary to discourage other residents from teasing, or trying to force fasting children to eat.

Feasting offers opportunities for celebrating a child's religious identity with traditional food and drink, helping to reinforce positive, happy aspects of fulfilling religious obligations which may sometimes seem arduous.

This chapter introduces some brief examples of aspects of daily care associated with religious belief and observance. Examples of some everyday practices connected with dress appear in Chapter 9.

Diet

Roksana, the 9-year-old Muslim girl who suffered conflict about eating meat (see above) would have been forbidden to eat food which was not *hallal* ('lawful'). To be *hallal*, meats must be derived from animals killed according to the *shari'ah* (Muslim law) while the name of Allah is invoked. *Haram* (forbidden) foods include any pork products. All such meat-based foods as burgers, soups and tinned meats as well as cooking fats must be derived from *hallal* slaughtered animals. No blood may be eaten, nor any creature which itself eats meat or had died before *hallal* butchery took place. *Haram* foods are considered to be bad for the body, and therefore bad for the spirit. Foods which are permitted but not recommended are *makrah*, and include certain birds. Fish is permitted.

If there is doubt about meat, it is best to offer a vegetarian diet to Muslim children. Vegetables are *hallal*, as they are seen to be clean and nourishing. Prepared food such as bread, biscuits, cakes, pastry and confectionery may contain animal fat.

Food is a gift from Allah, and Muslims wash and give thanks before and after eating.

Muslims may not consume any substance which can intoxicate or interfere with the clear functioning of mind and body. Thus alcohol and drugs are *haram*, and may neither be given to nor sold by Muslims. Some prepared foods such as liqueur chocolates and trifles may contain alcohol.

Healthy Muslims over 12 are required to observe the month-long fast of *Ramadan* between dawn and dusk (see Chapter 7).

Like Muslims, many Jews observe strict dietary laws, *kashrut*, based on the biblical Book of Leviticus. Many creatures are prohibited, including pigs, rabbits and horses (and all derivatives). Only animals with cloven hooves which chew the cud are permitted, and these must be slaughtered by a trained *sochet*, whose duties include salting meat to remove any remaining blood. Only then is it *kosher* ('permitted'). (Many Muslims accept *kosher* meat as *hallal*.) Birds of prey are forbidden, but such seed-eaters as poultry are *kosher* if slaughtered by a *sochet*. Only fish with both scales and fins are *kosher*. Shellfish, shrimps and other seafood are forbidden.

Milk (including all derivatives) and meat may not be eaten together, whether mixed into one dish (for example, as cheeseburgers, lasagne, or cream in a casserole) or served on one plate (including a sandwich with meat and butter). Milk products may not be consumed within several hours of eating meat, for example in dessert, confectionery or beverages. Orthodox and some other Jews cook and serve milk and meat products with different utensils and cutlery.

A special meal is eaten every week on the Sabbath, when the father of the family speaks blessings over a glass of wine and two *hallot* loaves. The most important meal of the year is at *Pesach* (Passover), when symbolic foods are arranged on a *seder* plate, representing the experience of Jews who were slaves in Egypt. Lionel Blue (1986) (a rabbi) recalls how his grandmother 'gave me spoonfuls of horseradish to remember the slavery of Egypt and the bitterness of exile. As I grew to like the taste, my theology never got sorted out.' Other foods link the liturgical year and Jewish history with flavours, for example: 'We celebrated the triumph of Esther with poppy seed cakes and the triumph of the Maccabees with nuts.'

During the eight days of *Pesach*, only unleavened bread may be eaten, familiar in the UK as *matzah* biscuits, readily available at delicatessens and supermarkets, and commemorating the hasty preparations of the Jews for their flight (Exodus 12). All foods containing wheat and other grains (except *matzah*), oats, pulses, rice or millet are forbidden. Strictly observant households keep a special set of crockery, cutlery and cooking utensils for this period. Practitioners are advised to obtain advice from observant Jews.

Yom Kippur ('Day of Atonement') is spent largely in the synagogue, and Jews fast from sunset to sunset. Children under 13 usually fast for part of the time.

For Hindus, voluntary regular fasting is undertaken, usually by women, probably on one day every week (every day of the week is sacred to a deity). Fasting may also be practised on festival and other special days: for example, unmarried girls may fast at the festival of *Jaya Parvati* in July to ensure a suitable marriage. Fasting usually implies abstention from certain foods and taking one light meal a day; some Hindu women eat a salt-free diet for one month every year. Young children are not usually expected to fast.

Most observant Hindus are vegetarian. A non-vegetarian should not accept the sacred thread, the tenth *samskara* (see Chapter 6). A mother in the UK explained that her sons had not taken the sacred thread, 'because they eat meat. In these things, I think you have to stick to everything. If they take the thread they have to give up meat. I don't want to force them. It's something they must choose' (quoted in Aylett 1992, p.17). Even when meat is eaten, no beef product should be offered to a Hindu, since the cow is sacred, a symbol of motherhood and the provider of essential milk and dairy produce. Pork is also usually avoided because in India the pig is considered to be 'unclean'. Fish is usually acceptable to non-vegetarians. Eggs, a symbol of life, may not be eaten by strict Hindu vegetarians. Some may prefer not to eat cheese made with animal rennet ('vegetarian' cheese is available nowadays from most supermarkets).

Diet is linked with the whole balance of the body and emotions, and Hindus regard choosing appropriate foods as a part of religious duty. Some 'hot' foods are considered to raise the body temperature and excite emotions, while 'cool' foods are calming and increase cheerfulness and strength. Alcohol and drugs should be avoided.

Although Sikhs are not prohibited from eating meat, many do adopt the Hindu attitude towards vegetarianism, including abstinence from eggs. Non-vegetarians are forbidden to eat animals which have been slaughtered by a *hallal* butcher, and few eat beef, respecting the reverence for the cow in

India. Some also abstain from pork. In the UK, Sikhs may be less strict about diet: this is a matter of individual conscience and belief. Alcohol and drugs are prohibited, especially for *amritdhari* (initiated Sikhs). Although in the UK Sikh males do commonly drink alcohol, females are more likely to follow tradition. For example, a study of Sikh girls in Nottingham found that 60 per cent of respondents were content to refrain from drinking alcohol, 'because they believed it to be unhealthy, unacceptable for Sikh women and a bad example for women to set for their children' (Drury 1991, p.195).

As for Hindus, for Sikhs fasting is abstention from certain foods, and is not commonly practised by any but the very devout, perhaps on the first day of the Punjabi month.

Rastafarians set much store by a healthy, nutritious diet, and this is regarded as a sacred matter. They observe the prohibitions of the Mosaic Law (Deuteronomy 14:3–21), including pigs, rabbits and sea creatures without both scales and fins. Many birds and insects are also regarded as 'unclean', and Rastafarians may not eat any creature which died a natural death, or touch the carcasses of prohibited animals. Contact with any flesh is regarded as defilement, and vegetarianism is common, based on the diet of the biblical prophet Daniel (Daniel 1:8–16). *Ital* (clean, pure) chefs are renowned for their use of fresh ingredients and excellent cuisine. Overall cleanliness is essential. Salt is regarded as unhealthy and used sparingly, if possible unprocessed.

Rastafarian parents are constantly careful that their children should not be in contact with polluting foods or conditions, and check ingredients of prepared foods to ensure that no 'unclean' substance is included. They may prefer children not to eat in restaurants or friends' homes. In the UK, both Princes and Princesses learn kitchen and culinary skills from an early age.

In accordance with the Nazarene Oath, Rastafarians abstain from alcohol, and may extend this to any product associated with grapes. Some abstain from any fruit of the vine, including melons and tomatoes. Smoking herbs, including marijuana, contributes to prayer and worship: biblical authority is cited, linking the herb to *kaya*, the tree of life, representing the wisdom given to Solomon.

Buddhists are subject to no special dietary rules, but are very often vegetarian because of the precept against taking life. The precepts are not rules, and Buddhists are free to follow their own consciences – for example, if a vegetarian needs to eat meat to sustain life (perhaps because no other food is available); some would eat meat to show courtesy to meat-serving hosts. Sensitivity should be shown to the preferences of children who might not assert their wishes. Buddhists are discouraged from taking alcohol or drugs, in order to keep the mind clear and alert.

For Christians, diet is a matter of personal decision. Adherents of some denominations (for example, Quakers) may be particularly attracted to vegetarianism as a way of living out beliefs in non-violence and respect for all life, but there are no rules. Some Christians abstain from certain foods at times of fasting, for example a child might give up chocolate for Lent. Others (such as Mormons) prohibit consumption of stimulants like tea and coffee. Special foods are associated with festivals (see Chapter 7). Some members of some denominations are teetotal (for example, the Salvation Army, Methodists, Baptists and Quakers).

Cleanliness

Both social and religious practices in several religions involve attention to cleanliness in order to avoid pollution. For lay Buddhists there are no special rules about ablution, but Hindus, Muslims and Rastafarians are required to conform to strict codes. For Hindus, such bodily fluids as saliva, sweat, mucus, urine and menstrual blood are regarded as 'polluting', and *puja* and cooking must always be preceded by washing. A menstruating female may not perform *puja*, but she may cook (see Chapter 8). Family members may not attend social or religious activities at times of birth or death, and must wash after a funeral. After defecation, Hindus wash the soiled area, using the left hand (the right is used in eating). After eating, the mouth is rinsed with water. Feet must be washed often. Shoes are regarded as particularly defiling: they are not worn in the house, and must never touch books, especially scriptures. Sandals may be worn in houses in the UK, but never in the kitchen or worship room. Showers are preferred to washing in still water.

Muslims also take great care to avoid pollution and maintain cleanliness and hygiene. The Qur'an specifies: 'Surely Allah loves those who repent and keep clean' (2:222). Running water is required to wash away all impurities. *Wudu* must be performed before worship. Shoes must never be worn in a place of worship, and should not be worn in a house. Like Hindus, Muslims use the left hand for washing and the right for eating, and it is essential to wash after defecation and before and after eating. Females may consider themselves to be 'unclean' during menstruation or for 40 days after giving birth; they abstain from fasting, performing *salat* and touching the Qur'an, and end the period by taking a ritual bath and cleansing their clothes and rooms.

Strictly observant Jews also regard menstruating females as ritually 'unclean'. Contact with men is forbidden, and Orthodox males may avoid contact – even shaking hands – with any females except their wives lest they be contaminated. The period of 'uncleanness' ends with a ritual bath.

Rastafarian males also avoid contact with menstruating females, and might, for example, be reluctant to shake hands with women other than their wives. This is in accordance with the Nazarene Oath. (Leviticus 15:19–30; 18:19). Empresses (adult females) may be excluded from the kitchen in order to prevent pollution. Emphasis is placed on purity and freedom from pollution at all times.

Hair

Several religions adopt hair styles to identify adherents: Rastafarians wear dreadlocks in accordance with the Nazarene Oath (Numbers 6:1–6) to signify consecration to God, together with African identity. In art, dreadlocks are linked with a lion's mane: Princes and Princesses are depicted as young lions, to represent their courage. Dreadlocks are cleaned constantly, in recognition of their religious significance, where possible with such natural elements as aloes and hibiscus leaf; it is acceptable to use commercial shampoo provided that this is as pure as possible. Water must be pure and hot. Such natural oils as coconut and olive are applied to stimulate healthy growth. Dreadlocks must not be brushed or combed because hairs may be broken. Dreadlocks may not be touched by non-Rastafarians, so practitioners need to discuss hair care with parents or co-religionists. The head is usually kept covered in public to avoid pollution by touching.

One of the five signs of a *Khalsa* Sikh (see Chapter 9) is *kesh* (uncut hair), for which another sign, *kanga* (a comb) is carried. Uncut hair was often associated with holiness in India, but was sometimes allowed to become matted and unclean; *kanga* reminds Sikhs that both their lives and their hair should be clean and orderly. *Kesh* represents acceptance of the gifts of, and the intention of working with, El Onkar ('One God'). *Kesh* is usually confined within a turban.

Although most Jews in the UK wear their hair in contemporary fashion, Hasidic Jews observe certain traditions. Boys' hair is often not cut until the age of 3, and hair next to the ears is never cut, but worn in *payas* (long fringes or sidelocks); the remaining hair kept very short, and beards are grown as soon as possible. Hasidic and very Orthodox Jews do not shave. Hasidic girls usually wear their hair long until marriage, when it is cut very short and covered, sometimes with a wig.

The heads of Buddhist, Hindu and Muslim babies (usually boys) are shaved as part of welcoming and naming ceremonies (see Chapter 6).

QUESTIONS

● Should children known to you observe any rules or customs connected with diet, cleanliness and/or hair care, associated with religious belief?

- If so, are they enabled and encouraged to do so?
- Can any difficulties about diet be overcome?
- Do children known to you understand the significance of such observances?
- Do you understand the significance of such observances?
- Do you ensure respect for them, for example by preventing other children from teasing or bullying?
- Do you feel uneasy about or hostile to any such observances as vegetarianism, fasting, using the left hand to wipe the bottom and the right hand to eat?

SUGGESTIONS

With colleagues and children:

- Discuss one another's ideas about the questions above.
- Learn about rules and customs associated with diet, cleanliness and hair care.
- Learn about different diets, and experiment with different foods.
- Ensure that all children known to you learn to respect one another's customs and preferences.
- Ensure that colleagues understand and respect the significance of diet, cleanliness and hair care.
- Include pictures, descriptions and stories about customs in life-story books.

Summary

Everyday care of the body is for many people an essential expression of worship, whether or not integral to prayer, *puja* or *salat*. Aspects of diet, cleanliness and hair care may hold deep significance.

Failure to respect these and ensure that children observe them may cause offence to families, and anxiety and conflict for children. Children may not feel confident to express wishes and needs to practitioners, while they may experience guilt at failing to obey parents and/or a deity.

Involuntary messages conveyed through everyday care may conflict with intended communications if practitioners are not fully alert to attitudes and practice (their own and those of other adults and children).

Practitioners may experience anxiety about or hostility towards such customs as vegetarianism and fasting; help and advice can easily be obtained.

Part 4

Spirituality, religion, abuse and neglect

Part 4

Spirituality, religion, abuse, and neglect

11 Abuse and neglect

Spiritual abuse and neglect

The UN Convention on the Rights of the Child requires attention to children's spiritual development and well-being (see Chapter 1). All and any forms of abuse and neglect may be seen as implying a failure to protect and nurture the spirit integral to the whole child.

This chapter explores associations between abuse/neglect and spiritual well-being, with reference to definitions of spiritual and religious rights, qualities, needs and values discussed earlier. Children respond to abuse in many ways which may be seen as demonstrating spiritual distress. Teaching associated with religion can lead to harm, for example through misunderstanding. However, children who have suffered abuse can find strength through contact with religious organisations.

Abuse, neglect and spirituality

A number of Articles in the UN Convention include direct reference to either spirituality or religion (but never both – see Chapter 1). Briefly, the Articles referring to spiritual development or well-being are no. 17 (information, materials and the mass media), no. 23 (disabled children), no. 27 (standard of living), no. 29 (aims of education) and no. 32 (child labour); those referring to religion are no. 2 (non-discrimination), no. 14 (freedom of thought, conscience and religion), no. 20 (care of children unable to live with their own families) and no. 30 (the right to practise minority religions).

Attention to either spiritual or religious nurture is required in no other Article. Bradford (1995) discusses religious and spiritual implications of some other Articles, but there appear to be inconsistencies within the document. This chapter assumes that the spirit of the convention implies attention to spiritual and religious well-being, whether or not this is stated. This argument may at the very least be deduced from Article 2 (these rights apply to all children irrespective of, among other aspects of their lives, religion) and Article 27 (every child has a right to a standard of living adequate for all forms of development including spiritual).

Failure to respect the right of all children to full implementation of these specific Articles and, by implication, of all Articles in the convention, itself constitutes neglect of spiritual and religious well-being.

In the context of this discussion, it is notable that Article 19 (protection from abuse and neglect) specifies only 'physical and mental violence, injury or abuse, neglect or negligent treatment', whereas Article 27 (standard of living) lists 'physical, mental, spiritual, moral and social development'. It is reasonable, perhaps essential, to assume inclusion of 'spiritual, moral and social' in the aspects of life to be protected under Article 19.

Corinne Wattam (1995) summarises aspects of the UN Convention relevant to investigations into alleged or suspected abuse, interpreting Article 19 broadly as: 'the State has an obligation to protect children from all forms of maltreatment perpetrated by parents or others responsible for their care'. With reference to 'assessment of behaviour which is said to be bad for the child', she cites Article 14 (freedom of thought, conscience and religion) and Article 15 (freedom of association and peaceful assembly) (p.180). This point is not discussed, but may imply that practitioners should be aware of possible conflict between concerns for children's welfare and rights to these freedoms.

Wattam does not note a further possible area of conflict implied in Article 16 (protection of privacy), which prohibits 'arbitrary or unlawful interference with ... privacy'. While practitioners may be expected to be acting lawfully when investigating allegations of abuse, great care and self-awareness are necessary to prevent such investigations from becoming 'arbitrary', intrusive and thus themselves a form of abuse. Article 16 also protects children against 'unlawful attacks on ... honour and reputation', which may result from investigations of abuse or of offending.

Infringements of these rights are illustrated in Kennedy (1995a). On privacy, a list of 11 forms of abuse associated particularly with children who have some disability includes force feeding, medical photography, opening mail, lack of privacy and personal clothes, and toys being used communally. Deprivation of visitors might be regarded as infringing Article 15 (freedom of association). Kennedy found that disabled children were often regarded as 'even more likely to make false allegations of abuse', or if they are abused, 'sexual abuse of disabled children is OK, or at least not so harmful as abuse of other children', and even the opinion 'it is impossible to prevent abuse of disabled children' (p.130). She quotes a man with cerebral palsy who supposed that he had been abused because '"why bugger up a normal child, when I am defective already?"' (p.128).

QUESTIONS

- Do you think that failure to implement all or any of the UN Convention Articles in itself constitutes neglect?
- Do you think that children should be protected from spiritual as well as other forms of abuse?
- Do you think that all forms of abuse involve abuse of the spirit?

SUGGESTIONS

With colleagues and children:

- Discuss one another's ideas about the questions above.
- Write a new Article setting out children's right to protection.

Some effects of abuse

The observable scars of children who have been subject to physical abuse (including neglect and sexual assault) are accompanied by wounds to the emotions, mind and spirit. Children also suffer invisible assault, unaccompanied by visible clues but nonetheless desperately needing careful attention from adults. Physical and emotional abuse attract far more attention than cognitive and spiritual abuse. (Crompton 1995, pp.334–5)

This appears to be the sole reference to a possible association between abuse and the spirit in the 28 papers in *The Child Protection Handbook* (Wilson and James 1995). Yet once practitioners engage with the idea (in training and informal discussion), they find much of relevance to their work.

Deeply considering implications of abuse for spiritual well-being, Colin (a social worker) asked me: 'If someone's spiritual development is impaired, once the cause is identified and removed has spiritual development been tainted? And if so, what to do?' He added: 'how to make sense of our confusion?' His question reminded him vividly of an unloved girl whom he now saw as *dis-spirited*, and he described how she rarely smiled as she constantly, fruitlessly sought attention from her family. Colin associates spirituality with 'positive movement, light, involvement, emotional congruence', which he wanted 'to pour in' to the girl who was 'a shell, no life or verve'. But 'the parents had the lock to the bottle top' (see Chapter 2).

'Beth' (a senior practitioner in a hospital) visualised the body language of children who have been abused as 'dragged down, slumping, exuberance crushed', illustrating the phrase 'his spirit was crushed'. Thinking about the topic for the first time, she considered that the spirit can be abused if, for example, children are constantly 'put down', their fantasies rejected or adults are intent on making them pliable and obedient (see Chapter 2).

These examples illustrate vividly some effects associated with abuse in its many forms. Quoting Salo (1990, p.80), Janet West (1996) refers to the 'damaged goods syndrome', including low self-esteem, lack of trust and expectation of trickery, and further notes: 'residual guilt, generalized fear of strangers and situations ... and inability to cope with anger and depression'; despair might be added to this list. She describes several types of abuse, including, first, neglect, and adding that 'Children can be abused emotionally ... physically, sexually and during ritual and organized abuse.' (pp.40 and 41)

Problem areas that may be exhibited by abused and troubled children include:

- emotional and behavioural disturbances, including behaving older or younger than the child's chronological age;
- psychosomatic and psychosexual disorders;
- interpersonal difficulties;
- trust issues;
- knowing what is appropriate behaviour;
- poor self-esteem;
- the child may find it difficult to distinguish and express appropriate emotions. (Janet West 1996, pp.40–1)

Possible responses by disabled children to abuse include: self-blame, anger, hatred, lack of confidence, bitterness, fear, powerlessness, guilt, rejection, isolation, depression (Kennedy 1995a, pp.146–7). Children who have been abused often experience and express guilt, sometimes long into adulthood. Disabled children who have been abused may direct their responses in two directions: guilt and fear (see p.145). Few of these responses are confined to disabled children, and Kennedy's (1995a) summary has much to offer practitioners in all fields.

Hanks and Stratton (1995) note that 'children often believe that if only they behaved in a different way or engaged in more of the same behaviour, the adults would stop maltreating' and as adults wonder 'why and how it was that they would run towards the ... adult and greet them warmly even though they were fully aware of the painful relationship and afraid of it' (pp.90–1).

Disabling society/disability	Possible response	Abusing society/abuse
'I'm not the child my parents wanted.'	**Guilt**	'I've caused it.' 'I'm abused because I'm disabled.' 'I liked it.'

Associated with these are responses linked with fear:

Of social situations	**Fear**	More abuse
Of not hearing (deafness)		Touch/closeness
Of appearing stupid		Injury/harm
Of making a mistake		Pregnancy
Of failing		Someone finding out

It is a short step to depression, the self-hating sense of badness, and despair:

'I'm useless.'	**Depression**	'I hate myself.'
'I'm stupid.'		'I'm bad/dirty.'
'I'm defective.'		

Source: Based on Kennedy (1995a), pp.146–7.

Children who have been sexually abused are often regarded, and regard themselves, as guilty, responsible for whatever has happened to them. Children may be unable to tell even 'safe' adults because they fear confirmation of the judgement of collusion and guilt they have already passed on themselves, perhaps because they have enjoyed unusual adult attention or sexual pleasure.

QUESTIONS

- Thinking of the body language of children known to you, do you recognise the descriptions given by Colin and 'Beth'?
- Do you think Janet West's list of problem areas in behaviour exhibited by children who have been abused has any links with spiritual well-being?
- Thinking of disabled children known to you, do you recognise the responses and conflicts described by Margaret Kennedy?
- Do you think all children who have been abused experience such reactions, especially guilt, self-blame and fear?

SUGGESTIONS

With colleagues and children:

- Discuss one another's ideas about the questions above.
- Describe ways in which children's body language can express spiritual distress, neglect or abuse.
- List ways in which children's behaviour can express spiritual distress, neglect or abuse.
- List children's responses to abuse, including guilt, self-blame and fear, and consider how these can cause conflicts for children who are associated with a religious group.

Responses to religious teaching

In 1995, Margaret Kennedy, as co-ordinator of CSSA (Christian Survivors of Sexual Abuse), presented a *Submission to the National Commission of Inquiry into the Prevention of Child Abuse* (Kennedy 1995b). The CSSA was founded by 'a Roman Catholic survivor who was told by her priest that *she* should go to confession to confess *her* sins of impurity' (p.1).

Blaming the female for assault by a male is far from modern. The great Hindu epic *Ramayana*, for example, narrates the rejection of Sita by Rama after her rescue from the demon Ravana. Although Sita has resisted all attempts on her virtue throughout her long ordeal, Rama accuses her of infidelity: '"For when Ravana saw your captivating, divine body, he would not have held back for long, when you were dwelling in his own house."' Sita protests her innocence and undertakes self-immolation: '"As my heart never wavered from Raghava [Rama], so may the fire, the witness of all people, protect me."' When Sita is delivered alive, Rama accounts for his actions by claiming. '"It was necessary that the lovely Sita should enter the purifying fire … for she had lived for a long time in the inner chambers of Ravana."' Without the demonstration of her purity, '"good people would say of me, 'That Rama … is certainly lustful and childish.'"' He announces that he had always known of Sita's fidelity: '"Ravana was unable to violate this wide-eyed lady, for she was protected by her own energy."' Sita's innocence is proved, and she is rewarded, not for fidelity itself, but the public demonstration, by reunion with her husband (O'Flaherty 1975, pp.198–204).

Virginity before and chastity after marriage are highly prized in most religious traditions, and involuntary relinquishment of 'purity', whether or not it involves actual 'deflowering', may be no protection from censure and punishment, often administered internally, by the child herself as she applies the strict teachings of her religion to her fall from perfection.

Children who have been abused are often subjected to the fire – purifying or otherwise – of investigation and court hearings. Those who are associated with a religious organisation may be faced with other ordeals. Kennedy (1995b), for example, notes the Christian emphasis on endurance: 'Since Jesus suffered, we too must suffer ... There is a connection between Jesus carrying His cross, and us carrying ours. To carry one's cross nobly and quietly is honoured as "saintly."' A survivor '"always thought the more pain you endured, the better"' (p.12).

Forgiveness is also highly prized. Jesus commanded: '"love your enemies, do good to those who hate you, bless those who curse you, pray for those who treat you badly"' (Luke 6:27–30). Christians are exhorted to '"turn the other cheek"' and to forgive '"70 times seven"'. A survivor "felt that forgiveness was demanded of me both by God and the Church. Was that not the true test of a Christian – the ability to forgive? In effect, I was seeing myself back in an abusive situation, in which someone bigger, stronger, and in authority over me was demanding something from me that I was unable to give"' (quoted in Kennedy 1995b, p.16).

Bill (a social worker) suggested to me that religious belief associated with, for example, forgiveness, can 'skew assessment of risk because the worker is too keen on believing in good in everyone'. He commented on the retributive aspects of the Bible, not least the warning of Jesus that anyone who causes a child to sin '"would be better ... to have a millstone fastened round his neck and to be drowned in the depth of the sea"' (Matthew 18:6).

For the Christian child, guilt can be exacerbated by the 'inability' to forgive: '"There was anger; fury might be a better word; hatred, grief, bitterness, resentment ... I felt guilty about these feelings; anger and hatred are not Christian"' (quoted in Kennedy 1995b, p.15). Conflict about acceptable, 'correct' feelings and responses is not confined to members of any Church or religious group.

Children who are associated with religions which worship a male deity (especially if, as in Christianity, he is endowed with qualities of perfect fatherhood) may meet problems in reconciling feelings about the abusing earthly father and the ideal heavenly parent:

> Abuse, particularly sexual abuse, raises questions about the nature of the 'family', and about what a 'father' is and what the paternal role is. Religious language often depends on a positive view of the value and trust placed in fathers, parents and family. For an abused child (or an adult with childhood experience of abuse) there may be real difficulties in this type of theological language which may have an effect on the child's spiritual life. For the abused child confusion may arise between the language in which the spiritual life is presented and the experience such language aims to represent.
>
> Feelings aroused by the abuse may not be fully recognised but may lead to strong reactions against traditional language which represents God as father or as protector, or indeed the range of 'family language'. (Armstrong 1991, p.4)

Children are taught to please and placate both the deity and their fathers (and other powerful males). Failure to achieve this may bring at least displeasure, at worst punishment. Failure to please the deity may result in the greatest punishment: separation from him in hell, however that is conceived.

It may be impossible to reconcile divine and earthly fathers, so the very endeavour to earn approval from one leads to conflict with the other. A story about the Jewish boy Jesus, when aged 12, caused his parents appalling anxiety after the annual visit to Jerusalem for the Passover. When Joseph and Mary set out for home, he remained behind. Since they were travelling with a large party, Jesus was not missed until the end of the day. After three days of anxious searching, they found the boy in discussion with teachers in the Temple. Questioned by his mother, Jesus asked: '"What made you search? Did you not know that I was bound to be in my Father's house?"' (Luke 2:41–52). This is in no way a tale of abuse: Mary and Joseph did not understand, but neither did they punish their bewildering son. However, the story illustrates the possibilities for misunderstanding and conflict inherent in religious teaching which employs familial terms. 'Meg', for example, was deeply hurt by the accusation that 'You'll do anything for your heavenly father but nothing for your earthly father.' Much of her energy was spent earnestly trying to please the former and placate the latter, and the impossibility of reconciling these important parts of her life caused confusion and distress.

Many children are taught that the deity loves and protects them. Children brought up within a Christianity-based culture may wonder how a loving, protective God could accept the death of his son without intervention. Children who have been abused, whether by their fathers or other powerful males, may wonder why the all-powerful deity fails to protect them. This failure means either that the deity lacks the ability to protect even one small child, or that he does not choose to exercise his power in such a way – terrifying and disastrous alternatives. Perhaps they are being tested, to prove their endurance in suffering and fidelity to religious codes. More likely they feel convicted of sin, confirmed in the belief that 'all have sinned and come short of the glory of God'. Certainly, trust in both divine and human power and protection is destroyed:

> 'Where *was* God when I was abused?'
> 'I knew that I had committed a terrible sin of some kind, and that I was evil: I was going to Hell.'
> 'I'd say to myself, if I'm good from now on, God will stop him doing these things to me. So whenever he's come into my bedroom, I knew I must have been bad.'

Worst of all, perhaps:

There is much pressure on the child survivor or adult to *heal quickly* because people have prayed for them, and want to see the power of prayer. In order for those praying to feel good, it is better for the survivor to say they *do* feel better, in order not to suffer further blame. (Kennedy 1995b, p.13)

'Failure' to be healed may lead to further pressure:

One survivor told us [CSSA] how she suffered terrible depression and went for healing. The depression did not go away, and the explanation was, 'You must be blocking God's healing by some sin you have committed.' (p.12)

An adult may use the word 'love' while engaged in an act of abuse, sexual or otherwise. Physical punishment or chastisement may be justified by: 'I'm doing this for your own good, because I love you.' If love is a tenet of the child's religion, what messages are received about the intentions and behaviour of the 'loving' deity and co-religionists who apparently permit and perpetrate such acts in the name of love?

Children who are not associated with formal religious belief and observance may nevertheless regard themselves as bad, even evil, and use religious imagery.

Toby (aged 9) was referred to Janet West (1996) for play therapy because of:

- Outbursts of extreme temper, recently holding a knife to his mother.
- Vicious fighting.
- Engaging in daredevil escapades.
- Trying to jump out of a window saying he wanted to die.
- Being involved in petty thieving (especially sweets).
- Being suspended from school for violent behaviour.
- Sometimes curling up like a baby.
- Calling himself 'bad', identifying with his second name Nicholas – Nick – Old Nick [a name for the devil]. (p.4)

As a baby and young child, Toby had been severely neglected, and possibly abused. He had moved between numerous addresses with his mother, between hospital and foster care, and at the time of referral, again lived with his mother under a Supervision Order in a relationship which was approaching breaking point after two-and-a-half years (West 1996, p.4).

The first stages of play therapy were dominated by expressions of his 'bad', angry feelings through the evil personification in the film series *Star Wars*, Darth Vader. Janet West (1996, p.7):

guessed from his interest in a film about the malevolent dealings of Old Nick, and from what Toby had said about himself and his forenames that he had identified himself to some extent with strong negative forces, and I considered it was no coincidence that he had chosen to work with Darth Vader and other powerful figures. (West 1996, p.6)

Later, however, Toby chose to be a good, brave knight, 'often the rescuer with good prevailing; had he been intrinsically "bad" we might have had a different scenario' (pp.6 and 7). And if Toby had had no opportunity to play out the conflict between Darth Vader and good knights, his life scenario might have been bleak indeed.

QUESTIONS

- Do you think that children who have been sexually abused are impure and should confess sin?
- If you don't think this, have you met other people who do think so?
- Why do you think some people believe this?
- Have any children known to you met this attitude after they have been abused?
- What effect did this attitude have on them?
- Do you recognise the possibility of conflict for children whose religious teaching emphasises the powerful, protective role of a male deity?
- Can children known to you express anger with and disappointment in the deity who appears to have failed them?
- Have children known to you expressed a belief that they are bad or evil?

SUGGESTIONS

With colleagues and children:

- Discuss one another's ideas about the questions above.
- Tell stories from religious or other traditions in which children/adults who have been abused in some way have to expiate their 'sin' and prove their purity.
- Make up stories about children who have been abused in some way who experience conflict in feelings and/or feel bad/evil.
- Make up stories about children who express anger with a powerful deity.

Spiritual strength

Having noted some commonly experienced effects of abuse (in whatever form), it is useful to recapitulate some definitions of spiritual needs, qualities and experiences (see Chapter 2 and 3). The key words in Bradford's (1995) summary of human spirituality are *love, peace, wonder, confidence, relatedness*. The care workers placed 'love and understanding' in the centre of their chart (see p.43), listing as spiritual needs to 'give meaning to life, be aware of the mysteries of life, develop own beliefs and get acceptance for them'. The four core qualities of spiritual experience explored by Nye and Hay are sensing a changed quality in awareness, value, mystery, meaningfulness and insight, and these writers discuss the importance of trust, privacy, a special place, relationship and delight and despair (Nye 1996).

If any part of the child is harmed, the whole child suffers. How much more is this so when the concept of spirituality is introduced? Neglect of and assault on mind, body and emotions inhibit, maybe for ever, the ability to experience the growing awareness of meaning, the terrifying glory of mystery, mastery of the self within the world, and development of wisely trusting and loving relationships. What more devastating abuse can there be?

Frances Cattermole (1990), however, demonstrates that spiritual growth may continue within a context of suffering and distress. Her summary of points which recurred during a seminar of youth leaders and young people (organised by the National Council for Voluntary Youth Services) includes:

- We all have singular experiences, sometimes tragic, with which we grapple. Our spiritual development takes place as we use time and space to reflect on these experiences.
- Spirituality is a struggle to make sense of existence by getting underneath the veneer of the superficial to explore the depths of reality.
- Spiritual development is the process by which we learn to cope, learn how to discover our place in the world. It occurs as we are introduced to the crisis points in life, e.g. birth, death, unemployment, handicap, personal relationships, under the watchfulness of someone who cares. (p.8)

Crisis leads to growth, and the spirit both gives and receives strength through struggle.

In discussing the importance of spirituality and religion in social work, several practitioners offered examples of profound experience in the lives of children who had suffered abuse or other desperate difficulty and distress. Some examples are given below.

Norma (a social worker) spoke of her own unhappy childhood, which had included two periods in residential accommodation. In the depths of unhappiness, she had experienced God entering her life, and has since offered the benefits of her faith through her work. She considers that it is essential to be able to forgive both others and oneself, which may have much significance within the context of abuse. She recalled a boy (aged 16) in a penal establishment. For his own protection he was in a cell alone, and he was contemplating suicide because his life seemed hopeless. However, he began to read the Gideon Bible in his cell, and although he didn't understand it, found that it gave him peace. He mentioned this to a prison officer (a Christian), who arranged a visit from the chaplain. This was followed by a visit from Norma, then a probation officer, who was wearing the Christian 'fish' symbol, like the chaplain. The boy said, 'I think God's got his hand on me,' and was able to talk about faith and other matters about which he could not have spoken before, including 'deep down hurting things'.

The opportunity to talk about spiritual/religious matters with a practitioner was also helpful to a 17-year-old girl whose response to a very painful childhood was that her problems must be her own fault and that God must be angry: 'If there's a God who's in charge of things it must indicate that I'm bad.' She felt rejected by God as well as her family. Because she was able to talk about such matters with Kate (a social worker in a child/family unit), who was a Christian, the girl began to see that she was not responsible for her problems, and to progress on her spiritual journey.

Practitioners do not always feel confident to engage in such discussions. Kate recalled an occasion when a child told her, 'I've become a Christian'; a colleague with her said later, 'I'm glad you were there – I wouldn't have known how to respond.' Yet practitioners are used to receiving information on many terrible and distressing matters.

Marlene (a social worker) worked with a girl (aged 17) whose many problems and anxieties (including an absent father) were expressed in such symptoms as eating disorder and recurrent depression. The girl knew that Marlene was a Christian, and felt able to talk about her idea of God as a father during her own father's absence, and her confusion about how to relate to her father should he return. The girl began to attend a church, and was eventually confirmed. Her self-esteem improved through involvement with the accepting congregation. Marlene in no way influenced her decision, but saw that the girl was helped to make decisions by being able to discuss the matter with no fear of ridicule, and with every confidence in her worker's interest and understanding.

Norma spoke of a girl who had been sexually abused by a family member during childhood. At 18 she was baptised into a Church, and gave testimony that she had never expected to feel so loved again. She was coming to realise that the abuse had not been her fault, and that God and other Christians could love her.

'Beth' (a senior practitioner in a hospital) described a girl (aged 14) who had been sexually abused as a child. She had not revealed this until the age of 14, when she began to harm herself. She was desperately seeking 'something to cling onto', and found her place in a church whose firm hierarchy gave her a sense of security. She was convinced of redemption, salvation and God as a good, chosen father, in contrast to her own abusing parent. When she absconded from local authority accommodation, she would go to a church member.

These and other examples illustrate how a church (or other religious group) can offer abused and unhappy children sanctuary and new hope. Acceptance by people who do not condemn and who represent a deity who does not blame the child enables emergence from the trap of self-blame and repugnance, the belief that she (or he) is unloveable, unlovely and incapable of love.

Children sometimes seek answers to unanswerable questions by writing to God, the ultimate authority. Although they can never find answers, asking the questions may help to clarify confusion, to find 'a place to be comfortable in'.

Kennedy (1995b) suggests:

> There is great potential for child survivors to benefit from 'speaking' to God about their pain, anger and hurt via special liturgies and worship. Such worship must allow the child to *be real*. All emotions, beliefs and feelings should be accepted and incorporated into the liturgy and worship. If a child or adult wishes to say that they hate God, then so be it. This allows them the space to vent the hurt and pain against God, whom they often perceive has let them down, and betrayed them just as their perpetrator has.

Enabling this can be very strengthening, while failure to understand the need directly to address the deity may add to distress:

> Secular people fail to understand that God in children's and adults' lives is seen as a total entity – a person or being one *can* talk to, and therefore in the midst of the pain of abuse, one needs to be able to *talk to* God! If this is not facilitated or allowed, then a channel by which to ventilate and express more pain is blocked, causing additional frustration. Christian children can be asked, 'What would you *really* like to tell God?'

Kennedy offers a possible response:

> 'I want to tell God that I hate him, that I believed he'd care for me, and he didn't. He let me down. I want to ask God why he didn't *do* anything if he's so powerful, and ask God why he didn't *do* something. I want to be angry.'

This might take place in a church or other place of worship, or within a small, specially convened group. A liturgy or form of service could be prepared with the child. Kennedy understands that:

> Secular workers will find this an alien idea – even contrary to their own beliefs. But CSSA believes that Christian children who are abused may need such a space before God to be real; in a way, to confront God just as one may confront an abuser. There can be enormous benefits if done sensitively and carefully. (pp.26–7)

Although as Kennedy notes, abuse is exacerbated by the attitude that the abused person is impure and should confess sin, the sense of guilt and responsibility, and the sensation of being soiled and damaged might be helped by a rite of passage during which feelings could be expressed, and after which a new phase of life might start. There is relevance in these ideas for all children, of any or no religion.

It is essential for practitioners to receive excellent consultation and support in dealing with these problems, enabling access to their own spiritual strength (see 'The needs of practitioners' in Chapter 12).

QUESTIONS

- Do you feel comfortable if children tell you about spiritual or religious experience or anxiety?
- If not, what makes you feel uncomfortable?
- How could you become more comfortable to engage in such conversations?
- Could any children known to you be helped by conversation about spiritual/religious matters or connection with a religious group?
- The examples of children gaining strength from association with a religious group given here are all drawn from Christianity; how do other religions help children who have been abused?

SUGGESTIONS

With colleagues and children:

- Discuss one another's ideas about the questions above.
- Consider ways in which religious groups can help children who have been abused or have had other experiences of distress and rejection.
- Help children to write letters to a deity asking questions and/or expressing feelings.
- Devise a rite of passage which could help an abused child express

feelings and fears and then pass on to a new stage of life.
- Make up stories about children who gain strength and new life after abuse, showing how they express and manage energy-draining feelings.

Summary

Following discussion of spiritual distress, this chapter introduced ideas about connections between abuse identified as physical, sexual and/or emotional, and abuse of the spirit, bearing in mind the requirements of the UN Convention on the Rights of the Child that attention should be given to children's spiritual development and well-being. Abuse in any form detracts from spiritual well-being, and is thus abuse of the spirit.

When some commonly observed effects of abuse are compared with definitions of spiritual needs, qualities and values, they can be found to have many points of meeting – for example, with regard to the development/deterioration of trust, relationships, self-esteem and confidence. Guilt, fear and depression, even despair, may develop to the exclusion of other more positive emotions.

Some abuse may be associated with religious teachings which, however intended, can cause confusion and distress, including anger towards a deity.

Spiritual strength can also result from abuse, as when children receive acceptance and love from religious groups which help them to grow away from the sense of guilt, shame and unworth. It may be helpful to devise some form of ceremony or rite of passage during which the child can express emotions and through which movement to a new phase of being can be achieved and marked.

It is essential that practitioners receive excellent consultation and support during work with children who have been abused.

12 Abuse associated with religious and ritual practices

Intentional abuse

Chapter 11 introduced ideas about associations between abuse and neglect, and aspects of spiritual well-being and religious teaching and belief. For the purpose of this chapter, these associations can be regarded as informal or unintentional, in that perpetrators of abuse are not regarded as deliberately inflicting spiritual harm or using a religious context to enable or itself serve as part of the abuse.

However, there are several ways in which abuse can be intentionally connected with religious organisations and/or practice, or some form of ritual with quasi-religious characteristics. It is not the purpose of this chapter to discuss these forms of abuse in detail: to do that would require reference to substantial specialist texts and, where possible, further reading is recommended. The discussion is necessarily brief, and intended only as introductory.

When the subjects of children and spirituality are linked, the effect is often to suggest that experience is essentially positive, connected with insights which change the view of the world for the better and lead to strong and fulfilling relationships with other people, the whole of creation and a deity. Chapters 4 and 11 illustrated how spiritual experience in childhood can be deeply disturbing and/or may be adversely affected by abuse and neglect.

It is recognised that abusive adults who have no concept of the spirit or soul cannot be held guilty of deliberately assaulting the child's spirit. Yet any abuse, whatever the effects intended by the perpetrator, harms every aspect of the whole person.

However, there are adults whose association with a religious (or quasi-religious) organisation indicates that they do profess belief in a spiritual dimension. When they abuse children, they must, in accordance with their own beliefs, be abusing the spirit.

Sometimes abuse takes the form of persecution and oppression associated with hostility between religious groups, whether these are entirely different religions or sects of the same religion. Here, questions must be asked about the beliefs of the groups, each of which may consider members of the others to be damned, perhaps without souls.

Most controversial is the matter of abuse allegedly perpetrated by satanist cults. If cult members profess belief in supernatural beings, it may be argued that a concept of spirit/soul exists and is deliberately associated with the many physical, mental and emotional forms of abuse. Material in this section may be disturbing to readers who have not previously engaged with this topic.

Practitioners who work with children who have been abused are likely to experience exhaustion and possibly illness, so it is essential to ensure that excellent and reliable consultation and support are available.

Abuse informally associated with religious organisations

From time to time, the news media are excited by the scandal of a priest or other holder of status in a religious organisation who is found guilty of child abuse (usually sexual). This may take place in residential establishments in which perpetrators work or for which they are responsible. Abuse may also take place on group holidays (for example, with Scout or Guide camps linked with a church), in perpetrators' own homes or elsewhere. Although the examples below refer to Christian situations, the discussion is relevant to any religion and denomination.

Margaret Kennedy (of Christian Survivors of Sexual Abuse) found that 'There is a very strong belief that sexual abuse does not take place within Christian homes,' and that 'it is often not seen as necessary for any sort of parish policy on Child Protection'. Far from young people's groups such as Scouts, Guides and church choirs being used as safe forums for safety and prevention programmes, 'Unfortunately it is the experience of CSSA that in these very groups, the leaders can be the abusers' (Kennedy 1995b, p.2).

It can also be difficult for adherents of a religion to believe that co-religionists could be guilty of abuse, perhaps because they are impressed with the apparent goodness and moral rectitude of the alleged abuser, who may hold high status within the particular group, and may be seen to fulfil religious obligations with devotion. Refusal to countenance the possibility of co-religionists committing any sin or crime, especially sexual abuse, may also reflect a fear that adherence to the religion itself is no protection: that anyone may become either a victim or, even more frightening, a perpetrator. Disturbance may be caused for practitioners who, as members of a religious group within which abuse has been alleged, are subject to suspicion and hostility because they do not collude with the argument of automatic innocence.

In 1991, the National Children's Bureau published *Taking Care: A Church Response to Children, Adults and Abuse,* based on discussions with members of several Christian denominations (Armstrong 1991). The publication includes: information on abuse and responding to abuse; practical learning activities for use with groups; discussion papers on issues for church communities, pastoral work and worship; frameworks for reviewing church activities with children and young people, and detailed references to sources of further help and information. Since publication of *Taking Care,* individual denominations have issued their own guidelines, for example:

- *Child Abuse: pastoral and procedural guidelines* A Report from a Working Party to the Catholic Bishops' Conference of England and Wales on cases of sexual abuse of children involving priests, religious and other Church workers (1994).
- *Protecting our Children: guidelines on child abuse for clergy and lay people* The Anglican Diocese of Southwark (1994).
- *Safe to Grow: guidelines on child protection for the local church and its youth leaders* Baptists (1994).
- *Safeguarding Children and Young People* Methodists (1994).
- *Safeguarding Children from Harm: protecting children from abuse; Guidelines for parents, elders, overseers and all who work with children and young people in Britain Yearly Meeting* Religious Society of Friends (1996).

(augmented from Kennedy 1995b, p.27)

Kennedy comments: 'It is clear that the media attention on clergy abuse facilitated a proliferation of Guidelines in 1994. While the first looks exclusively at clergy and other Church personnel molesting, the remainder excluded clergy molesters entirely' (1995b, p.27).

Abuse within a context where children are taught that they should feel safe destroys the roots of trust. If the context includes religious teaching and responsibility for spiritual well-being, immense spiritual damage is implied: at the very least, how can people who have been abused physically within a religious environment dissociate the sins of the perpetrators, including lies, from teachings about right behaviour in the sight of the deity which may now be seen to be 'false', especially if the perpetrator is not apprehended and receives no punishment, whether temporal or divine. Teachings about endurance and forgiveness in Christianity, for example, may cause confusion for children who are suffering at the hands of the very people who reinforce these messages of morality and right living: 'Does God mean me to endure *this* and forgive *him*?'

Children who have been thus abused may take action, reporting the abuse in the hope that it will be stopped, but that very action may feel like betrayal, and bring with it fear of reprisal, whether by the perpetrator or an outraged deity who has allowed the abuse to continue without intervening. Revelation may not be made until abuse itself is long past and the children are safely adult – 'safe' in a physical sense. The very fact of the delay in disclosure indicates how deep the emotional and spiritual disturbance is.

In 1993, a Roman Catholic monk was sentenced to seven years' imprisonment following revelations of sexual offences against a number of boys in a community home where he had worked. Some of the disclosures were made twenty years after the offences. A report by Frederick Lawton (1993) (a retired Lord Justice of Appeal) published in *The Tablet Catholic Weekly* wondered: 'Why did adult men years afterwards decide to inform the police of incidents which had happened when they were boys?' The same article refers to a Christian (Anglican) vicar 'sentenced to four months' imprisonment for sexually assaulting 20 years before a girl aged 13 who had been baby-sitting for him'. Lawton considers: 'As the charge was one of assault and not unlawful sexual intercourse, the injury to the girl ... cannot have been serious.' (Cited in Kennedy 1995b, p.3)

Lawton fails to appreciate the effects of any assault on a young girl, let alone the devastating impact of betrayal by a man of God, someone whom she should have had most cause to trust. Moreover, he appears to consider that events so long in the past should have been forgotten, should have ceased to affect the lives of the children once they became adult. Is there also a suggestion that assault by a person of the cloth, whatever the denomination, is in some way less harmful than by one who has not been ordained? He comments that the monk had stopped offending, apparently of his own volition. Lawton finds it 'reasonable to infer that this was after he has been to confession, had been given absolution and had performed some penance', but there is no evidence for this speculative comment, just as there is no evidence that the monk 'had stopped offending'. He asks if justice required 'that offences committed so long before should be punished with imprisonment?'. The implication appears to be that a sin, confessed and expiated within a religious congregation, should not also be treated as a crime in the secular context (for further comment, see Kennedy 1995b, pp.3–4).

Bill (a social worker) referred to the efforts religious organisations sometimes make to hide perpetrators, to 'make them better', perhaps taking them away from the diocese and counselling them, but not always keeping them away from children. He recalled the trial of a clergyman charged with sexually abusing children in a choir; the judge blamed the children for seducing him!

Abuse within the context of religion may not have any physical manifestation. Teaching about punishment for sin, if deliberately terrifying, can cause anxiety and fear beyond the child's coping capacities. Bill's sister had attended a convent school briefly, coming home full of terror because of preaching about hellfire.

Aspects of involuntary spiritual distress have been discussed in Chapter 4. Adults sometimes deliberately stimulate such disturbance, perhaps with the motive of saving children from present sin and eternal punishment, but meanwhile causing present suffering and possible revulsion from such unpalatable means of salvation.

Anxiety is often expressed about practices of new religious movements and cults, including mind-control techniques to separate adherents from families and maintain dominance by leaders. Young people may be attracted to some groups whose activities cause concern to relations and others. Ian Howarth (1994) (General Secretary of the Cult Information Centre) seeks to correct several popular misconceptions about cults, offering such clear comments as: 'People don't join cults. They are recruited.' 'Cults intend to retain a hold on people for life, or for as long as they are valuable to the cult.' 'Normal people from normal families are recruited into cults.' 'Cult members are sincere (sincere victims, but sincere).' 'Cult members are victims and need to be treated with love. They ... need help, not hostility.' Howarth lists characteristics of cults in general, and further defines two groups, *therapy* and *religious* cults. He also notes techniques of mind control. Although he finds that the average age at recruitment is in the low 20s, practitioners may have concerns about younger people (pp.33–4 and 32).

Robert Towler (1994) (Director of INFORM) describes the service provided by INFORM, which offers information to anyone concerned about cults. Since INFORM is in touch with many cults, it 'is often able to mediate between an enquirer and a movement, getting people back in touch with one another ... and generally putting pressure on movements to behave reasonably and compassionately towards ex-members or the families and friends of current members'. Towler finds that 'Of those young people who choose to join a new religious movement, the vast majority leave again of their own free will, either very quickly or within two years at the most.' He strongly advises concerned people to become well informed about 'the group, its origins, its history, its beliefs and its practices, and maintain as much contact as possible with your son or sister or friend, affirming the person without either affirming or deriding the group they have joined, only asking and gently questioning' (p.24). (See 'useful organisations' for details of support networks.)

Whatever the situation, betrayal of trust and misuse of authority and power are compounded by association with religion: how can the adult who purports to represent a loving, just, protecting deity commit such acts?

QUESTIONS

- Have you heard of any cases of abuse by clergy or other people in a position of trust within a religious congregation?
- If so, what did you feel about the perpetrators?
- If you are associated with any religious congregation, do you think your co-religionists could abuse children in any way?
- If you don't think this, why do you consider your co-religionists to be different from other people?
- Do you know any children or adults who have been abused, in any way, by clergy or other co-religionists?
- Does your religious congregation take any steps to protect children from abuse, including education, and guidelines for adults?
- What do you think could be the effects on spiritual well-being of children being abused within the context of a religious congregation?

SUGGESTIONS

With colleagues and children:

- Discuss one another's ideas about the questions above.
- Notice comments in the media when adults connected with religious organisations are accused of abusing children.
- If you feel anxious about observances of any established religions, obtain information and question representatives.
- If you feel anxious about new religions/cults, obtain information and advice from such groups as INFORM.

Oppression, persecution and sectarianism

The intention of this brief section is to draw attention to the importance of experiences of persecution and oppression associated with religion in the lives of many children. The issues implied by these topics are too many and too great for the few paragraphs available here, and practitioners are encouraged to pursue these and other ideas with colleagues, children and families.

Practitioners who work in areas populated by representatives of several religions and/or denominations may know the problems and suffering caused by intolerance of beliefs and assaults on, for example, places of worship and cemeteries. Membership of a group which suffers overt persecution may stimulate both fear of the persecutor and bonding with co-religionists' but it may also lead to resentment of parents and community leaders whose beliefs and attitudes may be seen as involving children in troubles which they themselves have not initiated and do not wish.

Practitioners who work in areas where the population is mainly Christian (or nominally so) may consider that oppression is found only where other religions are substantially represented and intolerance is expressed through public violence. However, physical and highly visible abuse are not the only ways in which children may suffer religious intolerance.

'Beth' (a senior practitioner in a hospital serving a mainly white population) was appalled by the attitude of a nurse feeding a Muslim baby who was forbidden to eat pork, in accordance with her religion. The nurse expressed exasperation at the requirement to arrange a special meal, considering that, since the food was mashed up, the parents would not know what she had eaten, and the baby would certainly be unaware of the contents of her dinner. Although several religions were represented in the area, it appears that no training in religious beliefs and observances had been arranged for hospital staff.

The nurse's attitude was based, perhaps, on a combination of overwork and ignorance; this is understandable, but is no excuse for neglecting, even abusing, the right of the child and family to respect for their religious beliefs. Moreover, exasperation implies strong emotion, raising the question of why the nurse felt this way about what might be seen as a small inconvenience in the course of a working day. Her supervisor, discussing the incident, might wonder if the nurse had some prejudice about Islam and/or other religions, and if so, what was the basis of such prejudice, and how might it affect her work with other children?

Older children may be forced into emotional and spiritual conflict by attitudes of staff which are at best unthinking and at worst actually cruel. As mentioned in Chapter 10, Ahmed et al. (1986) noted the suffering of Roksana (aged 9), a Muslim girl in care, who 'ate meat contrary to parental injunction. She did not wish to be different and that suited staff greatly,' but later, 'she expressed anxiety and feelings of guilt, she worried about betraying her mother and wondered about punishment from God' (p.59). Roksana was particularly vulnerable to emotional and spiritual conflict since, as a faithful Muslim girl, she had been trained to be obedient and submissive to adults in authority, and hence to the staff who wished her to eat *haram* (forbidden) meat.

The potentially deep and long-lasting effects of such feelings (see Chapter 4) raise concern for all the Roksanas who endure such guilt and anxiety alone, without recourse to an adult who can both remove the physical stimulus (in this case the forbidden meat) and provide understanding.

While staff who expect children to eat prohibited food or transgress other religious observances (see Part 3) are not, presumably, deliberately oppressing their charges, failure to learn about and respect such practices is a form of neglect.

The *Looking After Children* questionnaires (DoH 1995) acknowledge the possibility of oppressive behaviour by both adults and children, asking, under 'Identity', for example: 'Does the child get picked on by other children and/or adults (eg because s/he is looked after by the local authority, because of size, race, disability, gender or for any other reason)? What are the carer(s) doing to help the child cope with other people's prejudices?' (question ID6, age 3–9).

Although religion is not specified as a subject for being 'picked on', it must be assumed under 'any other reason'. The omission of a direct reference seems strange when religion (and spiritual) development/well-being are mentioned in several Articles in the UN Convention on the Rights of the Child, and when attention to religious welfare is required in the Children Act 1989. Since in ID6 (and the equivalent question for other age groups) the compilers thought it necessary to list 'size', 'race', 'disability' and 'gender' it would seem to have been prudent to add 'religion', to prompt those practitioners for whom religion is not an important aspect of life.

Also hidden within these questions are considerations of the prejudices not only of 'other people', but also the carers and children themselves. Holding prejudices and being a perpetrator of oppressive or even persecutory behaviour is itself detrimental to children's spiritual well-being.

Children may be teased and bullied for wearing special clothes: for example, the Hindu sacred thread or Muslim cap. Even when children are not distinguished by their clothing, their parents may be: female members of a substantial Plymouth Brethren community in one city were easily identified and well known by their dark-blue headscarves. The children were privately taught in their own school. Although they were not bullied by other children, they were to some extent objects of amusement, regarded as different within the city.

Young children may be taught to identify differences, which may lead to dislike, even fear. Bob (a senior practitioner) remembered his childhood in a small English town, when Protestant children walked to church on one side of the road, Roman Catholics to mass on the other. Although he had Roman Catholic friends, he was not allowed to bring them home. Bob felt excluded from such fascinating events as the Corpus Christi Procession, denied the chance to explore other faiths and denominations. What fears underlay the attitudes of parents who thus 'protected' their children? And what fears were instilled into the next generation? While Bob felt cheated of the chance to learn and explore, other children may have learnt attitudes which in some contexts lead to full-scale violent sectarianism.

To be subjected to oppression because of religious affiliation is clearly a form of abuse which attacks every aspect of life, especially the spiritual. For children, innocent of any acts, the passive matter of parentage may lead to active suffering. For example, the experiences of 'Michel', a fictional Jewish child, illustrate the experiences of real children. Michel's father dies in a concentration camp during the Second World War, and having been fostered by a Roman Catholic, Michel is placed in a Jesuit boarding school. As he learns more about his Jewishness, he tortures himself spiritually about his beliefs and identity. He assumes increasing responsibility for the suffering of his father, who couldn't hide from the Nazis '"because of me. He was afraid for me because I was so little ... he must have hated me."' His friend tries to comfort him, but Michel has a greater terror. If his father died because of him, he, the innocent child, was guilty of condemning his father to hell. '"They're in hell! ... They're burning in hell because they're Jews!"' Later, Michel sees himself as punished because not only is he a Jew, responsible for crucifying the Christian's Jesus, but worse, he has taken communion during Roman Catholic mass; '"Jew! Accursed of God! Hypocrite! Damned for sacrilege and false communion!"' (Lewis 1967, pp.336, 337 and 483; see also Chapter 15).

Intolerance may be exacerbated by apparent confusion between religions. A (real) Jewish boy in a public school was given an insulting nickname and thoroughly disliked, not least because of his hard work, achievement and Semitic appearance. The intolerance was increased not because of his religious beliefs, but because, on the contrary, he was seen to attend the school chapel. Whether or not he practised Judaism at home, his failure to be demonstrably observant within the school lost him any chance of respect.

An Arab boy in hospital in Jerusalem for cardiac surgery 'requested a Jewish skullcap and kosher diet'. He had been terrified by horror stories that 'his heart would be taken out and given to a Jewish boy' (Goodall 1994, p.30; see also Chapter 13).

Much suffering may be caused by lack of knowledge and understanding, especially when information about religious beliefs and observances is obtained exclusively from the mass media, and based only on the most florid and extreme aspects of the religion. But suffering is also caused deliberately by adults and children who choose to assault, verbally or physically, those whose beliefs differ from their own.

QUESTIONS

- Have you ever felt oppressed because of your religious belief and/or affiliation?
- Have you ever met other people who felt oppressed because of their religious belief and/or affiliation?
- Have you ever taken an oppressive attitude or action, whether deliberately or because of ignorance?
- If so, how do you feel about that? How could you guard against further such acts?
- Are any children known to you experiencing teasing, bullying or other problems because of their religious affiliation?
- If so, what do the children feel about their experiences?
- How can they be strengthened to cope with such attitudes?
- What are the attitudes of your agency/establishment towards them?
- Do any children/adults known to you express oppressive attitudes towards people affiliated to different religions/denominations?

SUGGESTIONS

With colleagues and children:

- Discuss one another's ideas about the questions above.
- Check every aspect of the conduct/policy of your establishment/agency to ensure that no oppressive practices are in operation.
- If there are examples of spiritual abuse associated with failure to respect the religious beliefs and observances of children and families, either because of ignorance or deliberate cruelty, consider how such problems can be avoided, and develop a plan to ensure this happens.
- Consider ways in which children perceive the acts and attitudes of adults, and how they may cause anxiety, confusion and distress.

Abuse intentionally associated with ritual practices

The topic of ritual abuse stimulates strong feelings and controversy. Many practitioners are convinced that ritual and/or satanic practices exist; others are equally convinced that descriptions of such practices are based on imagination or on such stimuli as videos and books, or are misinterpretations of children's words, drawings and play. These responses are introduced here by definitions from two sources:

Ritual abuse is the involvement of children in physical or sexual abuse associated with repeated activities ('ritual') which purport to relate the abuse to contexts of a religious, magical or supernatural kind. (McFadyen et al. 1993, cited in Hobbs and Wynne 1994, p.216).

Organised Abuse is: sexual abuse where there was more than a single abuser and the adults concerned appear to have acted in concert to abuse the children AND/OR where an adult has used an institutional framework or position of authority to recruit children for sexual abuse.

Ritual Abuse is: sexual abuse where there have been allegations of ritual abuse associated with the abuse, whether or not these allegations have been taken any further or tested in the courts.

Satanic Abuse implies: a ritual directed to worship of the devil. 'Satanist' carries the same implications. Allegations may not indicate the intention of the ritual or indicate that it is focussed on the devil, so it seemed more accurate to use the broader 'ritual abuse' for all the cases in the study. If 'satanic' is used it refers to the perceptions of people in the study. (La Fontaine 1994, p.3)

The appellation 'satanic' appears to have been introduced in press reporting of alleged abuse in Orkney in 1991.

In 1994, when Jean La Fontaine published research findings on *The Extent and Nature of Organised and Ritual Abuse*, she found no evidence to justify further research or concern. Her government-funded study was commissioned because: 'A number of cases of the sexual abuse of children had been accompanied by allegations that the victims had also been subjected to bizarre rites, referred to, variously, as witchcraft, satanism or devil worship', a view contested by 'a variety of persons and groups whose scepticism derived from a range of different perspectives on the problem' (p.4).

La Fontaine's 12 conclusions include criticism of communication with children by adults, including social workers and foster carers, and of the collection, recording and transmission of information derived from interviews. She had already expressed the opinion that:

The testimony provided by younger children was fragmentary or the meaning of what was said was unclear. Children's words were interpreted and the sense rather than the words might be reported. Drawings and play may be used to produce supplementary material but that must also be interpreted to show its significance. Behaviour is also used as evidence. In several cases, it was the behaviour of the children rather than what they said which first seemed to call for an explanation. It was assumed among foster parents, and to a large extent among social workers, that the degree of disturbance the children showed was evidence that they had suffered something more severe than the 'usual' forms of sexual abuse. This view appears to be contrary to the psychiatric orthodoxy, although one consultant seemed to share it. (p.26)

La Fontaine also suggests that:

Satanic abuse as an explanation of the children's state evokes a strong emotional response. Believing in it made it possible for foster-mothers and social workers to care for very damaged children with patience and sympathy. The belief has also encouraged fears of an unknown evil among child protection workers and foster-parents and seems to generate an obsessional desire to find out about what happened and who the perpetrators were, which added to their own stress and obscured the children's needs ...

Demonising the marginal poor [abusing parents] and linking them to unknown satanists turns intractable cases of abuse into manifestations of evil. (p.31)

This report raises important questions about social work practice and communication with children (in all circumstances, not only in relation to such allegations). However, the essentially covert nature of the alleged practices under discussion, the deep secrecy emphasised by other practitioners and writers, suggests that La Fontaine's research does not necessarily remove the need for concern.

Also in 1994, Valerie Sinason (a consultant child psychotherapist) published *Treating Survivors of Satanic Abuse*, a collection of 34 papers by established and respected members of a number of professions, some well known in social work practice. Most references in the present section are taken from this book, which can provide a substantial introduction for practitioners who have little or no knowledge of this controversial issue.

One contributor to Sinason's compilation is Tim Tate (a journalist), whose controversial book, *Children for the Devil*, was published in 1991, following concerns raised in 1987 when he had been contacted by a psychiatrist who was anxious about allegations made by a patient about what appeared to be rituals associated with regular abuse, and murder, of boys (Tate 1987, p.xi): Tate had previously broadcast a television documentary about child pornography, including a list of British paedophiles, in *The Cook Report* (1987).

In 1997, Tim Tate produced a programme in *The Death of Childhood* series on Channel 4 on child abuse since Cleveland in 1987. The second programme (produced by John Williams) introduced the events of, and comments on, the three major cases associated with allegations of ritual abuse: Broxtowe (Nottingham) in 1987, Rochdale in 1989–90, and Orkney in 1991. In that programme, barrister Peter Joyce suggested that 'Satanic abuse was a diversion which was in grave danger, at times, of making us take our eyes off the ball', that is, of distracting attention from actual sexual abuse. Liz Kelly (North London University) considered that 'Abusers got the message that the more crazy things you do with children, the more the children will not be believed and you will be safe.'

My own interest was aroused when a social worker spoke of intensive involvement in one of the major cases. I had not followed reports of the case, and I heard the account of what had happened to both children and practitioners with horrified astonishment. Later, it was difficult to remember what I had been told because the impact had been so great. This reaction is common: for example, Leslie Ironside (1994) (a senior child psychotherapist), who worked with a severely abused and traumatised boy: 'began to realise how difficult I found it to remember what Tom had said or done. Normally I felt quite able to write up sessions with children and consider that my own struggle to recall work with Tom throws light on the "indigestibility" of the presenting material' (pp.91–2). Phil Mollon (1994) (a consultant clinical psychologist and psychotherapist) considers that 'hearing about ritual abuse is in itself a significant trauma which evokes emergency defensive measures [comprising] … vigorous efforts to deny, misperceive or in other ways avoid the impact of the account' (p.136).

Some years later, I met another practitioner who had been involved in the same case as my first contact; a question in a training exercise we were sharing stimulated a distressed response which led to discussion of feelings about the investigation and associated events, by then some time in the past. Conversations with practitioners in several fields have indicated that information and concern about cults and rituals are widespread.

Whether adults who take part in rituals believe in and worship satanic powers, or use the behaviours described below to intimidate and control vulnerable children, spiritual and religious abuse is implied, and those implications must be discussed.

As Sinason learned for the first time about satanic abuse, she also learned about secrecy and danger (Sinason 1994, p.14). The first chapter in her compilation is entitled 'Going through the fifth window', taken from a quotation 'The house has five windows: through four the day is clear and still. The fifth faces a black sky, thunder and storm. I am standing by the fifth window' (Tranströmer 1983, cited by Sinason 1994, p.4). She found herself 'standing by the fifth window' when consulted by Anders Svensson, a Swedish psychologist who had been 'asked to assess a severely handicapped woman of 44 ("Ingrid") who was suddenly found to be severely bruised, hallucinating and afraid of windows'.

Svensson contacted Sinason initially to obtain copies of her papers on work with sexually abused handicapped patients. Later he asked 'for her evening home number as he did not feel safe calling from his work. She gave it, as something powerful about secrecy and danger had been communicated, and told her secretary to let her know of any call from Sweden as a matter of emergency.' Gradually, Ingrid's descriptions of what had been done to her led to a realisation that she had been a victim of ritual abuse. Sinason and Svensson learned about other cases in both the UK and Sweden. As Ingrid lost her fear and was believed by Svensson, she became stronger: "'I am handicapped but I am not mad ... They are mad. It is my legs, my body.'" Fear for the practitioners could also decrease as secrecy was reduced by sharing discoveries and understandings with others (pp.14–21).

Fear and secrecy are common adjuncts of abuse in whatever form, controlling the child and ensuring, through the resultant collusion, that abusing behaviour can continue as the child has been forced into complicity. The child who does not report or 'confess' appears to consent.

Organised abuse depends on controlling children and perhaps adult participants through fear and maintaining invisibility. Children themselves may contribute to the control. Wild and Wynne (1986) studied child sex rings in Leeds. They found complex social organisation:

> In these rings there was no recognition of satanic or ritualistic abuse. However, the powerful forces which bound the children together in secrecy were understood as well as the way the children themselves could appreciate and use power. One important lesson ... was just how effectively the secrets were kept. (Hobbs and Wynne 1994 p.215)

Hobbs and Wynne (consultant community paediatricians) joined with other professionals from a variety of disciplines to study 'cases of child abuse that included ritualistic elements'. They found that:

> By providing an opportunity to share disturbing and at times frightening information, the group has enabled a clearer understanding to emerge. The work feels very much like a starting-point in an extremely complex area where most professionals tread with cautious reluctance. However, the children's accounts encourage us to continue. (p.216)

Once again, professionals of considerable experience and standing write about fear and the need to combat the potentially paralysing response to such disturbing material through sharing both information and reaction. They are prepared to engage with such personal as well as professional disturbance because of 'the children's accounts'.

Mollon (1994) describes his reaction to revelations about her childhood by a patient, Helen:

> a mixture of shock, disbelief, horror, dread and terror – including fear for my own safety. I experienced it as an assault on my sense of reality; and I suggest that this is what satanic abuse is – an assault on reality and on the child's sense of reality, an attempt to destroy and possess the child's mind. (p.139)

Whether or not that attempt is successful, revelations by victims of this form of abuse may be regarded as fantasising, hallucinating or lying. Ingrid stated strongly, '"I am not mad"', strengthened by the belief of others. Mollon finds that it is particularly difficult for victims to reveal:

> supernatural experiences and powers associated with satanic activities. My clinical experience suggests that this is a common issue in working with satanically abused patients; their fear is that they will be regarded as mad – the dreaded scenario is of finding the courage to tell and then being disbelieved. (p.139)

Alan Cooklin (a consultant family psychiatrist, honorary senior lecturer, Clinical Director of the Children and Families Psychotherapy Directorate and Chair of the Institute of Family Therapy) comments on a stage of work with Karen:

> From this point on I felt that Karen knew that she knew what she knew. The question of feeling 'mad' and not believed no longer seemed such an issue. However, I am convinced that to be 'believed' is a critical need for anyone who has been through this kind of abuse. (Cooklin and Barnes 1994, p.125)

Practitioners, too, may meet disbelief, and their observations and opinions may be discredited. Allegations of ritual/satanic abuse are so controversial and stimulate so much emotion that practitioners may experience conflict and distress within working relationships. Colleagues may regard them as hysterical, foolish, following a personal obsession, mad (which can be particularly disturbing when the horror of listening to survivors' accounts leads those who hear them to question their own sanity: 'Can I really be hearing this? I thought I'd heard everything and was unshockable but this is beyond belief. So if I believe it, even for a moment, am I in danger of being sucked into a world of madness?'). In the television film *Flowers of the Forest* (Eaton BBC2), a social worker who removed children from home because she suspected ritual abuse was portrayed as increasingly obsessed and unbalanced, volatile and impulsive. Notably, she smoked frequently and nervously. She was shown as dominating a weak and vacillating senior officer, and eventually battling with a colleague for control of the children.

Joan Coleman (1994) (an associate specialist in psychiatry, and co-founder of the Ritual Abuse Information Network and Support – RAINS) summarises the motivations and practices of satanic cults. Basing her summary on reports from British survivors, she finds: 'the religious aspect seems to be supremely important for some members; for others, the quest for power, sexual gratification or financial profit may dominate. All these can overlap, but control over the members is essential if perpetuation of the cult is to be achieved and secrecy maintained' (p.244). Structures are hierarchical and dominated by people who often hold powerful and high-status positions in everyday life as well as within the cult (p.243). Practices include ceremonies, denigration of Christianity, and indoctrinating children; membership usually begins in childhood, and continues for life. Significance is attached to certain dates, colours, symbols emblems, insects and numbers, for example (pp.244 and 248).

Coleman reports that abused children are trained from an early age to be perpetrators. Her patients:

> have described how as 4-year-olds they were made to poke objects into the orifices of younger children and to assist in torture. Initially, they may be very reluctant, but some of either sex, as they grow older, seem to find it increasingly easy to sexually abuse and inflict pain on the younger children. Some girls grow up more afraid of their elder brothers than of their fathers. (p.250)

Children of cult members can expect little if any affection from their parents; rather, they are prepared for full participation in cult practices. They may be:

> abandoned, then 'rescued' and told that Satan has saved them from death. One survivor described being left alone, naked and cold, at the age of 4, for three weeks in an underground room, while her mother went abroad. Her only company was the corpse of a woman she had seen being killed. She was given water but no food; she was told that if she was hungry enough she would eat the rotting flesh of the woman. She was finally taken out by her father, who then sodomised her. (p.250)

Severe punishments may be inflicted for failure to fulfil instructions and complete tasks (p.250).

Effects of involvement in such cult practices include dissociation, which children can achieve from an early age as 'the only way they can survive' (p.250). Multiple personalities may develop and be used within the cult; triggers for particular personalities or behaviours are programmed from any of a multiplicity of stimuli (for example, certain words, melodies, voices) (p.251). For this reason, children in the process of being rescued from cults are prevented from receiving contact and messages of any kind from people suspected of being cult members.

This section began with a definition of ritual abuse as 'the involvement of children in physical or sexual abuse' (McFadyen et al. 1993). However, it is clear that all aspects of life are abused. The UN Convention refers to 'physical, mental, spiritual, moral and social development' (Article 27). The forms of abuse discussed above attack not only the body, but also the mind: for example, by the 'assault on reality and on the child's sense of reality' and the 'attempt to destroy and possess the child's mind' (Mollon 1994, p.139). Interference with thought is at least invasion of privacy, at worst torture and destruction of the self.

If children are, as many practitioners believe, abused in this total form, they suffer assault of the spirit. However temporal the power of cult members, distortion of every aspect of life is involved, and the context of assault is spiritual. If children are forced to use language and participate in ceremonies which represent worship of supernatural powers or desecrate the sacred practices of Christianity (are the practices of other religions also desecrated?), spiritual life is twisted and perverted, directed towards destruction. Every aspect of healthy life must be infected, for where are trust and love, self-confidence and joy, respect for life and connection with the world?

The term 'soul murder' has been used in connection with gaining complete domination over a victim (Shengold 1989, cited in Goodwin 1994, p.6). This raises a complex theological question: can a soul be killed? Many adherents of religions believe in a life after death in which the soul or spirit moves to heaven or hell, and in the context of such beliefs, children who participate in satanic cults would be considered to be damned, especially if they remain members throughout life. If such cults really do worship a concept of devil and revile a concept of godhead, there is a clear implication that the soul has been 'lost'.

The UN Convention requires respect for 'freedom of thought, conscience and religion' (Article 14), 'freedom of association … and peaceful assembly' (Article 15) and 'freedom of expression', including 'freedom to seek, receive and impart information' (Article 13). All these are violated by this form of abuse, as described by the practitioners quoted above. If children are controlled within such cults, they are prevented from developing the ability to learn about and develop religious belief and adherence. They are also prevented from developing the moral sense represented by the law of the UK and of many religions – for example, the prohibition on killing, torture, sexual connection with children under 16 and animals – and they are encouraged to lie.

Socially, the implication is that children are inhibited from developing relationships with peers, and from learning about the varieties of relationships within families which are most usual within the culture of the UK. Keeping secrets, participating in forbidden practices and developing massive defences of dissociation prevent open friendship and membership of informal and organised groups within the community (even where children join such groups, their participation is tainted by the 'double life'). The ability to play is also severely disturbed (see Kelsall 1994, pp.94–9).

Neil Charleson was appallingly abused from the age of 14 in a residential establishment for children with learning disability. In his 20s he was free of both school and abuse, but the damage could not be repaired: 'The only people I went to bed with were people who I wanted to show how much I hated them' (Charleson and Corbett 1994, p.68). What greater abuse of the spirit can there be?

QUESTIONS

- Have you ever heard of ritual/satanic abuse?
- How does this summary make you feel? If you are distressed, share your feelings with someone you trust.
- Do you think that such things really happen in the UK?
- If you don't think so, what do you think about people who claim to have been abused in this way? Do you think they are lying?
- If you don't think so, what do you think about practitioners who work with and write about the experiences of people who claim to have been abused in this way?
- If you do think that such things happen, what do you think about people who assault children in these ways?
- If you suspected that children known to you were suffering/had suffered this kind of abuse, what could you do? To whom could you speak about your anxieties?

SUGGESTIONS

With colleagues:

- Discuss one another's ideas about the questions above.
- If you find that there is concern within your agency/establishment, invite a practitioner with knowledge of this subject to speak with you.
- Obtain reading material and discuss, with a supervisor, remembering the disturbing nature of this topic.
- Study the criticisms of social workers and foster carers in La Fontaine (1994), and discuss how interviewing and communicating with children can be improved.

The needs of practitioners

- Working with troubled children ... can be shattering and draining.
- It behoves [practitioners] to
  - Ensure their holistic needs are met by paying attention to their own body, emotions, mind and spirit.
  - Work on their own painful issues in a supportive environment.
  - Take responsibility for re-creating themselves.
- The intact, fully functioning [practitioner] will give a better service to the child. (West 1996, p.211)

Janet West is writing for and about play therapists, but her advice is relevant to all practitioners. She quotes Crompton (1990, p.117): 'in order to work effectively and to pay the cost, workers need training and preparation and the same kind of listening and respect they offer the children' (cited in J. West 1996, p.213). Play therapists and other practitioners:

> have to be able to empathize with, feel into, accept and understand what the child is conveying, often wordlessly. Therefore workers have to be free and open within themselves to experience whatever needs to come up. It is important that they are receptive to unconscious and conscious aspects of the whole child – spiritual, emotional, physical, cognitive – so it is imperative that they pay attention to these aspects of themselves. (p.213)

Noting reactions to these strains, West identifies how: 'Spiritually, play therapists can go to the depths, their faith apparently shattered, as they feel assailed from all sides with negativity and a spiritual vacuum.' She advises that 'People working holistically need to take care of themselves and pay attention to their whole being', offering ideas about the care of body, emotions, spirit and mind. She proposes the following exercise:

- You are challenged to find time for, and do, something that
    - is good for your body
    - allows emotional outlet
    - your mind enjoys and finds satisfying
    - takes you further into your own quest for (inner) values.
- Enjoy holidays from work.
- Go kindly with yourself. (p.213)

Writers in Sinason (1994) note the extreme strains of working with children who have suffered abuse in connection with rituals. During her association with Anders Svensson, Valerie Sinason became so frightened that a colleague observed: '"You look ill. Whenever I see you – you have just had a phone call from Sweden that makes you ill." Only then did she realise that she ... was keeping a secret.' This led to sharing 'the secret' with other colleagues, and insights into the differences between 'the dynamics of confidentiality and secrecy ... in this case we had gone beyond keeping confidentiality. We were keeping a secret and being struck dumb with terror' (p.18).

Practitioners must have access to colleagues whom they can trust not to treat them as if they are mad. As the practitioner bears the horror of revelation, essentially avoiding any reaction of disbelief, so must the horror be passed on and endured by a consultant and support group. Mollon (1994) concludes his account of 'The impact of evil' with an acknowledgement: 'I am grateful to Mr

P. Casement for his crucial support with almost unbearable clinical work described here.' He also thanks Dr Joan Coleman, 'who was inspired, with others, to set up the Ritual Abuse Information Network' (p.147).

Stress may be experienced if abuse has been (or is alleged to have been) perpetrated by people holding positions of trust, or respected, within a religious organisation with which practitioners are associated. The practitioner's own trust may be lost, or co-religionists who cannot believe in the guilt of one of their number may blame the practitioner for being associated with the profession which has 'caused all the trouble'. Thus the religious congregation, which should offer access to both spiritual strength and social support, may in itself become an additional arena for conflict and anxiety.

Bearing such strains affects not only the individual but also family members and friends. Practitioners should not neglect personal relationships and responsibilities because of professional involvement, however caring and demanding.

Whatever the form of abuse, whatever their specialisation and intervention, practitioners have both a need and duty to be alert to their own responses in every aspect of life, including social and moral, to find for themselves and their families the compassion and care they offer the children with and for whom they work.

QUESTIONS

- How do you care for your whole self when you are involved in work with children who have been abused?
- Do you consider that you are thoroughly healthy in all aspects of your life and relationships?
- If so, how do you manage it?
- If not, how could you care for yourself better?
- If you have to receive distressing, even horrifying information, who can you consult?
- Have you ever been involved in a professional situation which caused you to be ill?
- If so, did anyone notice that your illness was linked with a particular case?
- Were you able to trust anyone enough to share the whole story?
- What would you do if colleagues told you about a situation which worried them so much that they were becoming ill?
- If you learned that a member of a religious organisation with which you are associated had been accused/was guilty of abuse, how might you be affected?

SUGGESTIONS

With colleagues:

- Discuss one another's ideas about the questions above.
- Plan a network which could offer support in cases where spiritual/religious well-being is of particular importance.
- Note ways of being more aware of one another's signs of stress so that illness connected with particular events and cases can be identified quickly.
- Plan other ways of helping one another with strain and distress.
- Follow the advice of Janet West, and use the exercise reproduced above.

Summary

This chapter has introduced ideas about some forms of abuse which are intentionally or informally associated with religious and other ritual practices. If, as I believe, all abuse implies abuse of spiritual well-being, this applies especially to that which takes place within the context of a religious (or quasi-religious) organisation.

Through raising questions about some practice issues and introducing the work of several specialists, it is hoped that practitioners will be enabled and encouraged to explore these matters, as appropriate, on behalf of the children with and for whom they work.

Abuse may be deliberately perpetrated by clergy and other people whose position within a religious organisation should indicate that they are worthy of trust. It can be difficult for co-religionists to accept the possibility that colleagues are capable of, for example, sexual abuse, thus children may not be provided with appropriate safeguards. Religious organisations may believe those adults associated with them, rather than the children.

Some people are anxious about the power of cults (especially those with residential communities) over young people who join them and are inhibited, or prevented, from contact with family and friends.

Although oppression and persecution connected with religious affiliation are not the most common forms of abuse, children can suffer through acts of unthinking or deliberate failure to respect beliefs and observances, especially in everyday care.

Some practitioners have experience of abuse associated with ritual practices and/or satanic cults, a topic which is regarded variously with deep anxiety, or with disbelief.

Whatever the form of abuse, practitioners are subjected to extreme strain, and must be provided with excellent and reliable consultation and support, in order, really and always, to listen to the children.

Part 5

Children and death

13 Spiritual and religious care

Children and death

Although relatively few practitioners work with children who are seriously ill and/or dying (for example, in a hospital or hospice), many have contact with children who have been bereaved.

For instance, a group of practitioners (mainly from residential settings) attending in-service study on loss and bereavement were reluctant to discuss death since none of the children with whom they worked had been bereaved. They preferred to focus on loss through separation from living parents. However, when permission was given to change focus, one spoke of 'Lina', whose mother had died. During her mother's lifetime, Lina had been unable to live with any other member of her family. Now she could return to her father. The practitioner reported that Lina showed no signs of grief or mourning for her mother. No one, it seems, had considered the range of deep and troubling emotions which might follow the death of an unloved and unloving parent, including anger, betrayal, frustration, guilt, and fear that the 'bad' characteristics of the parent might be 'inherited' by the child.

It may be tempting to accept that children who express no sadness feel no sadness. Susan Jacob (1993) (a nurse), for example, describes the reactions of Linda (aged 16) to the death of her alcoholic, sexually abusive step-father in a car crash; Linda herself had been driving: 'When Linda was informed of [his] death ... she experienced a sense of joy and relief' (p.1,790). It is to be hoped that someone was alert for later reactions of shock and guilt. Responses to bereavement are neither simple nor time-specific. Practitioners in all settings may encounter reactions to losses past and recent which are expressed, and not expressed, in many ways (see also 'Play' in Chapter 16).

Practitioners may be so used to thinking about separation that they ignore

181

the impact of death, which may be regarded as irrelevant to their work. Yet children may lose people belonging to several categories of contact or relationship, for example: grandparents, parents, siblings (including those unborn through abortion or miscarriage), neighbours, peer group members, teachers, social workers or carers (day, foster or residential). Pets are especially prone to be short-lived and often offer children their first experiences of grief, and maybe funerals.

Experiences of death within the family and separation from living relations may not be uncommon when divorce often inhibits, even prevents, contact between children and at least one parent. For example, 'Joe's' parents separated, and he went to live with grandparents. When his grandmother died, Joe was not taken to the funeral, and his grandfather would not tell him anything about what had happened. He moved to an aunt and uncle's, where he displayed much insecurity and low self-esteem. A half-brother later died, leading to an unsuccessful reunion with one parent, then return to his aunt and uncle. The multiplicity of desertions by his living parents and his dead grandmother and brother led to constant anxiety that he would be left again, which would lead to more moves, and that perhaps he was unworthy to be loved and cared for. Joe attended a child and family clinic for a while, but did not derive lasting benefit, and no further service was offered. Joe's aunt sought support and help, but could gain none from any source available to her.

Death may occur in several ways, including abortion, accident, childbirth, euthanasia, illness, murder, natural disaster, old age, suicide, terrorist attack or war.

Dramatic events such as the mass murder of schoolchildren in Dunblane in 1996, the killing of individual children, crashes on school outings or accidents on holiday are highly publicised and usually soon forgotten by the public. But for the children and families who have been bereaved, whether family or friends, the impact remains for ever. Practitioners may be involved during the crisis or later, meeting children for whom the bereavement has become an ineradicable memory, conscious or buried.

Val Clark (1996a) suggests that the most significant deaths for children are those which are sudden or violent, and 'the death of a peer ... because of their untimeliness. People with whom one has a special relationship (whether family or not) are often greatly missed and a teacher's death may be particularly distressing.' Significant effects, including shock, may also be associated with the first death in a family or the clustering of several deaths together. The deaths of pets are significant if the animals are much loved, the first or long-lived pets, or again, if the death is sudden or violent.

For the purposes of this chapter, dying and bereavement are not considered separately. Children who die often leave bereaved siblings, and dying children may themselves be bereaved. Because this book focuses on spiritual and religious matters, this chapter does not seek to examine the whole subject of working with bereaved and dying children, but rather to introduce some ideas about spirituality, religion, death and bereavement, referring substantially to the work of Martin House, a hospice in West Yorkshire.

Material quoted from Martin House is derived mainly from two visits in 1996, when several members of staff gave generous time and attention, and from *Caring for Dying Children and Their Families* edited by Lenore Hill (1994a) (Head Nurse at Martin House). Particular thanks are due to staff who gave permission for their thoughts and memories to be incorporated into this chapter; the identities of children and families have been disguised.

Reference is made also to a video of Garvan Byrne talking with Mother Frances Dominica at Helen House in 1985 (the first children's hospice in the world). Other material is drawn from *Interventions with Bereaved Children* (Smith and Pennells 1995) and other texts.

Martin House

Martin House was opened in 1987, purpose built on the edge of a small town in West Yorkshire, with low red brick buildings and steep gabled roofs. The central living/dining room is used by families and staff and all help with preparing meals and washing up in the kitchen. Many children and their families have benefited from the services of the multi-disciplinary staff. Most of the children suffer from progressive disorders, muscular dystrophy, for example. Others have such illnesses as cancer; cystic fibrosis; metabolic, renal, liver or heart disease. In short, children with life-threatening, life-limiting or terminal disease may be offered care, together with their families.

The chapel at Martin House is a peaceful circle of simplicity and light. Clear windows show the sky and frame the herbs and shrubs which surround all the buildings of the hospice. The chapel is linked to these by a roofed passage. On the communion table stands a cross in the form adopted as a symbol by the Order of the Holy Paraclete based at St Hilda's Priory, Whitby, North Yorkshire. The sisters were invited to establish a house at Martin House at the suggestion of paediatricians who were impressed by the example of Helen House. One nun, Sister Caroline, is a chaplain.

Within a large roundel in the centre of the cross is the symbol of Martin House itself, a house martin, soaring freely above hilly meadows. A postcard of the cross explains: 'Remembering a son who found a damaged Housemartin and restored it to health'. The boy himself died but it is symbolic that his compassionate act, not his death, is remembered in this way.

The postcard also refers to a quotation from the Bible, (Matthew 25:34–40), the parable of the sheep and the goats which celebrates the lives of people who care for others: 'when I was hungry, you gave me food; when thirsty, you gave me drink; when I was a stranger you took me into your home, when naked you clothed me: *when I was ill you came to my help*, when in prison you visited me'. This links with the other symbolic 'martin', Saint Martin, a Roman soldier who gave half his great military cloak to a beggar.

Children's hospices (of which there are 11 in the UK at the time of writing) are not substitutes for other forms of care; rather, they intend that their services should be complementary to and co-ordinated with hospital and community care. Hill (1994b) notes that the aim of all staff 'is to meet the families just as themselves. They offer friendship and service not professionalism and direction' (p.179). Although Martin House hospice has connections with an order of nuns, there are no requirements of religious adherence or restrictions on it. Chaplains offer services in the chapel and personal contact with children and families, but a conversation with Sister Caroline, for example, does not depend on accepting her religious beliefs.

While families may choose for their children to die at Martin House, the main use is for respite. The whole family (including pets) can spend time together, relieved for a while of, for example, 'changing dirty nappies, feeding, which may take two hours for one meal, and washing and ironing the clothes. They can still enjoy time cuddling or playing with their child, or spending time in the multi-sensory room or the jacuzzi' (pp.180–1).

Martin House also enables couples 'to spend time talking and listening to each other, and doing "normal" things such as playing, shopping or going on trips out with their well children'. Sometimes the ill child may remain in Martin House for up to two weeks while the rest of the family goes on holiday or perhaps decorates the house. Essentially, 'The children, sick or well, love to visit, and every effort is made to ensure that they enjoy their "holidays" with us.' Time is easily filled with 'busy activities, games, painting, model-making, as well as trips out to local places of interest and the cinema', which 'help to enhance the quality of life' (pp.180 and 181).

The emphasis in Martin House, in accordance with the philosophy established at Helen House and in other hospices, is indeed on life – both the greatest abundance of life possible for the ill child and care for the continuing lives of bereaved siblings and parents.

Spiritual care

'Spiritual care is an important part of whole care; you don't care for the body without caring for the spirit.' Lenore Hill is clear that caring for the spirit is integral to the philosophy and practice of Martin House, firmly based on holistic principles. She considers that 'Religious care is only part of spiritual care', reinforcing the view of former chaplain Michael Kavanagh (1994):

> The term 'spiritual care' can conjure up images of religious functionaries of one kind or another, doing religious things. This may lead others within the caring professions to see such care as being a specialist field within which they themselves may have little competence … [However,] all those involved in the care of a child in the context of his family can exercise spiritual care … [exploring] how people make sense of their lives. This quest is one that concerns us all, and is therefore not simply the province of those who are 'professionally religious'. (p.106)

Trying to make sense of life and death is a common preoccupation when facing one's own or someone else's death, especially when the dying person is a child.

Attention may focus on the experience of dying, and beliefs about life after death. Bereaved children at Camp Winston residential groups (a support programme in Gloucestershire) are encouraged to ask a doctor any questions they wish, including about spiritual matters:

> it is obviously important for the doctor (and indeed all camp co-ordinators and volunteers) not to adopt any particular religious stance. It is more helpful to generate a selection of alternative answers. The child will then usually choose the answer that best fits their cultural and family beliefs while recognising that other explanations exist.
>
> Spiritual questions have included the following:

- Where do people go to when they die?
- If people go to Heaven, can they see you all the time? …
- Will people ever come back?
- What do you eat in Heaven?
- Why do people have to be buried or burnt? (Stokes and Crossley 1995, p.182)

An important aspect of work at Martin House is with bereaved siblings, whose parents are often too involved in their own feelings to have attention to spare. They need opportunities to express grief, misunderstandings about where the dead child is, guilt about bad feelings, perhaps because they fear that they bear some responsibility for the death, perhaps because they feel that they should not enjoy life. They need permission to ask questions, to express feelings and to carry on with their own lives.

Dying children also have questions. Some are afraid of what happens next, some have a strong sense that it will be wonderful. A dying girl said: 'I don't know where I am, but this is so beautiful.' Part of caring for dying children and their families is acknowledging that death will come, and helping to engage with fears and hopes. Janet Goodall (1994) (a retired paediatrician) writes on 'Thinking like a child about death and dying', offering illustrations of children's experiences. For example:

> A 5-year-old, very experienced after more than three years of cancer therapy, developed paraplegia and became blind in one eye. His friend had died of leukaemia. He asked his mother, out of the blue, 'Is it going to happen to me like it happened to David?' Her first shocked reaction was to say, 'Don't be silly, of course not', and then to wish for the ground to swallow her up.
>
> Later he asked her directly, 'Am I going to die?' and this time she had the courage to say 'Yes, we're all going to die and because you're so poorly, it looks as if you're going to die first, but it won't be today and we'll be with you'.
>
> At 5 years old he could match his own state to his old friend's and so expect the same outcome, but he did not yet have a mind mature enough to range very far ahead. His mother's answer satisfied him without then feeling the need to ask, 'When will it be?' Not long afterwards he died quietly, still at home, with his parents present. (pp.23–4)

The boy's sisters (aged 4 and 10) also benefited from their parents' ability to engage with truth. As their brother's health deteriorated, they were told: 'Marc's body was like a house that was falling down and one day he would move out and leave it behind.' When Marc died, 'they chose to sit with [his] body, letting the fact sink in that he had really gone. The older one commented later, without distress, that he had seemed "peaceful, but different"' (p.24).

Children may take courageous initiatives to achieve truthful communication. Paul (aged 12) visited Helen House for respite care twice with his parents. The third time, booked by Paul himself, he stayed on his own. The parents would not allow staff to initiate discussion with Paul about his illness, but accepted that 'if *he* initiated the discussion we could not break our rule about never deceiving or lying to a child' (Frances Dominica 1996, p.104).

Once his parents had left, Paul said: '"I got cystic fibrosis real bad. I'll probably be dead this time next year. What's it like?"' If the staff member had prevaricated or the answer had been 'other than brief and to the point he would have been the other side of the garden kicking a football around'. Paul returned to the conversation over several months as and when he chose: 'Our role ... was to be open and ready to enter into dialogue and to follow his lead' (p.104).

Paul's need for truth and his ability to accept it was demonstrated elsewhere, too, although his parents were never able to respond. In hospital, he asked a paediatrician who was carrying a batch of medical notes, '"Are you going to have a meeting about me?"', and revealed that he had made a yellow mark on the cover of his notes. He asked: '"Can I come to the meeting?" He did, and this was the start of much more open communication between patient and professionals' (p.105).

Of equal importance is the recognition and strengthening of the will to live as abundantly as possible. Garvan Byrne, who died at 11, was filmed in conversation with Mother Frances Dominica during a stay at Helen House. He speaks of his strong faith and the fullness of a life which to people who did not know him might have seemed circumscribed: '"I do thank Him for what I've got – I can walk, I can do lots of other things. It doesn't matter how handicapped you are or how sick. You always succeed in something. God gave each of us a gift. It's keeping it going and practising it each day and thanking Him for it."' Despite his strong belief in life after death, his pleasure in earthly life made him reluctant to die: '"I love my family and my home and life so much, I don't want to go yet"' (Frances Dominica 1996, p.111).

Staff at Martin House talked of children who, like Garvan, demonstrated spiritual strengths. Hazel spoke of 'Sean', whose doctor expected him to die soon from a degenerative disease, but who lived for several years, making numerous visits to Martin House. Sean's movement was severely restricted, but Hazel recalled that 'the spirit to live was unbelievable'. Despite minimal mobility, he was pursuing a course of academic study.

Sean's spiritual and emotional capacities were equally developed. During one of his stays at Martin House, a relation died. Sean was heartbroken, and expressed anxiety about whether the relation had known of his love, which he feared he had not been able to show. He worried also that his family was now suffering bereavement as well as anxieties about Sean himself.

Sean was reluctant to talk about his own death, and it was sometimes difficult for staff to acknowledge that he chose not to discuss this. His death demonstrated the spiritual strength shown in his life. However good the relationship with staff, children may not wish to discuss illness and death, and it is important to recognise and respect their reticence. Frances Dominica (1996) noted: 'Children may prefer not to talk about death – their own or anyone else's. "It helps me to talk about it but I don't see why a child or person should be forced into having to talk about it, not if they don't want to" commented a ten-year-old' (p.104).

Hazel had invited Sean to a party, but on that day he was admitted to Martin House for terminal care, and was unconscious. A little while earlier, Sean had visited local shops, and although ill, had chosen and bought a present for Hazel. Immediately after the party, Hazel visited Sean, bringing him some balloons and saying: 'I've brought the party to you.' Sean died next day.

Hazel remembers Sean's great spirit to live, and his laughter: 'he often laughed at our stumblings to communicate with him because he knew that we loved him and wanted it to be right for him; his face would light up'.

Friendship and joy in relationship is also demonstrated between children. 'Luke' and 'Lucy' were close friends. When Luke died, he was laid in the Cold Bedroom (see below), where his family could spend time with him. Lucy went to the room on her own, without telling anyone. She left an open letter, in which she wrote about their friendship and asked Luke to be with her when she eventually died too.

Spiritual qualities, needs, rights and experiences have been discussed in Chapters 2 and 3. A parent whose son had died wrote: 'suffering may produce good effects in children, including patience, courage, the ability to withstand pain, an understanding of their parents and early maturity' (Bayly 1984, p.102). However, ideas about spiritual distress, betrayal, deprivation and abuse have also been introduced in Chapters 4, 11 and 12, and these may be experienced by children who are seriously ill, dying and/or bereaved no less than by others. The same parent wrote:

> Children … often struggle to cope with suffering just as adults do. Who can explain the pain of an infant sister to another child in the family, or the helplessness and strange behaviour of a brain-damaged brother? Guilt can compound these struggles. Most children, at some time or another, think or say to a parent or sibling 'I wish you were dead!' If death later occurs, the child may be torn by guilt. (Bayly 1984, p.102)

This family had:

> learned the hard way that spiritual needs must be met. Our son was three years old when his five-year-old brother died of leukemia. My response was to smother him with affection; his mother's was to withdraw from him. Approximately four years later, we were driving to church one Sunday when he said, 'I wish I wouldn't think that first thing when I wake up every morning.'
> 'Think what?' I asked.
> 'I hate God.'
> Later, when he was 10 years old, this same son lost his 18-year-old brother. My wife and I did not recognize his needs or know how to meet them. When he became a teenager, he rebelled and moved far from Christianity. (We thank God that he has wonderfully returned.) (p.106)

Indeed, the needs of siblings are easily ignored, perhaps unrecognised, as parents concentrate first on caring for the sick or dying child, and later on their own grief and other emotions. Sisters and brothers may be placed with grandparents to leave more space, physical and emotional, for the ill sibling. But this detracts from their own care, and may lead to: 'overwhelming sadness, jealousy, anger, resentment and fear. They feel "left out" or second best, some become withdrawn and irritable, others openly aggressive and hostile. They are reacting to the losses and tragedies that suddenly invade their once secure and loving families' (Hitcham 1993, p.20). Needs for love, relationship and trust may thus be betrayed at a time when the opportunity to share feelings of sadness and fear might lead to increasing spiritual and emotional strength, understanding and confidence.

Fear of death (one's own or that of other people) is common in adults, and may be assumed to begin in childhood, although it may not be expressed explicitly or may be covered up with a giggle and fantasies about ghosts. For example, a young woman remembered four years of childhood as a period of terror, 'afraid of death and of life for that matter, and subject to severe panic attacks which nobody seemed to notice' (Robinson 1977, p.111; see also Chapter 4).

QUESTIONS

- Have any children known to you died or been bereaved?
- Did they receive appropriate understanding and support, for example to express their feelings, not only immediately after the death but also from time to time as the need became evident?
- If you think that spiritual care is important, how can it be offered to dying and bereaved children?
- Do you think that spiritual care is the concern only of ministers of religion and other chaplains?
- Are children known to you enabled and encouraged to ask questions about death?
- Are children known to you enabled and encouraged to remain silent if they wish?
- Can you engage with children's fears and misunderstandings?

SUGGESTIONS

With colleagues and children:

- Discuss one another's ideas about the questions above.
- Consider the questions asked at Camp Winston, and discuss possible answers.
- Collect euphemisms for death; for example: 'passed over', 'gone through death's door', 'popped his clogs'.
- Consider ways children can communicate about death.
- Read texts which describe children's beliefs about and understanding of death.

- Consider the fears and anxieties about death which children may experience.
- List agencies which may offer help to children who are dying and/or bereaved.

Religion

By no means all the families who are associated with Martin House adhere to any religious belief, but the impending and actual death of a child often concentrates attention on ideas about a deity and/or future existence of some kind.

In her study of schoolchildren who had been bereaved, Val Clark (1996b, p.38) found six particular trends in their responses. One was that 'belief in God (or a divine spirit or life force) and the concept of a loving and just God seems to be challenged by bereavement'. Among the girls interviewed in depth, she found that two accepted the dichotomy and struggled with how it might work, while a third rejected 'any notion of a loving God because of the death of several loved ones ... recently'. Another finding is that some 'seem to have a definite sense of the deceased with them. They talk to them, feel them with them at certain times and may even imagine them ageing in their minds'. Clark found: 'an uncertainty about having a sense of the presence of God or a divine spirit but a strong belief that God or a divine spirit can or may be present at times of distress, especially after a death' (p.38).

Parents may feel betrayed by a deity whom they have tried to please, or punished because of some fault or failure, including genetic inheritance. They may feel anger and despair, and ask: 'How can God do this to us?' Some families may reject the deity who has thus failed to provide love and protection, while others turn to religion for support, perhaps seeking assurance of continuing life and future meeting with their children. Some parents choose diverging paths, one perhaps increasing involvement in religion, while the other rejects all idea of religious faith. Such divergence may eventually impose (or perhaps reflect) strains which may lead to separation.

The beliefs and attitudes of parents and children radically affect the ways in which families relate internally and manage the period of illness, eventual dying, death and aftermath (Kavanagh 1994, p.107).

Facing the truth with children is of the greatest importance, and teaching associated with religious belief may sometimes conflict with this and appear to constitute betrayal. A child whose family held strong Christian beliefs died rapidly and in terrible pain: 'Mummy, I've asked Jesus to take my pain away and he isn't doing it.' Ministers of religion can demonstrate insensitivity to children and families, saying, for example: 'It must have been meant', or even 'It must be a punishment.' When a child died from a genetically transmitted illness, the minister who officiated at the funeral assured the family that they would never again have to endure such an experience, whereas it was very likely that others of their children would suffer the same illness. This led the Martin House staff member to query her own faith; at first she doubted whether God would intervene, then she felt that 'He doesn't do it to them anyway', considering that God neither imposes nor inhibits the onset of illness.

'Sue', a devout Christian, liked to attend morning service at a church near Martin House. Her disabilities rendered this difficult, but she was helped and encouraged to attend. At Easter, when Hazel took Sue to church, no one welcomed or otherwise acknowledged them. When the congregation exchanged the kiss of peace, not one person turned to either Sue or Hazel. After the service, the minister was distributing Easter eggs; ignoring Sue herself, he asked Hazel: 'Is she allowed one?' She turned the potentially humiliating incident into a joke with Sue.

Sue had strong faith and a great respect for ministers, and Hazel felt deeply hurt on her behalf. However, Sue was able to laugh at the whole incident and relate an earlier experience when with 'Ben', also in a wheelchair, a woman had asked, 'Do the wheelchairs want communion?'; Ben had responded brightly: 'I don't know, shall we ask them?'

Although Sue and Hazel seemed unmarked by the incident at the time, they discussed it later, not least because Hazel was very upset. Sue proposed that the minister should be asked to make some comment to the congregation about being kind. However, she later decided not to attend morning service at that church, preferring to travel to evening service in another town, and demonstrating that her humorous courage had masked distress.

Sue would talk quietly and with deep interest about her religious faith, and showed not only great concern to emulate other family members in belief and behaviour, but also sensitivity to the strain on her parents occasioned by the need for physical care. For example, Sue would try to tolerate discomfort at night in order not to disturb her mother. Hazel considered her to be 'one of the most caring Christian people I've ever come across', an example to the people in church who had shown no care for or sensitivity to her. Sue was very pleased when she said this, an encouragement in her efforts to be a good Christian. Hazel summarised the church experience as 'very isolating and sad but Sue rose above it and I've got to learn from her'.

Janet Goodall (1994) encourages practitioners to be aware of how important religion can be to dying children and their families:

That the event of reasoning ability can for some quench simple faith, including many who care for children, should not negate the importance of this aspect of their lives for those whose spiritual awareness remains very much alive. It has been known for the trust in God expressed in dying children to rekindle faith in some of those who tend them. It is not uncommon for dying adolescents, whether or not they have had such thoughts before, to begin a search for spiritual certainties. We can fail them by overlooking this as a possible source of anxiety, though now help is offered will obviously vary with circumstances, culture and creed. (pp.29–30)

Practitioners may be expected to attend naturally to the religious and spiritual concerns of children within the context of a specialist establishment such as Martin House. Garvan Byrne, for example, discussed his beliefs with Mother Frances Dominica at Helen House hospice in full confidence that he would be respected:

'Garvan, is making your communion important to you?'
   'Yes, and it was a very joyful experience, my first Holy Communion, and meeting Christ in Holy Communion I found was a great joy and very, sort of, mysterious, very peaceful. It was the only time I could seem to talk to Him about my deepest problems, and have a really good talk to Him about them and what I felt and ask Him for his help. He always answered me back, and my way of praying is just praying with an open heart to Him so that I get the open answer back. Yes, it was a very important time and my very first time was extremely the most happiest day of my life, I think, that very first day I took it and His coming to me was very special.'
   'What do you think happens to your body when you die?'
   'I will leave it behind. This is only a reflection, this is only something, a sort of tag to say this is Garvan, this is me … The real me will go up to God.' Frances Dominica 1996, pp.110–12)

Boy and nun shared a context of religious belief, observance and vocabulary which enabled both questions and answers to be understood.
   However, seriously ill and dying children and their families spend more time in hospitals (including out-patients' clinics) and their own homes than in hospices. Practitioners may be involved through the hospital or clinic, day or foster care, or in the course of fieldwork with families. Responsibility to attend to religious and spiritual concerns is not confined to a special establishment. Goodall (1994) notes that practitioners may fail children 'by overlooking [the search for spiritual certainties] as a possible source of anxiety' (p.30).
   Goodall also notes the importance of providing help appropriate to culture and creed. The comments and illustrations above, for example, have referred to aspects of Christianity. Every religion teaches its own beliefs about the destiny of the individual after death (see Chapter 6). For example,

a Hindu family observing beliefs about *karma* and reincarnation would not be beset with doubts about the reason for a child's death or the possibility of future existence. Reba Bhaduri (1990) combined understanding of the beliefs of a Muslim family with learning from the Hindu law of *karma* which brings 'a sense of containment rather than control' to enable a child, Siraj, to receive hospital treatment for an illness from which his older brother, Saleem, had died. His parents refused to allow him to attend the hospital, which they considered had killed Saleem. Reba Bhaduri resisted pressure from medical staff to pressurise the grieving parents, knowing that any attempt to gain control would achieve only further resistance. Rather she visited the whole family regularly for some time, recognising the effects of Saleem's death on every individual. Eventually, Siraj's parents willingly took him to the hospital to receive medical treatment, which saved his life.

Lack of attention to children's religious experience can have dramatic, even tragic results. Goodall (1994) offers this example:

> Professor Robin Becker tells how a young Arab boy was admitted to a Jerusalem hospital for cardiac surgery, but to everyone's surprise, during the preoperative assessment, he requested a Jewish skullcap and a kosher diet. Sessions with the child psychologist helped him to show, through his drawings, the terrible anxiety which had led him to set aside his own religious adherence ... his companions on the ward had fed him horror stories, saying that he was fooling himself to think that his surgery would be corrective. Instead, his heart would be taken out and given to a Jewish boy. It took some time before he was finally, and with relief, restored to a Moslem lifestyle. (p.30)

This boy was deliberately misled; perhaps his companions intended only to tease, perhaps they had a more malign purpose. Fortunately, his reaction was bizarre and observable enough to attract appropriate help. It is all too easy to imagine equivalent anxiety stimulated and fed by religious disinformation and misunderstanding but neither overtly expressed nor recognised.

Children's attitudes towards death are largely learned from those of adults, especially if they hold some religious belief. Some Muslim children, for example, described death: '"Muslims believe that when we go to sleep the soul goes away to God. If God doesn't want us to live the next day, He tells the angels not to put the soul back"' (Year 7). The same group said that in Hell '"If you're thirsty, you have to drink blood and pus. It's quite horrible, but that's what it says in the Qur'an"'. Shanaz (Year 5) believes that:

> 'If you're good you go to Heaven and have a wonderful house, with clothes and shoes. You're with your mum, and she says, "I love you – you said your prayers to Allah". If you're bad, you go to the fire, and there are snakes here and here' (gestures under arms and over shoulders) 'and you can't move, and you call out

for your mum, but she's not there. She's up with God, and she looks down and says, "Shame! Shame! You didn't pray to Allah. Shame! Shame!"'

Usma (Year 5) accepts her father's view that:

'Paradise is a place where you're free and everybody's brothers and sisters, nobody's mum and dad, you all are friends and everything. You're all the same together, there's nobody that's less good or anything, but everybody's the same. Nobody's less and nobody's more.' (Ipgrave 1995, pp.22–3)

Failure in understanding can lead to errors which may be perceived as deliberate affronts. Although families choosing the services of Martin House are mainly Christian or profess to be uninterested in any religion, staff are keen to extend their service to the many religious traditions represented within the nearby conurbations, recognising the need to learn about beliefs and observances of every individual and family as well as every religion and denomination.

QUESTIONS

- If you are associated with a religion, what do you and your co-religionists believe about death?
- Does religious belief help you to face the idea of your own death?
- Does religious belief help you to help bereaved and/or dying children?
- Are you aware of the religious beliefs of children and colleagues?

SUGGESTIONS

With colleagues and children:

- Discuss one another's ideas about the questions above.
- Learn about beliefs about death in the religions represented within your locality.
- Discuss how local centres of worship receive children who are ill and/or dying: for example, is there easy access, do ministers and congregation welcome or ignore children?
- Suggest how centres of worship could improve service to ill, dying and bereaved children.
- Consider the story of the Arab boy who pretended to be a Jew because he was afraid; discuss whether children in your locality could experience similar fear because of religious (or other) associations.

- Consider the story of Rheba Bhaduri and the Muslim family; identify ways in which religious beliefs and/or philosophy of life can be used in service of children who are dying or bereaved.
- Consider how religious belief or misunderstanding can stimulate fear.
- Identify how you could gain greater understanding of children's beliefs and help to dispel fears and anxieties.

Ceremonies and symbols

An essential focus of religious belief and observance is the rite of passage, the ceremony which follows death, usually known as 'the funeral'. Every religion approaches this in its own way, including reverent disposal of the body; in the UK this is conventionally through cremation or burial. Practitioners in any way involved with dying or bereaved children need to know about attitudes to death and funeral rites in their culture (see Chapter 6). They may, for example, help families arrange the form of funeral they choose, and negotiate with ministers of religion or funeral directors. It is easily possible to arrange a funeral without reference to a deity or after-life, focusing on the life of the person who has died, for example playing favourite music (for advice, contact the British Humanist Association, see Useful Organisations).

Children associated with Martin House may die there if they and their families wish, or at home or in hospital as appropriate. The funeral is usually in the home locality, whether the ceremony is religious or secular, but may be held in the chapel at Martin House. One funeral which was designed and organised by the main participant, the deceased, is remembered with respect and love by the staff at Martin House.

'Maria', a devout Christian, was nearly 20 when she died, after several years' association with Martin House. She chose to die and have her funeral there, where she had many friends. A very intelligent person, she had many interests, such as watching sporting activities which required the physical strength she could never possess. She thought deeply on many subjects, including termination of pregnancy because of genetic risks; she explained that if her mother had aborted her, she would never have been born; she considered her life well worth living. She had 'great inner strength and faith'.

Maria entered the final stage of her illness at home, and was admitted to hospital. Lenore had promised that she should die at Martin House, and Maria was transferred from the hospital, although she was not expected to regain consciousness. However, as the ambulance approached Martin

House, Maria opened her eyes and remained conscious and lively for several days (which included a religious festival). Maria's funeral was in the chapel. On her coffin was placed a cherished souvenir connected with her favourite sport interest, and the music was the signature tune of a popular television sport programme.

This story, cherished by Martin House staff, illustrates the deep importance of attending to the funeral, the rite of passage which follows death. It may be that other young people facing death would like to be involved in creating their own funerals. Children who are bereaved may participate in arranging funerals, for example choosing music and flowers. Michael Kavanagh (1994) suggests that 'Part of the preparation for dying can … include symbolic acts of preparation or the planning for the funeral', which might reflect 'the sense they have made out of their illness in terms of readings or choice of hymns and music … it is important that whoever is conducting the service is aware of these requests' (p.114).

At Martin House, an annual service commemorates children who have died and seeks to represent the beliefs of all the families attending. Lenore asks that everyone should understand that a contribution which may seem strange to one family may be just right for another. A Jewish family expressed gratitude for a Jewish contribution: 'It might have been included for us'; Lenore answered: 'It was.' The service seeks to acknowledge 'the pain as well as the hidden hope that it also present. Hence the choice of hymns and readings reflects both pain and hope' (Kavanagh 1994, p.120).

A commemorative ceremony is also an important element of the Camp Winston residential events for bereaved children. ('Winston', mentioned below is the bear mascot of the camp):

After supper we hold Winston's candlelight ceremony … a simple ritual which allows participants to connect with some of the feelings of deep sadness that may rarely surface. Each child and team leader are given their own hand-crafted Winston candle and it is explained that Winston likes to light a candle on special occasions to remember people who have died. Sometimes he remembers funny events, sometimes difficult memories, sometimes happy times and also sad times. It is explained that one of the beliefs that Winston holds is that it is 'all right to cry'. One by one, everyone is invited to light their candle and given the option to say 'I'm lighting my candle for — and the thing(s) I would like to remember about them are —.' …

Eventually, when all the candles are lit, some music is played which gives time and physical comfort to reflect on the feelings that have been aroused. Plenty of tissues and physical comfort are available throughout the ceremony. The fact that team leaders also participate in the ceremony can provide a useful role model for children who may not have seen adults cry.

One by one, each candle is blown out and the ceremony reaches its conclusion. The children are encouraged to keep their candles, as they may then decide to light the candle on important occasions, for example birthdays, Christmas, anniversaries. Children can also choose to light their candles to mark important personal events, for example one boy decided he would light his candle each year to mark the beginning of the fishing season as this was an activity he had always shared with his dad.

The opportunity to feel and express emotion within a simple ceremony and using the ancient symbol of light enables the children to become noticeably 'more relaxed and calm' (Stokes and Crossley 1995, pp.182–3 and 184).

At Martin House, a weekly interdenominational service is held in the chapel. Those who attend may find peace or inspiration, consolation or a sense of community. One service brought the healing force of shared laughter. Bet, who was blind and self-harming, spoke little but could sing the theme from a favourite film. When the chaplain stopped speaking for a moment, Bet called loudly: 'Where's he gone?' Everyone laughed. A staff member commented that it is important for families to laugh without feeling guilty, not least because neighbours and relations are inclined to expect that their lives should be full of gloom and doom. The little incident within the safe context of the service provided an opportunity to share a smile and relax.

On the table in the chapel stands the cross decorated with a soaring martin, symbol of Martin House. Other symbols are used in the annual memorial service: the service sheet reflects the pain and hope of the journey of bereavement with pictures of butterflies and rainbows; flower bulbs 'have been particularly valued as they are a practical outworking of the mystery of death and new life' (Kavanagh 1994, p.120).

On a window sill in the Cold Bedroom stands a small model of a hand within which rests, in safety, a little girl; it was carved in coal by a miner in memory of his daughter. The Cold Bedroom:

> can be chilled down to keep a child's body cold. After the parents have washed and dressed the child, and whenever they are ready to do so, the child is carried to this room. He is placed in a bed or cot, with a favourite duvet cover and favourite toys. Many other items may be placed in the room by families. These are as various as religious symbols, flowers, football scarves and firemen's helmets. The family has unrestricted access and can pick up the child, or talk to him for as long as they wish, although for some families this available time is constrained by religious beliefs. (Hill 1994, pp.182–3)

Families can take time to say goodbye to their dead children and to plan the funeral. Even when children have died at home or in hospital, the Cold Bedroom at Martin House can be used, and the whole family can stay in the hospice.

Children and families are encouraged to bring any symbols and artefacts connected with religion to Martin House at any time, but it is fairly rare for anything to be brought. Most common are probably rosaries, crucifixes and statues brought by Roman Catholic children. A Muslim family brought holy water from Mecca for use in care of their sick baby, and with the instruction that the water should not be touched by menstruating staff.

QUESTIONS

- Have you ever arranged or attended a child's funeral?
- Have children known to you attended a funeral?
- Were they able to play any part in the arrangements?
- What do you think about memorials for children?
- If you are associated with a religion, what are the rites of passage and ceremonies which follow a death?
- If you are not associated with a religion, what form do you think a funeral should take?

SUGGESTIONS

With colleagues and children:

- Discuss one another's ideas about the questions above.
- Learn about the rites of passage and ceremonies associated with death in the religions represented in your locality.
- Consider ideas about ceremonies which might be designed for children who are not associated with any religion.
- Discuss ways in which ceremonies, such as the Camp Winston candlelight meeting, can help children who are bereaved.
- Consider ideas about spiritual well-being, needs, rights and values, and apply them to children who are dying and/or bereaved.
- Identify ways in which spiritual well-being in relation to children who are dying and/or bereaved is nurtured in your establishment.

The needs of practitioners

Lenore Hill finds that working with dying children and their families is 'a challenge to our own beliefs' which can have tremendous impact on every aspect of life; there is 'a deep sense of something spiritual when someone is dying'.

The work is spiritually draining. One staff member spoke of a child dying in uncontrollable pain. She prayed that the pain might be relieved – 'Please God, don't let it happen' – but had to realise that 'He's not magic, He's just as distressed as you are, it makes you question a lot.' Staff cannot hold any part of themselves back, because only through being close to families can they earn and keep trust. A staff member recalled sharing a spiritual experience with a dying girl and her parents: she felt a great surge of painful, spiritual love for, and oneness with, the child and family, and both child and adult were able to speak of their feelings for one another.

While staff work as a team, individual practitioners form close relationships with particular families, maintaining contact throughout involvement with Martin House, which includes visiting families' own homes (Hill 1994a, p.180). After a child dies, further contact may be extended to bereaved siblings and parents. No staff member is expected to begin a new attachment until strength has been recouped.

Practitioners never become accustomed to the deaths of the children whom they come to love. However, talking about death helps them to gain confidence in understanding their own feelings. People who are not used to working with dying or bereaved children may be less confident. Staff at Martin House had been taken by surprise when one boy wanted to ask advice about sex. The Family Planning Association agreed to provide a course, but a representative confessed to fear of being with dying children, in case one died. Such honesty is essential to help allay fears and enable communication with children. Perhaps it is helpful to think in terms of 'children who are dying/bereaved' rather than 'dying/bereaved children': the dying/bereavement is only part of the whole child.

Practitioners need regular opportunities to share experiences and feelings on all aspects of their work, not least to examine their own fears and confusions, together with the joys and developing understanding of life and death which must accompany involvement with children who face these great questions.

Summary

Practitioners in any field may have contact with children who are seriously ill, dying and/or bereaved. This chapter has introduced ideas about spiritual and religious considerations, largely based on two visits to Martin House hospice, and a book about it (Hill 1994a). Spiritual and religious care involves attention to many aspects of children's beliefs, including fears and anxieties, and to the attitudes and responses of other people. Ceremonies and symbols have great significance at times of passage, such as death.

However limited and short the life expectancy of individual children, attention to spiritual aspects of their whole care – including love, trust, relationship and wonder – is essential. Children who have been bereaved need similar attention in order to enable spiritual well-being.

Practitioners also need attention to their spiritual well-being, recognising both the enrichment and the depletion of contact with children who are dying and/or bereaved.

14 Suicide and termination of pregnancy

Choosing death

Two aspects of death with spiritual and religious implications for children are suicide and termination of pregnancy.

Although many practitioners may consider that these matters do not concern them because they do not work in specialist clinics, young people who have attempted suicide may be treated on hospital wards and referred for social work service. Children in residential or penal establishments, for example, may attempt, or may have already attempted, suicide. Children whose siblings or schoolmates have attempted or committed suicide have been bereaved, and families may need help in engaging with and expressing feelings of not only grief but also shock, anger, fear, perhaps guilt. Adults may find difficulty in permitting children to be informed about the suicide, and if they do know about it, to express and discuss feelings.

Termination of pregnancy can have intense and long-lasting effects which may lead to spiritual growth and strengthening, but may also lead to entrenched bitterness and sadness, maybe depression and illness, especially if no counselling service is available.

Matters concerning death voluntarily chosen for oneself or another are fraught with conflicting and deeply held opinions, often connected with religious belief. It is essential to understand the beliefs which underlie the attitudes and behaviour of children and families, even when they profess no religious belief.

Suicide

Material in this section is drawn mainly from *The Long Sleep: Young People and Suicide* (Hill 1995).

Practitioners involved with young people who wish to end their own lives may perceive this as expressing spiritual desperation. In terms of the discussions of spiritual experience, values, distress and abuse in Chapters 3, 4, 11 and 12, a young person who reaches the point of attempting, or achieving, suicide may be deemed to have suffered at least neglect of spiritual well-being. Young people who kill (or attempt to kill) themselves may be supposed to experience the despair identified by Nye and Hay as the opposite of delight (associated with the core quality 'sensing value' – see Chapter 3), the negation of spiritual enlivenment. Other spiritual needs have also been ignored or neglected, whether deliberately or through indifference.

Some causes of suicide include:

- **loss** – absence of emotional warmth and security and such accumulated losses as breaking up with a boy/girl friend, death in the family, argument;
- **abuse** – humiliating situations which demolish self-respect are common precipitants to suicide attempts;
- **depression** – including deep unhappiness;
- **difficulty in communicating.** (based on Hill 1995, p.53)

Here are negative counterparts of love, peace, wonder, confidence and relatedness (Bradford 1995) and the senses of awareness, mystery, relatedness, meaningfulness and insight (Nye 1996, see also Chapter 3).

Loss and sadness are inevitable experiences which every person must learn to engage with and grow from; but Hill's list identifies experiences of terrible loneliness, self-doubt and despair. Frances Cattermole (1990) suggests: 'We all have singular experiences, sometimes tragic. Our spiritual development takes place as we use time and space to reflect on these experiences'; both sad and happy times come within the range of spirituality. However, spiritual development can occur best 'under the watchfulness of someone who cares' (p.ii); young people who contemplate suicide may have lacked both watchfulness and care. Even where responsible adults are caring, the inner agony may not be perceived, as expressed by the young woman who from the ages of 8 to 11 'was afraid of death and of life … and subject to severe panic attacks which nobody seemed to notice' (quoted in Robinson 1977, p.111; see also Chapter 4).

Practitioners who hold certain religious beliefs may regard suicide as sinful. Parents, siblings and other relations may also hold firm views. Susie found that her parents' beliefs held her back from suicide:

'My mum always told me that if you killed yourself it was a really bad sin. But my parents also told me that once you were Born Again you were saved and you wouldn't go to Hell. But there was always this nagging doubt in the back of my head. If I hadn't had this religious dilemma I might have thought – get on with it.' (Hill 1995, pp.88–9)

Kate Hill comments:

Susie was unclear whether suicide would qualify her for eternal damnation. The fear that it might helped, for some time to curb her self-destructive impulses. Religion may act as a buffer against suicide in various ways. The social life of the church, the belief that suicide is a sin or the fear of a punitive God might all keep suicidal feelings in check. (p.89)

Discussing the attitudes and influence of religious institutions, she notes:

Active involvement in religion does appear to insulate some individuals against suicide but participation in religion has been waning in the UK for several generations. For centuries, the church's refusal to bury suicide victims in consecrated ground within its cemetery walls provided a mark of religious disapprobation. Now, for most, religious values and institutions no longer shape attitudes to suicide. A generation gap accounts for the recent shift in thinking. Parents are more likely to judge suicide in religious and moral terms, whilst their children regard it in terms of individual rights. Liberal norms, of a secular bent, encourage acceptance of suicide. The exact influence of a more permissive cultural milieu is hard to fathom but the European countries which experienced the sharpest drop in church membership, between the 1960s and mid-1980s, suffered sharper increases in youth suicide. (p.89)

Hill appears to be writing exclusively about Christianity; practitioners concerned with young people whose families are associated with this and any other religious tradition need to learn about not only the expressed attitude of the young person, but also the beliefs of the particular religion and denomination, which may vary widely. Young people and their families who do not profess any form of religious belief may nevertheless be deeply, perhaps unconsciously, influenced by such beliefs. When working with surviving siblings, for example, it is essential to know if the family believes that the dead child is being punished, for example in hell.

Young people contemplating suicide may be influenced by an image of hell, or indeed heaven. Susie, brought up in a strict fundamentalist Christian Church:

'had an image of little demons dressed in black. I used to lie awake all night thinking about it. I had nightmares when I was a kid – monsters and fires and things. I used to think a lot about this hell business. As I got a bit older I thought: it can't be this fiery pit. That's too childish. I thought Hell must be like a grove; like lying awake all day in a grove. Heaven was a big green field with pink cherry blossoms, with lots of people singing.' (Hill 1995, p.130)

Susie's visions of hell and heaven are remarkably similar in their evocation of rural tranquillity, representing escape from the pressures of everyday life, including bullying at school and isolation caused by her family's religious convictions, leading to a state of perpetual miserable anxiety.

Maxine 'knew I wouldn't go to heaven, but I imagined I'd be alone – not with other people tormenting me. Because I used to be really bullied at school by the boys' (quoted in Hill 1995, p.132).

For Cheryl, too, the prospect of existence after death was heavenly – freedom from the unbearable strain of daily life:

Prior to her first suicide attempt at 13, Cheryl's misery and fear about the deed she was contemplating brought about an uncharacteristic interest in a compassionate God. This allowed her to reason away some of her worst anxieties about suicide:

'I started to think about Christianity, missing out the big chunk about not taking your life. I thought God will understand, because he's seen how this family operates. He'll know that I can't survive this, and the world is too frightening and people are too cruel.

Death was a state where there was no tension, where everything was fine. It was just the end of trauma, the end of being upset and of crying and having to live with these horrible people. It would stop this racing round in my head and it would have just been sleep and I'd be going to Heaven.' (Hill 1995, p.132)

The idea of post-death existence imagined by these girls is characterised by a vision of the ideal life for which they long: freedom from pressure, conflict, anxiety and family rows, and a long rest in privacy. The evocation of heaven, or hell, recalls the privacy sought by Joanna (aged 10) in her imaginary garden, 'where it was always sunny and peaceful, in contrast to the gloominess of home life and endless chatter of her noisy sisters', which 'provided both peace and the company of imagined friends whose presence she could control'. Joanna 'lacked confidence in herself, and also spoke about her deep fears of death and annihilation' (Nye 1996, 2/16–17). (This girl did not seek death, but was aware of its inevitability, and linked it with fear; see Chapter 4).

For young people who attempt or commit suicide, death may appear to be the only escape from an intolerable existence. Susie remembered that her mother:

'had two miscarriages and I thought, I wish I'd been one of those miscarriages. I was going round all day wishing I was dead. I really wanted to die. I prayed to God every day: "Why don't you give me an illness and just let me die?" I'd wake up and think – "I'm still here." I was really disappointed to wake up alive.' (Hill 1995, p.132)

Susie presents herself as a child who has been bereaved, both of the siblings who are never born and of her own childhood. For Susie, religious belief only adds to daily conflicts and burdens, and her prayers are those of an old person in desperate pain who has born all the reverses that life can devise.

Bereavement by suicide raises many painful emotions, including guilt ('Is it my fault?'), anger, ('How could he do this to me?') and fear ('Might I feel as desperate as that one day?'). Questions about a deity who has failed to protect or may punish the person who has died may also be raised.

Children whose siblings or schoolmates kill themselves may not feel able to engage with – still less express – such feelings, which may be buried, fester and emerge in apparently inexplicable depression, delinquency or illness. Anxiety may be raised if the suicide is connected with pressures about school work and examinations. Suicide, attempted or achieved, requires attention to the spiritual despair of the young person, family members and friends (including schoolmates and teachers). Practitioners need to consider ways in which spiritual well-being has been impaired, and how it can – literally – be revived.

QUESTIONS

- Have you ever known and/or worked with young people who attempted to or succeeded in committing suicide? If so, how did you feel about this?
- Do you know how the young people felt?
- Are there any ways in which they could have been helped not to commit suicide?
- If they are still alive, are they likely to try again?
- How did/do their siblings and other family members and friends (including schoolmates) feel about the suicide attempt, whether or not it was successful?
- Have any children shown inexplicable behaviour changes which might be connected with unexpressed anxiety about a sibling/schoolmate who has committed suicide?
- If you hold religious beliefs, what does your congregation teach about suicide: for example, is it a sin?

SUGGESTIONS

With colleagues and children:

- Discuss one another's ideas about the above questions.
- Consider aspects of suicide which can be linked with ideas about spiritual well-being, distress, abuse and neglect.
- Discuss the beliefs about suicide held by religions represented within your establishment.
- Consider how to help children whose siblings have committed suicide.
- Consider how to help children whose schoolmates and/or friends have committed suicide.
- Consider the ideas suggested by Kate Hill about possible connections between loss, abuse, depression and difficulty in communicating and suicide, bearing in mind ideas presented in Chapters 3, 4, 11 and 12.
- Discuss how ideas about life after death, including concepts of heaven and hell, can influence decisions about suicide.

Termination of pregnancy

Material and background for this section was gathered partly from conversations with two practitioners engaged in counselling about termination of pregnancy. Although both were employed within the same health trust area, the policies and practices in their clinics differed radically. Pam (a social worker) saw applicants for termination only if referred by a consultant; of the team of three doctors, only one regularly referred women for counselling, but all applicants under 16 were (officially) referred. Anna (a nurse) saw all applicants on referral to the clinic, in which counselling was seen as integral to the total service.

Practitioners do not need to be employed in a specialist clinic to have contact with young people who are contemplating or have undergone termination of pregnancy. Both parents of the foetus may be known to field social workers and residential or foster carers. Conception may have occurred during rape or sexual abuse, or one or both parents may be accommodated in residential or foster homes, or a medical or penal establishment.

Siblings and schoolmates may be affected by the decisions and experiences of sisters and friends who become pregnant. Children may also be aware that their mothers have aborted potential siblings.

Termination raises many questions and conflicts for people whose beliefs about life, death, spirituality, religion and morality are firmly held. In the USA, for example, some 'pro-life' activists considered the murder of doctors performing abortions to be justified. Practitioners concerned in any way with young people considering, or having undergone, termination need to be clear and honest about their own attitudes and beliefs.

It is not possible in this brief section to consider the teachings of all religious and philosophical groups. Opinions differ, not only between but also within religions. It is essential to determine the individual's religious/philosophical background. As an example, a brief discussion based on Islamic teachings follows.

For Muslims, conflict focuses on different interpretations of the Qur'an. Some say: 'God creates life and He will provide for any children that are produced', using the same *sura* (verse) to prohibit both abortion and contraception (Wattam 1993, p.65). A *hadith* (saying of Mohammed) states that:

All creatures are God's charges and he who is dearest to his God is he who is most useful to his charges. The germ of every one of you is concentrated in his mother's womb in the form of a drop for forty days, then he becomes a clot of blood for the same period, then the angel is sent to ensoul him. (cited undated b, in Compton, p.27)

The process of foetal development described in the Qur'an is also quoted in Anita Compton's introduction to 'Abortion: Some Muslim perspectives' (undated b, pp.26–31), using the version of Ali A. Yusuf (1946):

12 Man we did create
    from a quintessence of clay,
13 Then we placed him
    as (a drop of) sperm
    in a place of rest,
    firmly fixed;
14 Then we made the sperm
    into a clot of congealed blood,
    then of that clot we made
    a foetus lump; then we
    made out of that lump
    bones and clothed the bones
    with flesh; then we developed
    out of it another creature.
    So Blessed be God
    the best to Create. (the Qur'an, cited in Compton undated b, p.26)

Another *hadith* states: 'the good deed most deserving of reward is to maintain ties of womb relationship, and the evil deed most deserving of punishment is aggression and severance of the ties of womb relationship' (cited in Compton undated b, p.27).

Yusuf al'Qaradwi (1960) considers that 'Islam ... does not allow doing violence to the pregnancy once it occurs', although: 'If ... after the baby is completely formed, it is reliably established that the continuation of pregnancy would necessarily result in the death of the mother, then, in accordance with the general principle of the Shari'a, that of choosing the lesser of two evils, abortion must be performed' (cited in Wattam 1993, pp.65–6).

Shaykh Abdullah al'Qalqili (1982) describes a different approach:

> The jurists give examples to illustrate the meaning of the excuse for abortion as in Ibn Abidin who says, 'like the mother who has a baby still unweaned and who becomes pregnant and her milk ceases and the father is unable to hire a wet nurse to save the life of his baby'. The jurists also state that it is permissible to take medicine for abortion so long as the embryo is still unformed in the human shape. The period of the unformed shape is given as a hundred and twenty days. The jurists think that during this state the embryo is not yet a human being. (cited in Wattam 1993, p.66)

Compton (undated) summarises opinions of four Islamic schools of law (Hanifi, Maliki, Shafi, Hanbali) representing a range of strict or liberal views. For example, some adherents of the Maliki school (developed in Medina) forbid termination altogether, others once 'animation' has taken place (ensoulment by the angel, described above) (pp.28–31).

Some Muslims accept UK abortion laws, citing such authorities as the opinion of a *mufti* that termination is not infanticide even when the foetus is past the 120 day period before human shape has been identified (al'Qalqili, cited in Wattam 1993, p.66), but for others the stricter interpretations of Muslim law prevail.

Practitioners engaged with Muslim girls, boys and their families need to learn about beliefs regarding the soul, sin, death and punishment. A girl might experience conflict within herself, wishing to be free of pregnancy, but attentive to the religious code of her family and community; she might wish to respect teaching about the sacredness of life, but be afraid of bearing a child; she might wish to terminate the pregnancy, perhaps in order to continue with school examinations, but fear the disapproval of family and religious leaders. Such conflicts might not at first be apparent, especially if a girl had reached the point of attending a clinic.

Crucial in all discussions of termination are definitions of and beliefs about what constitutes a human person, and whether humans in general and embryos in particular have souls. The British Humanist Association Briefing

'Abortion' in the *Conscience in Action* series asks 'What is a human person?':

> People disagree over abortion mainly because they have different views of what constitutes a human person. Those who oppose it see the embryo as a person while it is still at an early stage in its development. We submit that this view is not justified by moral considerations on the basis of present scientific evidence.
>
> A human person does not, and cannot, exist without the capacity for consciousness and awareness. This is the basic pre-condition for the moral status of personhood. All morally significant qualities depend on it. This capacity does not in itself make a person, but no being which lacks it can be a person. Only when this basic capacity is present does a being acquire a right to preservation comparable with that of a fully human person.
>
> In discussing abortion we need to discuss only the critical points in human development that relate to these basic criteria. (British Humanist Association, undated a, p.2)

The BHA defines moral grounds for abortion, finding that up to 12 weeks, 'there are no moral grounds for refusing abortion'. After 12 weeks, 'the fetus is becoming more firmly established … and it is right that the law does lay down criteria which have to be satisfied before an abortion can proceed' (p.3).

Later, 'the possibility of survival outside the womb becomes morally significant, not because of the inherent rights of the fetus but because of the impact of its destruction on all those concerned' (p.3). With regard to rights, the BHA considers:

> Certainly the human embryo deserves respect, because of its importance to human persons … The respect due to a fetus grows as the fetus grows in significance, particularly when it is loved. But respect carries no absolute rights comparable to the inherent rights of the people most involved with the fetus. (p.3)

A girl and her family who appear to adopt this line of reasoning may nevertheless have feelings deriving from, perhaps, religious faith practised in childhood but now rejected, or the beliefs of other family members. Tensions may arise between the girl and the father of the foetus, or her parents, because of differing views on the existence of the soul and the sanctity of pre-natal life.

Pam (a social worker) noted that for girls who get as far as asking for termination, the need to end pregnancy overrides other considerations, including doubts deriving from religious teaching. Anna (a nurse) found that religious/spiritual considerations were rarely introduced into discussions by younger women and girls.

For girls engaging with decisions about unwanted pregnancies, consideration of religious and spiritual implications may often appear to have no relevance. Yet the decision to end a life (whether regarded as actual or potential) is very solemn, and may have long-lasting consequences, emotional and spiritual. A girl may be able to grow through the experience of making such a decision, recognising that she has wielded power and faced (or not faced) responsibility. Her decision may later lead to regret, guilt and confusion about religious teaching and attitudes towards the sanctity of life. She should have opportunities to reflect on her action and to mourn the lost life.

The most common reaction after termination is relief, but adolescent girls often experience emotional problems, such as:

- feeling abandoned by the baby's father;
- feeling bitter towards parents who may have added pressure to terminate the pregnancy, keeping her dependent and lacking control over her own life;
- feeling alone with no one to talk to;
- feeling disillusioned;
- feeling bitter towards men and angry with herself for 'giving in' – especially true for those who felt pressured into having sex. (based on Baker 1985, p.99)

These sad, negative feelings may be difficult to express cathartically; rather, they may be suppressed, finding no healthy outlet, but turning inwards into depression or physical illness, or outwards in the form of behaviour which attracts criticism, maybe punishment, confirming feelings of lack of control, bitterness, anger and badness. If pregnancy and abortion result from rape or sexual abuse, such effects and responses may be exacerbated.

Although vocabulary usually associated with spirituality may not be used, practitioners may find girls engaged in spiritual crises as they recognise the implications of their decisions. Pam met 'Kerry' when she applied for a termination. Kerry was doing well at school, and appeared to be in control of herself and her feelings, certain that she knew what she wanted. Six weeks later, the girl was 'a wreck, in a heap', sobbing and crying, overwhelmed by guilt and loss, 'more spiritually aware without religious overtones, more sensitive to feelings' and very isolated and shocked by her own emotions. Pam found her to be 'a brave person who showed spirit to face all this on her own'. While preparing for the termination, Kerry's whole self focused on her one aim: to be free of the pregnancy, and with it worry and distraction from school work and examinations. Once this aim had been achieved, the girl had no defence against her overwhelming feelings. With the social worker, she was able to talk freely, engage with her new self and grow, emotionally and spiritually.

The service offered by Pam to Kerry is not always available: some authorities do not encourage or provide facilities for follow-up counselling. Yet Kerry's story demonstrates how post-abortion reaction can be devastating. By offering time to Kerry during the crisis, Pam could help her to recognise, understand and grow with her feelings and experiences. Had no such service been available, the girl might have passed into depression, perhaps physical illness, and after-effects might for long have remained dormant.

Writing for young people, Sharpe (1987) advises that:

> Having an abortion may not take long, but it is very different psychologically to an operation to take out a tooth. It is a deeper loss than that, and you may feel very sad as a result, even if you have definitely not wanted a baby and are relieved not to be pregnant anymore. Mourning such a loss is to be expected, but there is no set reaction, and some girls have abortions without such an emotional response. The crucial factor is to allow anyone who is pregnant to make up their own minds. They should have access to good counselling that provides information, time and support so that they can decide for themselves and take responsibility for whatever course of action they choose. (p.215)

If no support is available and the girl experiences the procedure as a lone ordeal, her suffering may be great. Vicky, for example, became pregnant (although using contraceptives) only a few months after setting up home with her baby daughter and new boyfriend:

> 'He didn't want to know, so I had to face telling my parents again and I decided I'd have an abortion, but I had to go private because of my doctor messing me around. It took me three or four weeks to get an appointment down at the hospital. By then it was too late. So I had to go down to Brighton to have it. I made his parents pay half and as I had money in the bank I had to use that. I didn't cope very well with it, and for months afterwards I went through a very deep depression, and I kept telling myself that I'd killed my baby. I've got over that as best as I ever will.' (pp.215–16).

The deep distress experienced by Vicky recalls the discussion of spiritual distress in Chapter 4. The young woman has been bereaved, and by her own choice. With no love or care, no one with whom to share her guilt and sorrow, she descends into depression and self-accusation. Her assessment, 'I didn't cope very well with it', is haunting; how 'well' is a girl in that position supposed to 'cope', and what constitutes 'good coping'? Her sad final comment is redolent of spiritual despair: 'I've got over that as best as I ever will.' Being able to express feelings and to share mourning, if the girl so wishes, is essential to every aspect of her own being. It is essential for those around her, too: for Vicky, in deep and apparently chronic depression, had a baby daughter who needed a healthy mother.

Although the aborted foetus may be regarded, medically and legally, as without life, Anna (a nurse) found that women who profess no religious convictions may want to know what has happened to it, 'to make peace with what has been part of them'. A non-denominational blessing is said in the hospital chapel, and foetuses are cremated at the local crematorium. When termination is at late term, usually because of abnormality in the foetus, a blessing may be said by the chaplain, and a name added to the hospital book of remembrance; an annual service is held for those grieving over loss in pregnancy.

Anne Baker (1985) (The Hope Clinic for Women Ltd, Granite City, Illinois) writes:

> One Catholic woman requested that the nurse … baptize the fetal material after the abortion. One of our Catholic employees showed the nurse how to do it, and when the time came, she carried out the request. In post-abortion counselling, the woman said she had felt a wave of relief and 'peace in my soul' after the baptism. (p.44)

Baker is clear that people may want and need 'to clarify their beliefs about God, ask questions and listen closely to the responses' (p.43). Anna found that regardless of their religious background, many women felt that they were committing an unforgivable action: while doing something right for themselves they had more universal moral reservations about termination. Baker suggests that practitioners may raise questions with women who are afraid that God won't forgive them, for example:

> 'Do you believe that God is ALL Merciful? All forgiving? All Compassionate?' If she answers yes, then why would God single her out as the exception? Why would He forgive all except her? … If she is religious, there is usually a high value placed upon having faith. You can talk about her having faith that God will forgive her. Most people also believe that God is All Wise and All Understanding. If your client does, then you can help her reason. (p.43)

Practitioners are often reluctant to engage in discussion of religious belief and spiritual well-being, perhaps because they do not wish to seem to intrude their own views. Yet in situations where life and death are the subjects of concern and decision, the client has a right to the opportunity to clarify beliefs, confess fears and be assured of an attentive, non-judging listener.

Religious faith may enable growth and deeper understanding of the individual's belief. One woman counselled by Baker belonged to a deeply religious family and:

> also did volunteer work with handicapped children 'for the Good Lord'. She

stated, 'I never thought I'd be having an abortion, but my husband and I have been praying a lot together over this decision. We feel that God has sent me this cross to bear because some time in the future I may be able to help someone else in my situation.' (p.43)

The section on suicide above quoted Susie's wish that she had been one of her mother's miscarriages, and her prayer to God: 'Why don't you give me an illness and just let me die?' (cited in Hill 1995, p.132). This section ends with a memory of 'Maria', who died after a life of physical weakness due to genetically transmitted illness. She was opposed to termination of pregnancy on the grounds of genetic risk because, she explained, had her mother chosen abortion, she would never have lived – a life she found rich and full (see p.195).

QUESTIONS

- Have any young people known to you contemplated or undergone termination of pregnancy?
- Have any young people or children known to you been associated with termination: for example, as siblings, boyfriends or friends of girls who have terminated pregnancies.
- Have any young people or children known to you been bereaved as a result of termination?
- What is your opinion about termination? Are you influenced by any religious teachings?
- Does your attitude towards termination affect your work with young people?
- What attitudes influence the opinions of young people?

SUGGESTIONS

With colleagues and children:

- Discuss one another's ideas about the questions above.
- Consider the extracts from Muslim writings. Discover and discuss the teachings of religions represented in your establishment.
- Consider how you could engage with beliefs and teachings which influence attitudes towards termination and conflicts which may be stimulated, both internally and between young people and families and communities.
- Define 'a human person', using the BHA briefing as a starting point: does 'a human person' have a soul?
- Discuss the concept of rights in relation to embryos, bearing in mind

the comments of 'Maria' (see Chapter 13), who relished her life, however circumscribed by genetic illness.

- Consider possible responses to termination by girls and family members, using Anne Baker's list and the experiences of 'Kerry' and Vicky as starting points.
- Identify services for termination in your locality.
- Plan an ideal counselling and support service, and compare this with services in your locality.
- Study Vicky's story, considering every aspect of her experience, especially her need to mourn, her guilt at killing her baby, and her deep and lasting depression. Discuss how her experience links with ideas about spiritual well-being and distress.
- Discuss situations in which religious belief has helped or hindered young people in making decisions about termination.

Summary

Discussion of two aspects of death which affect young people and their families – suicide and termination of pregnancy – has highlighted some spiritual and religious implications. Practitioners in all fields of work with and on behalf of children may be involved, since feelings and responses are not confined to specialist clinics.

Special attention is needed if adequate pre- and post-abortion counselling is not available. Responses such as sadness, mourning, anger and guilt may not be experienced by every girl, but if no opportunity is made for such expression at the appropriate time, suppression may lead to depression, illness and/or disturbing behaviour.

Similarly, children need opportunities to express feelings following bereavement by suicide. The desperation of children who are contemplating suicide may not always be recognised, and practitioners need constantly to be alert to signs of deep sadness, withdrawal and difficulty in communicating.

Practitioners need information about and understanding of beliefs regarding both suicide and termination, including sinfulness and punishment. They also need to be clear about their own and other people's views on the moment at which the embryo becomes a human person, and whether or not the embryo has a soul and/or rights.

Part 6

Communicating with children

15 Stories, myths and legends

The importance of stories

Religion and stories are inseparable – tales of deities and demons, martyrs and miracles, the eternal war between good and evil, the celebration of holy lives. Stories are transmitted in many ways, narrated by parents at bedtime and read from sacred texts by religious leaders during services. Simplified versions are written for children, while illustrations in paint and stone, wood and stained-glass adorn places of worship. Many festivals celebrate and perpetuate the great stories of religious traditions.

Not only do children consciously learn the myths and legends of their own religion and culture, they are also unconsciously influenced by the stories and images by which they are surrounded and which embody the values and beliefs of both their local community and encompassing society. Don Cupitt (1991) (a theologian) comments: 'So potent is story that in preliterate societies, in childhood and in religion most of the really important information is preserved and transmitted in story form. Stories simply stick in the mind better than anything else' (p.79).

Stories may be received and understood on many levels, from literal and concrete to complex symbolism. Understanding may change with experience, and any story may be understood in different ways by different people. Children understand stories in the context of their own experiences, and may not perceive meaning in ways intended or expected by adults. A boy (aged 5), for example, found in the folk story of Rapunzel (whose hair could be used as a ladder) reassurance: 'That one's own body can provide a lifeline' (Bettelheim 1978, p.17; see also Crompton 1992, p.137). Cupitt (1991) suggests that 'in symbolic guise at least, [stories] must confront the child with the realities of sex, violence, misfortune and death. If you have never been shocked by art, you will not be equipped to cope with life' (p.33).

Telling and sharing stories is a universal method of communicating, especially important when working with children. It is as essential for adults to listen and learn as it is to narrate. Through such sharing, adults can show respect for and interest in children's religious backgrounds, indicating respect for and interest in children themselves. Learning about children's religious and spiritual experiences and beliefs should lead to understanding of anxieties and fears, and should offer clues towards further communication. Sharing enjoyment, including amusement and fun, demonstrates recognition that religion is not confined to repetition of prescribed observances or rules about morality. Stories can be used in social work practice in numerous ways, including in life-story books.

It is not possible in this chapter to represent all religions equally, if at all. Practitioners are encouraged to regard these examples as models, and to learn stories from children, families and religious congregations within their own localities.

Creation myths

Stories which account for the beginning of this world convey messages about relationships between creating deities, humans and the rest of creation. The particular myth which underlies the upbringing of an individual child can have considerable power, even if the child and family profess no religious belief. Interpretations of myth change: for example, 'the Genesis creation narratives ... are now interpreted by many Christians in the light of the theory of evolution' (Davies 1994a, p.1). Thus ancient stories both represent understandings of the beginnings of life and death, and problems of existence within individual experience of the present world.

In the versions of the myth of Adam and Eve familiar to Christians, Jews, Muslims and Rastafarians, the earth is created by God, who issues a series of commands, and completes the work with two humans. Eve is created later than Adam: in one version she is fashioned from one of his ribs to be his companion. Both humans are superior to all other creatures. Life is peaceful and stress-free while they accept the regulations imposed by God and abstain from eating fruit from the tree of the knowledge of good and evil. Once they succumb to temptation and thus challenge the authority of the providing but constraining creator, their life in the Garden of Eden ends. The price of free will is work, procreation and death. It is also sexual shame, for their first act after eating the forbidden fruit is to fear their nakedness and cover their genitals (which act still informs attitudes towards sexual morality still prevalent in the UK) (Genesis 1–3; Qur'an 1/4:30–9).

Children whose view of the world is influenced by this story may receive strong impressions about authority and power: for example, the relative importance of male and female, and of human and non-human creatures. The story teaches about obedience and punishment, and proposes that life on earth for all the progeny of Adam and Eve expelled from the Garden of Eden (also known as Paradise) is dangerous and essentially less than perfect.

However, children may also perceive that only by challenging the authority of the all-powerful creator/provider parent can they attain independence, accepting the replacement of luxurious dependence with responsibility for their own lives.

A myth from Africa tells how the good spirit Mukulu created the first man and woman from two holes in the ground. He gave them land, tools, cooking vessels and grain, and instructed them to build a home, cultivate the soil and cook food. Instead, they hid in the forest. Mukulu repeated his instructions, this time to a male and female monkey, who obeyed him in every detail. Mukulu took the monkeys' tails and attached them to the humans, thus transposing the two species. In this story, disobedience to the creator results in dispossession not from a luxurious garden, but from a life of labour, while animals are raised to human status and responsibility (Ganeri 1994, pp.22–3).

A Polynesian myth attributes the creation of the earth and sky to creatures which other traditions appear to despise as low in the hierarchy. Old Spider, who lives above the sea, finds a giant clamshell which she cannot open until she utters a magic charm which enables her to slip inside. In the total darkness she finds a tiny snail, which she invests with magic powers and releases, then she sleeps for three days. This is repeated with a larger snail. The tiny snail pushes the clam shell further apart, and being placed on one half, becomes the moon. Old Spider then asks a caterpillar to push the shell wider open again, but the work is so hard that the caterpillar sweats and eventually dies. The sweat becomes the salty sea in the lower half of the shell – the earth. The top half is the sky, in which Old Spider places the larger snail, the sun (Ganeri 1994, pp.21–2).

A Chinese myth attributes creation to the offspring of the powers of darkness and light, *yin* and *yang*, a god called Pan Gu who was born inside a giant egg, growing for 18,000 years in darkness until the shell split, the light parts floating up to form the sky, the dark sinking to form the earth. Pan Gu stood between earth and sky, holding them apart for 18,000 years until he died. Then his breath formed clouds and wind, and his voice became thunder, while his eyes turned into the sun and the moon (Ganeri 1994, p.24). Here, the earth is created from the union of light and dark, which are complementary, not in conflict. The creating god himself provides the substance for earth and sky, sun and moon, from the shell in which he grows, and then his own dead body. This has parallels in other creation myths, and may be seen on one level as an allegory of the life cycle, new growth from dead matter, and the resurrection of the year.

Models of behaviour

Stories are deliberately used to teach ideals of behaviour according to the precepts of the religion. Cupitt (1991) reflects: 'a good religious story may persuade me that it is possible for me so to live that I can make my life make sense. And religion itself is the attempt so to live as to make life make sense, whatever happens' (p.15).

The lives of *gurus*, saints and prophets are narrated as models, exemplifying the virtues most dear to the narrator. Attitudes towards such virtues may change with changing times. Female Christian saints popular in the Middle Ages famously died to protect both virginity and religion, preferring torture followed by eternal life as brides of Jesus to marriage with pagan and violent kings. Their hideous sufferings are not longer extolled as models, although the basic virtues of fortitude and fidelity to one's own values and integrity remain, and may be tested at times of crisis.

The Hindu epic poem the *Mahabharata* includes a section called the *Bhagavad Gita* ('The Song of God'), in which Lord Krishna converses with the hero Arjuna on the basic beliefs, not least the virtue of selfless service.

While most of these stories are set in past times and/or distant lands, it may be difficult for children to distinguish biography from fiction. Some take seriously – and sometimes disastrously – adult advice to emulate heroic forebears.

Michel (aged 11), the eponymous subject of a novel about a Jewish boy torn between Judaism (he has been circumcised) and Roman Catholicism (he has been baptised and confirmed, and has taken communion), suffers almost fatal conflict as he tries to follow the example of saintly children. In a Jesuit seminary, he envies St Tarsicius (who at the age of 11 risked death at the hands of the pagan Romans) and St Saturninus, 'pushed by the enraged crowd before the statue of Jupiter and ordered to bow down and make sacrifice. Things were different today, a boy didn't have any chance at all. Christ had conquered the world, and the opportunities just weren't there any more' (Lewis 1967, p.323).

To compensate, Michel tests himself, expiating a supposed sin by standing 'on one foot with his arms outstretched at shoulder level, in the attitude of the crucifixion ... until the burning in his shoulders and leg became intolerable, and the sweat poured down his face'; only then 'he forgave himself'. Later, he keeps pebbles in his shoe, 'to mortify the flesh', and through the pain of an infected blister fantasises gangrene and amputation, becoming 'St. Michel, the one-legged hermit' (pp.320, 324 and 325).

The dangers of taking ancient (or any) tales literally and out of context is compounded for the confused and lonely boy by the horrific story of St Dominique du Val, who, Michel reads, was ritually killed by Jews; owing to his immense fortitude and fidelity, the chief murderer accepted both baptism and execution. For Michel, this tale brings double horror: he too is Jew, and therefore, he supposes, also capable of such atrocities; yet as a Christian, he may suffer for his faith (p.557).

As recounted in Chapter 4, Yvonne Stevenson, the daughter of an Anglican vicar, endeavoured literally to follow the models of her religion when, after a Good Friday service commemorating the crucifixion of Jesus, she decided to offer sacrifice by hammering a rusty nail through her right hand (thus also sacrificing her hope to play the violin). She 'put the nail in position, and raised the hammer. At that very instant the gong went for tea. It was a message from God, telling me to stop – just as He had told Abraham to stop before he slew Isaac' (in Islam, Ishmael is the son at risk). Just as one story led to trouble, another helped to justify escape, and imagining a conversation with her mother, grew in understanding: '"why do you agree to the saints and martyrs and to Christ suffering?' ... 'We don't agree ... and we don't want to add to suffering by causing more of it"' (Stevenson 1976, pp.43–4).

Other stories illustrate more accessible attributes, such as patience, honesty, love and kindness.

Festivals

The liturgical year is punctuated with celebrations and commemorations of the great stories of religious history, often closely associated with secular history. An example is the Jews' escape from Egypt, remembered at *Pesach*, when the story is told by the father of the family in response to four ritual questions asked by the youngest child at the *seder*.

Children may traditionally act versions of stories, for example the several tales associated with the conception and birth of Jesus narrated, pictured and enacted at Christmas (Luke 1–2, Matthew 1–2, Ganeri 1994, pp.50–2).

Jewish children celebrate the triumph of Esther, a Jew married to the king of Persia (now Iran) at a time when her people were persecuted. The chief minister, Haman, planned to kill all the Jews in Persia, but was foiled through Esther's brave intervention. The full story is told in the biblical Book of Esther. At the festival of *Purim*, the story is read in synagogue, when children stamp, boo, hiss and shake rattles at every mention of Haman's name. Then they may dress up and act the story. Special cakes eaten at *Purim* are called 'Haman's Ears'.

For brief accounts of other festivals and stories, see Chapter 7.

Spiritual experiences

Many stories based in religious traditions do not narrate past events, but seek to represent intangible experience, notably the eternal battle between good and evil, light and dark. While humans battle with earthly problems, supernatural beings fight, both here and in their own dimensions.

Some religions are populated with myriad deities and demons, angels and avatars, devas and djinns. The inner, human struggle to define and achieve a good life, and to define and resist evil is mirrored and acted out on a cosmic scale.

The Hindu epic poem *Ramayana* narrates the adventures of Rama (avatar of Vishnu), who is banished from his kingdom and loses his wife, Sita, to the demon king Ravana. Only with the aid of the monkey god Hanuman can Sita be rescued and Rama restored to his kingdom. While the *Ramayana* can be received as a brilliant 'action epic', full of physically dangerous and courageous adventures, it is also, and essentially, a parable of spiritual challenge, including sacrifice and humiliation, love and rescue on the journey to wisdom and fulfilment.

The life of Gautama Siddhartha illustrates the spiritual journey of the individual. Born a prince, he is protected from knowledge of the world outside his parents' palace in order to ensure his future as a great temporal ruler. The king has been warned that his son must never see anyone old, sick or dead. However, the prince sees an old man, a sick man and a funeral, and learns that this is the common lot of humanity. He leaves his wife, son and possessions and becomes an extreme ascetic. After seven years he has become emaciated and ill, but has not achieved the truth and knowledge he seeks. He meditates for 49 days and nights and becomes the Buddha ('The Enlightened One'), understanding that suffering is caused by discontent, the failure of people to be satisfied and at peace with themselves. He develops this teaching, and is joined by many other people, including his own son.

The parables of Jesus (the Jewish tradition of didactic narration) use images from everyday life vividly to illustrate spiritual and moral virtues. Some are reflexive, commenting on the reception of the teacher's words. For example, a sower broadcasts seeds: some on the path, where they are trodden underfoot; some into the air, where they are eaten by birds; some on the rock, where they germinate but die of drought, and some among thorns, where their growth is choked. Those in good soil, however, yield a fine harvest (Luke 7:4–15).

Stories about spiritual experience are by no means confined to religious scriptures. The popular *Star Trek* space fiction films (television and cinema) present moral as well as physical challenges in which decisions must be made in terms of a strict ethical code: for example, life in whatever form must be respected, and wherever possible protected. The stories test problem-solving abilities in which every aspect of the whole person, not least the spiritual, is engaged. A theme in the *Star Trek: The Next Generation* series is the quest of an android, Data, to define and attain humanity – in other words, to develop a soul (a notable episode is entitled 'The measure of a man'). This theme relates to the universal myths of non-humans, including fairies, mermaids and ondines, to achieve a soul, although the inevitable penalty is (physical) death. Other *Star Trek* stories examine the responses of children (Klingon and Beta-Zed, as well as human) to bereavement, and the development of individual personality (and therefore responsibility for the self and others) among members of the Borg, an ant-like corporate entity.

A strong storyline in the soap opera *Eastenders* in 1996 built conflict between good and evil represented by Sarah, the fair-haired, innocent, 15-year-old member of an evangelical Christian group, and Dan the dark-haired, sexually attractive drug dealer, struggling for control of Sarah's brother, Tony. Conflict reached a peak when Sarah, pretending to be 18, pursued her role of guardian angel in a Blackpool nightclub. Dan, demonic in red light, spiked her soft drink with a drug (ecstasy), causing Sarah to collapse.

Stories representing the battle between good and evil appear in every form. *Terminator II*, starring Arnold Schwarzenegger, presents two 'terminators' (superhuman machines), sent back in time, one to destroy and one to protect a boy on whose existence depends the future of humanity. He had been conceived (in *Terminator I*) during a brief encounter between an unmarried woman and a man from the future who died while protecting her and the unborn child. This man returns to the mother in a vision to advise her to protect the boy, with the help of the 'good' terminator. The battle eventually ends with the triumph of 'right', the good terminator having learnt from the boy that he must not kill people (although destroying the 'evil' terminator is definitely acceptable). In the final, deeply moral action, the good terminator chooses his own destruction, which, he understands, is essential if humanity is to survive without further threat from such machines. He sacrifices himself for the good of the people – all people – and the film ends with a strong message of hope.

Many books written for and popular among children engage with questions of ethics and morality (without reference to religion), and refer to the liberation and development of spiritual aspects of life (whatever the vocabulary used). Stories about disadvantaged children, for example, often focus on the ability to develop and demonstrate such spiritual attributes as courage, fortitude and creativity. The old favourite *What Katy Did* ('Coolidge') confines the young heroine to bed after an accident, with (we have to believe) no prospect of ever walking again. At the end of the book, the saintly Cousin Helen praises her: '"You have won the place, which, you recollect, I once told you an invalid should try to gain of being to everybody 'The Heart of the House.'"' Katy responds with expected modesty: '"I haven't been brave. You can't think how badly I sometimes have behaved – how cross and ungrateful I am, and how stupid and slow. Every day I see things which ought to be done, and I don't do them."'

This book may be old, but the sentiments, the expectations of behaviour, can be found in contemporary literature. For example, David, a 'golden boy' whose athletic career ends when his cancerous leg is amputated, achieves new courage with which to face death (Ure 1987).

Seeing meaning in stories

Stories which overtly or implicitly refer to religious beliefs, spiritual experience and/or ethical codes may not be received and understood exactly as intended by the narrators. For example, tales to explain the absence of a relation who has died can stimulate unexpected responses.

Jade (aged $3\frac{1}{2}$) regularly said goodnight to her great-grandfather, Whisky the dog and her hamster, although they had all died. She knew that they were stars. However, she mystified her family with the news that her great-grandfather had gone to London, then explained that 'during the day stars don't need to shine', so were free to have days out, and could be glad of cloudy nights for longer holidays (Needs 1994, cited in Crompton 1996, 4/35).

In contrast, after the death of his father, a boy (aged 4) had great difficulty in falling asleep. He demanded that all windows should be kept locked, and was reluctant to cross streets or be in the shade of trees. It emerged that his mother 'had told him that God had reached down from Heaven while his father slept, picked him up and taken him to heaven'; now he feared that God would take him too, if he slept (Torrie 1978, p.7).

Children's responses to stories are complex and individual, influenced in unpredictable ways by the attitudes (both overt and unconscious) of the adults who narrate the tales and offer the explanations. Both Jade and the boy, children of similar age, had been told lies in the form of imaginative stories intended to explain actual events. Jade developed the story into a lively, happy image of life after death continuing attractive aspects of her own life; there seems little doubt that she would be able, without stress, to relinquish that story as education informed her that dead people, dogs and hamsters are not transformed into stars.

The boy, however, had interpreted the story as a literal event whose implications terrified him. If he were to be told that the explanation of his father's death had been 'only a story', how would this child interpret other images and stories? Would they be rejected as lies or feared as literal, and how would he regard the adults who thus apparently abused his trust?

When considering the impact of stories in the context of social work practice, it is essential to be aware of both the intention of the narrator and the interpretations of the audience.

Stories associated with religious traditions may similarly have an unexpected and unpredictable impact. For example, narration about the resurrection of Jesus after crucifixion by someone who believed in his return to physical life might scare children who, having no former knowledge of the story, might expect to meet a living corpse.

The Hindu legend of Ganesha might equally raise anxiety for children unfamiliar with such characters and adventures. The god Shiva returns from a long journey without knowing that his wife, Parvati, has a son (whom she has formed from earth in his absence). When Ganesha, a sturdy boy, refuses to let Shiva pass, he is beheaded. Shiva soon learns what he has done, and substitutes an elephant's head, with which Ganesha is perfectly satisfied (see, for example, Ganeri 1994, pp.57–9; Jaffrey 1992, pp.171–4).

The story, which represents repair of damage and overcoming obstacles, can suggest also the terrifying prospect of being harmed by adults who should offer only protection, and of losing valued parts of oneself and one's life. The return of the unknown father who supplants the child as protector or companion of the mother has universal significance.

Any story may yield several possible layers of meaning A beautiful example from Christianity, with a Jewish setting, narrates the miraculous healing of Jairus's daughter (Luke 8:40–56). Jairus, an important official in the Jewish Temple in Jerusalem, comes in person to Jesus to beg help for his dying daughter. Although a messenger brings news of the girl's death, Jesus goes to the house. He stills the noisy mourners, saying that the girl is not dead but asleep. He allows only her parents and three of his closest companions to enter her room, where he takes her hand and tells her to rise. On her instant recovery, Jesus thoughtfully orders food.

An important message for children and families is the care and attention shown to the girl. Her busy, important father takes time to go in person to ask for help: the high-status male does not try to order or purchase service, but requests aid from someone whom he might well have regarded as of low, even negligible account. Then the busy, important healer comes to her in person. The attention of these powerful males is particularly remarkable, as female children had little status is biblical times. The father's love for his daughter appears to have been great.

For the carer, there are messages about communication. The noisy mourners are sent away: the sick child and her family need peace and privacy. Jesus makes direct contact, he touches and speaks to her. He sends for food: the body needs sustenance as much as the spirit. Diagnostic abilities are shown: Jesus ignores the report of death, and identifies how to heal the girl. Children are sometimes seen as beyond help because they are labelled as 'too disturbed', 'delinquent' and even 'evil' – they have 'died'. Yet even a 'dead' child can return to life.

The reference to food could suggest that the girl has suffered from an eating problem and been near to physical death from starvation. Jesus releases her, and restores normal appetite. One commentator (a Methodist minister) suggested that the 12-year-old girl is (like Sleeping Beauty) passing through the changes of puberty: this interpretation might imply the beginning of menstruation, attended by pain and confusion; if this were so, Jesus taking her hand would be particularly remarkable in view of the prohibition on touching females who are, or might be, menstruating. The story could then be seen as containing the powerful message that no child is too 'unclean' or socially/religiously unacceptable to receive loving contact from an adult carer. The story can also represent emergence from the state of childhood dependence (lying down) to the beginning of adult responsibility (rising up).

In the story of Gautama Siddhartha may be seen a similar theme of growth and development from childhood to young adulthood. His parents' attempts to prevent him from learning about old age, illness and death can not inhibit healthy development, including knowledge of the realities of life and death. The refusal to provide preparation for and education about these realities means that when he leaves the palace and meets them for himself, the impact is immense, and his new understanding and vision lead to the very outcome which his parents have sought to prevent: he leaves his home and, as all young people must, learns from his own experience and forms his own philosophy about how to live.

These examples are offered as a model for ways of understanding and seeing meaning for individual lives and circumstances of contemporary children in stories from religious traditions (see also Crompton 1996, 5/1–11).

Using stories in social work practice

An essential contributor to healthy development is imagination, itself definable as a spiritual attribute. In his introduction to 'A guide to the use of story in spiritual aspects of education' (*c.* 1993) Mike Newby writes: 'The experience of imagined reality through story enables a rehearsal of encounter with life's momentous scenarios, preparing the child for relationships, for adventures, for crises, for seeing himself as having a future which he must carve out for himself.' He defines story as: '"a living word" insofar as it speaks through our imaginative powers to our inner selves, awakening our participation in the spiritual contest of light and dark, truth and ignorance, virtue and vice, openness and hiddenness' (p.i).

He suggests that 'Properly understood, religious traditions embody shared communal responses to life's ultimate questions, and provide a language rich in symbolism by means of which the believer can orientate his life, giving it a worthy goal. Ancient religious stories are the seed-bed of this language, a language from which all modern reflection on life's meaning and purpose has developed' (p.ii).

Telling, listening to, sharing and creating stories is one of the most fundamental and important forms of communication, not least in the context of religion and spirituality. The services of many religions include readings from scriptures, often of stories about the founders and famous adherents of the tradition: the universal way in which children learn about their religious and cultural environment.

Such stories can inform practitioners about the religious and spiritual background, experience, beliefs and needs of children. The best source of information is children themselves, who enjoy telling stories to adults whose responses can communicate, for example, enjoyment of the stories and of new knowledge, and approval of the narrators' story-telling abilities. The very experience of sharing stories, of adults' willingness to learn from children, demonstrates both respect for their religious backgrounds and valuing of the children themselves.

Through sharing stories and noticing, for example, which tales are chosen most and least often, practitioners may gain clues about feelings, joys and anxieties.

Many stories associated with religious traditions are concerned with death, and illustrate beliefs both about death itself and the destiny of the dead individual. For example, Kisagotami, asks the Buddha to revive her dead baby. He tells her to bring him a mustard seed from a house where no one has died. Through visiting a number of households, Kisagotami learns that everyone has to die. Only then can she accept the death of her own child and, through healthy mourning, part from him and find peace (Goodwin

1991, pp.19–21). This story contrasts with the Rastafarianism belief that death is a punishment and signifies failure. A Jewish story portrays the prophet Elijah saving the life of a boy who had apparently died (I Kings 17:17–24), and the Christian story of Jesus healing Jairus's daughter, also apparently dead (Luke 8:40–56) is told above, as is that of the Hindu Ganesha, who is killed but restored to life by his god father.

Practitioners working with children who have been bereaved or are dying may find knowledge of appropriate stories useful. All children can find such stories helpful in beginning to learn about death and in finding opportunity to express anxiety, perhaps because of such 'explanations' as that given to the boy who believed that his father had been taken to heaven by Jesus.

When using such stories, practitioners need to be clear about their own beliefs, experiences and feelings, and also respect the images and beliefs of other people, recognising that for some a story may be regarded as literally true, while for others it is a metaphor.

A number of children and young people experience separation from their parents. Esther (the Hebrew Queen of Persia) and Mohammed (the founder of Islam) are orphans, well cared for by uncles; indeed, Mohammed suffers additional bereavement when his grandfather, with whom he lives after his mother's death, also dies (Collinson and Miller 1985, pp.85–6). The Hebrew Moses and Hindu Krishna are fostered to protect them from danger. When Moses is born in Egypt, the Pharaoh orders the death of every son born to a Hebrew woman. Moses is hidden in a waterproofed basket camouflaged by reeds at the river's edge, and guarded by his sister. When Pharaoh's daughter goes to bathe, she finds the basket and recognises the baby as a Jew. She fosters the baby, who is suckled and cared for by his own mother (Exodus 2:1–10). Krishna is born in prison after seven older siblings have been murdered by his uncle, who fears that a child of his sister will kill him. The baby, embodiment of the god Vishnu, is smuggled away to a loving foster mother, Yasoda (Ganeri 1994, pp.53–5).

Some stories depict children and young people achieving success despite bereavement and other potential disadvantages. The Hindu Ganesha is not disturbed by abrupt separation from his own head and its replacement by that of an elephant. Ismael and Isaac, in parallel Muslim and Jewish stories, survive near sacrifice by their father Abraham to become powerful patriarchs (Genesis 22:1–18; Qur'an 19:41–65; see Walshe and Warrier 1993, pp.56–7). The Sikh Guru Hargobind is only 11 when he succeeds his father, who has been assassinated. Menelik, founder of the Ethiopian Church and especially revered by Rastafarians, is brought up by his mother, Makeda, Queen of Sheba. As he approached manhood, Makeda sent him to visit his father, Soloman, King of Israel. Soloman tries to keep him, but Menelik insists on returning to his mother. Soloman sends Levites with him to instruct the Ethiopians about God. The Levites remove the Ark of the

Covenant from the Temple in Jerusalem, but are pursued by soldiers. However, the pursuers are prevented by a sandstorm from reaching Ethiopia, and thus Menelik brings the true faith to his people (Hanna 1996, 5/10).

Children in danger or distress are protected and rescued, not necessarily by their own parents. Just as the baby Moses and Krishna are saved from death, Jesus is hidden from the soldiers sent by King Herod to destroy all boys under the age of 2, and is taken into Egypt by his foster father, Joseph, and mother, Mary (Matthew 2:16–18). Ismael and Isaac are saved from death by divine intervention in the form of a ram caught in a thicket, while the future Guru Nanak, founder of Sikhism, is saved by a snake. After working in the fields, the boy falls asleep in the hot sun. To protect him from severe sunburn, a cobra spreads its hood to provide shade until he wakes. The child is saved by a creature which could have harmed him: a graceful parable about unexpected sources of aid (Bennett 1990, pp.28–9).

Children develop strengths and initiatives despite parental disapproval. Gautama Siddhartha achieves enlightenment only after refusing to accept the way of life determined by his father. When Jesus, at the age of 12, absconds from his parents' care, remaining in Jerusalem after the annual visit for the Passover (see Chapter 11), his worried parents find him after three days of extra travel and frustrated searching. The boy is calmly sitting in the Temple, listening to and questioning the teachers, and impressing everyone with his understanding and answers. Mary and Joseph, rather less impressed, communicate their anxiety. Jesus feels that they have not understood him, but accompanies them home and is 'obedient to them' (Luke 2:51). Maryam is told by the angel Jibrail that she will bear Allah's child. Afraid of her family because she is not married, the girl runs away, and her baby is born beneath a tree, attended by Jibrail. Fresh water flows near her feet, and she eats dates from the tree. On her return home, her family upbraids her and Maryam can not defend herself. However, when the baby speaks, explaining that his mother has been chosen by Allah, the family accepts the child and helps Maryam to care for him (Khattab 1987; Ganeri 1994, pp.48–9).

These brief references are offered as illustrations of the myriad stories which can enrich social work practice with children.

Stories are invaluable when simply told orally or read aloud, and much can be learnt from children's choices and ways of narrating and/or listening. Children may refuse to listen to particular stories, perhaps because of the actual content, perhaps because of associations with past narrations and narrators. Children enthusiastically inform adults if they tell familiar stories inaccurately, and such corrections can not only give confidence (because of evidence that adults listen, take note, and amend their versions), but also enhance a sense of connection with the tradition from which the stories are derived. Stories from religions can be found in beautifully illustrated books which emphasise the strength and beauty of the stories themselves, and express respect for their origins.

Coles (1992) found that stories associated with religion had considerable impact on many children with whom he worked: 11-year-old boys, for example, frequently expressed deep loneliness, 'because they were troubled by some of their "impulses", their lusty moments, their combative or envious or frustrated moments', and often turned to biblical characters 'to gain some perspective on their solitary selves'. Children used biblical stories or lessons from the Qur'an 'to look inward as well as upward', linking the great legends 'to their own personal stories as they explore the nature of sexuality, and regard with awe, envy, or anger the power of their parents, as they wonder how solid and lasting their world is, as they struggle with brothers and sisters, as they imagine themselves as actual or potential lovers, or as actual or potential antagonists'. Attending carefully to the children's narrations and responses, Coles learnt that 'The stories are not mere symbolism, giving expression to what people go through emotionally. Rather, I hear children embracing religious stories because they are quite literally inspiring – exciting their minds to further thought and fantasy and helping them become more grown, more contemplative and sure of themselves' (p.121).

Children whose families are associated with a religion are often named after a famous character – for example a deity, hero, heroine or saint. Appropriate stories might be included in life-story books, perhaps with comments about how like or unlike the famous subject the child might feel.

Original stories can be created by children with their families and/or practitioners – perhaps to help expression of problems and to explore solutions to them. For example, Alan (a social worker at Martin House hospice) developed ideas about story tapes to help parents and practitioners to communicate with children about illness and approaching death (see Chapter 16).

Many books written for children and young people explore themes of low self-esteem and lack of identity, both associated with spiritual health and vitality. 'The invisible child' (Jansson 1973, pp.103–19) tells of a little Moomin who, emotionally and spiritually abused, has become invisible. Placed by a wise 'social worker' with a foster family, she is helped gradually to become visible until only her face is unseen. Only when she feels anger because she thinks her foster mother (for whom she has developed affection) is being attacked can she express strong emotion, followed by healing laughter.

Children and practitioners can develop their own stories, discovering causes of and cures for their own 'invisibility' (Crompton 1992, pp.153–6; 1995, pp.346–9; 1996, 2/26–7).

Creating their own stories is also an excellent way of expressing and identifying fears and anxieties which may be distorting spiritual growth. Fear of punishment (directly divine or through some human agent such as a parent or religious leader) for some hidden sin may lead to a sense of worthlessness and the associated fear that if the sin is found out, adults who presently show affection will be horrified and withdraw. Children who have been sexually abused, for example, may be appalled not only by the abuse, but by an element of enjoyment, perhaps of physical sensation and/or unusual attention. If such reactions cannot speedily be 'confessed' and anxiety dispelled, the sense of sinfulness for colluding in wicked acts, and the lack of worth, may grow, inhibiting development of confidence, especially in relation to eventual choice of sexual partners. Some children may experience fear of delayed punishment after death, and there may be anger against not only earthly parents, but also a supposedly powerful deity, both of whom have failed to fulfil duties of protection (see Chapters 4, 11 and 12). Sharing a story about a fictional character can provide a safe context in which fears can be expressed, and often dispelled.

QUESTIONS

- Do you think stories from religious traditions can help children to understand and celebrate their own religions?
- Do you think stories from religious traditions help children to understand and respect other children's religions?
- Do you think that children known to you understand the difference between 'fact' and 'fiction'?
- Do you think it is ever appropriate to tell children fantasies about subjects (for example, death)?
- If so, how can you ensure that children understand the context of the story?
- Would you be alert to distress arising from a story?
- How can you help a child who is confused or distressed by a story?
- Do you encourage children to narrate stories to you?
- If children narrate stories, do you respond with interest and respect?
- Do you narrate stories to children? If so, are you alert to their responses?
- Do you provide books/tapes/videos/writing/drawing materials so that children can read/listen to/watch/create stories?
- If children create stories, are they and the stories respected?

SUGGESTIONS

With colleagues and children:

- Discuss one another's ideas about the questions above.
- Narrate creation myths from one another's religions and cultures.
- Discuss how creation myths influence individual ideas about society, life and death.
- Create new creation myths, perhaps about the future.
- Narrate stories from religious traditions which portray different models of behaviour.
- Discuss how such stories influence individual ideas about behaviour.
- Imagine a new hero or heroine whose qualities and achievements could be adopted as models for belief and behaviour.
- Narrate stories about fasts and festivals.
- Discuss how such stories influence individual ideas about religious belief and observance.
- Devise a new festival and create a story to 'explain' it.
- Consider the examples of stories about religious experiences; narrate stories from your own experience.
- Discuss how such stories influence individual ideas about belief and behaviour.
- Consider ways in which stories are used to influence children.
- Collect stories on various topics into a book with illustrations.
- Include stories about, for example, respected people in a child's religion (especially those with the same name as the child) in life story books.
- Collect videos of stories from religious traditions.
- Read books/listen to tapes/watch videos together.
- Create original stories.
- Read the section on 'Storytelling' in Crompton (1996, 5/26).

Summary

Through this brief exploration of some approaches to stories, myths and legends connected with religious tradition, practitioners are encouraged to learn, narrate and encourage children to narrate. Several ways in which such activities can be useful in social work practice are proposed, in both the final section and the Suggestions.

Further material about practice is introduced in the following chapter, which focuses on ideas about story-telling and other forms of communication in a particular context: children who are dying and/or bereaved. This chapter is intended as a model for practitioners to apply to other settings and situations.

16 Communicating about death and loss

Telling the truth

This brief chapter focuses on applying some methods of communication with children who are dying and/or bereaved. Material is drawn particularly from Martin House hospice (see Chapter 13) and from the video by Maureen Hitcham (a social worker with the Malcolm Sargent Team, Royal Victoria Infirmary, Newcastle upon Tyne), entitled *Somewhere over the Rainbow* and the accompanying handbook, *All about the Rainbow* (Hitcham 1993).

Fundamental to working with children who are dying or bereaved is the ability to listen, to be open to what is happening, and to face and tell the truth. Lenore Hill (Head Nurse at Martin House) makes sure that parents are fully informed about their children's condition, treatment and prognosis, and tries to help them tell the truth. She promises that she won't say bluntly, 'You're dying,' but encourages parents to realise that many children do know and are greatly helped if enabled to talk freely. Indeed, children can feel isolated if adults inhibit honest communication about death. Children themselves raise questions, and they don't ask if they don't want to know.

Sometimes parents inhibit children's ability to discuss their illnesses (for example 'Paul' in Chapter 13). Comments such as 'There's nothing to be frightened of' deprive children of the right to honesty and, perhaps, freedom of speech. Parents' fear may lead to denial of the reality of children's present suffering and inevitable death. Practitioners may not be able to persuade parents to relinquish the defensive/protective stance, and may be inhibited from responding directly to children who may be expressing anxiety and distress.

'Hugh' (a nurse) experienced a positive interaction with a child and parent which illustrates the importance of trust between child, parent and practitioner. In the presence of her mother, 'Alice' took Hugh's hands and said, 'Hugh, I'm dying.' He responded, 'And how does that make you feel?' 'Very sad; and how does that make you feel?,' Hugh answered, 'Very sad.' Hugh thought Alice had wanted her mother to be part of the conversation, to know that Alice knew she was dying and what she felt, but could not address her directly.

In *Somewhere over the Rainbow*, the mother of Michael (who died when he was 9) reflects that he knew he was dying but that 'everyone's afraid of asking the deep questions'; Michael and said, 'I know you can die with this leukaemia,' and had asked how you become a ghost. His mother said, 'we sat and talked about the most amazing things.' Shortly before his death, Michael had become very frightened. His mother asked, 'Are you afraid of dying, Michael?' 'It's worse than dying.' She thought he was frightened about where he was going, what would happen after death. This video illustrates also how siblings of seriously ill and/or dying children may be overlooked and deprived of parental attention, even affection. They, too, need to be included in conversations about 'amazing things' (see Chapter 3), and told the truth.

Janet Goodall (1994) emphasises the importance of telling the truth, answering questions and using clear language instead of those euphemisms which are either 'meaningless or mystifying' (p.17). Crompton (1990) discusses 'The cost of concealment' and the importance of saying goodbye (pp.28–39, see also her Chapter 6, 'Speak the truth in love', pp.63–7). Elisabeth Kübler-Ross (1983) notes: 'There are thousands of children who know death far beyond the knowledge adults have' (p.xvii).

A contribution to *Spiritual Needs of Children* (Shelley et al. 1984b) recalls Sarah (aged 3), dying of leukaemia: 'Tears flowed from her mother's eyes as she cradled the toddler in her arms. Sarah reached up and patted her mother on the cheek, saying, "It's OK, Mommy. God will take care of me"' (p.35).

Tina (aged 3), who was: 'in the terminal stage of cystic fibrosis, seemed especially anxious when she was readmitted to the hospital after a brief time at home. Her mother tried to reassure her that she would be coming home again soon, but Tina responded, "No, tonight I'm going to heaven with Jesus". She died that evening' (p.35).

Shelley et al. (1994b) find that 'Spiritual development is often accelerated in dying children who may display a wisdom beyond their years' and consider that:

A child's understanding of death is influenced by his experiences. A child who has seen an animal struck by a car on the road or has seen seriously ill or deformed children in the hospital may view death as mutilation. Those who have lost a close relative may see it as abandonment. Death may also be associated with immobility such as traction, restraints or non movement. Although they may be unable to verbalize their fears, they may be able to work them out by drawing or by playing with dolls or puppets. (p.35)

Painting and drawing

Children often indicate their awareness of grave illness and impending death through drawing and painting. For example, when shown a number of pictures by children suffering from serious illnesses, I at once chose the one which had been painted by an 8-year-old boy dying of leukaemia. Entitled 'Lonely king', it is in heavy black on a background of intermingled blues and browns. A little king floats helplessly above a house whose chimney belches a great stream of black smoke which dissects the figure. A substantial castle at top right is echoed by a ghostly castle at bottom left, while a cat and two mice turn away from the king, who is indeed lonely (Crompton 1992, p.ii).

John Allan (1988) (a Jungian psychotherapist) discusses 'Spontaneous drawings in counselling seriously ill children', and introduces Caroyl, a little girl dying of leukaemia, and her counsellor, Jodi (pp.93ff; also cited in Crompton 1992, pp.169–70).

Caroyl drew a monster who 'at first appears to be frightening to the tiny person who calls for help. Is this death calling for her?' The monster is sketched with dotted lines, which suggested to Jodi 'the breaking down of her own body boundaries due to the leukaemia'. The mouth is 'blood-red and seems smeared, possible signifying the need for an infusion of healthy blood'. The word 'help' flows from the figure's mouth towards the monster. Wondering if the person in the picture was calling to the monster for help, Jodi 'asked Caroyl if she ever felt like that figure', which led to 'a long discussion about how her family was coping, her wish to talk more, but wanting to protect them from more distress'. The picture also contains a house whose ground floor has no windows; Jodi wondered if this indicated Caroyl's sense that 'she had to keep something hidden or could not be "up front"'.

Allan (1988) offers guidelines, and considers that 'basic caring and a willingness to be open to the child's view will enable many to be effective in aiding a child on a journey through life'. Practitioners of all disciplines are encouraged to use drawing to aid expression and communication, which may also help grieving relations who may find comfort in sharing their children's work (pp.108–15).

Maureen Hitcham (1993) (a social worker) notes how much energy children spend on suppressing angry feelings, often leading to difficult, anti-social behaviour. She describes work with Stephen (aged 4), much of whose frustration and anger:

> was directed at the intravenous drip administering chemotherapy which made
> him feel so sick. He was very weak and was having difficulty in breathing but he
> enjoyed throwing things around the room and scribbling. He enthusiastically
> engaged in the following piece of work just two weeks before he died. I produced
> some drawings showing the outline of the drip with a figure next to it. Stephen
> scribbled fiercely over them saying how much he hated the drip. He also filled in
> the facial expressions [on the figures] before and after dealing with his anger. (p.43)

In the first drawing, with scribble over the drip, shows the figure with a
clenched mouth. The second drawing shows a smiling figure and the words,
'I don't like you drip. I would like to punch you because you make me feel
sick' (p.43).

Story-telling

Enabling children openly to consider truth – and with it fear – often entails
assisting parents to engage with their own fears about children's possible
responses. Alan (a social worker at Martin House) described how story tapes
can be devised by children, parents and practitioners. Tapes are available for
families to listen to as and when they wish, and further tapes can be made
as appropriate. Stories can be based on children's favourite toys, story books
or television characters who meet challenges and pursue adventures which
reflect the children's own experiences and feelings. For example, a character
could be propelled into another world (a universal theme) and encounter
parallel existences in which the child fulfils secret ambitions impossible in
real life.

A linked theme might be travelling to an unknown place to see what it is
like, with permission to return at will. The journey entails leaving and
returning to both home and body, representing a concept of life and death as
a continuous journey. Children who are dying may be told, within the story,
that it is possible to 'visit' a different form of being, and that they have some
control over when they choose to make the final move out of their bodies.
Alan considers that it is possible for children to be empowered to continue
to live until they feel ready to leave the body, and to have permission to die
when living in that body is no longer tolerable.

Families may choose to introduce ideas about dying, and perhaps the
concept of the soul moving into another form of life, through this medium.
Listening to story tapes, by engaging children's interest, increases
motivation to communicate, for example encouraging speech or, if
verbalisation is no longer possible, communication by sounds. Stories enable

three-way communication between children, parents and practitioners, providing a focus for all involved to consider ideas, understanding and feelings. Tapes also provide tangible material for parents and children to share.

Offering imaginative opportunities to express ideas and fears about dying and death is different from the evasive euphemisms which many adults employ to avoid some concepts of truth.

Children who have been bereaved need opportunities 'to tell their story of what happened as *they* understand it'. At Camp Winston:

> The older groups may often choose to simply explain verbally what happened; however, the younger children will usually use a variety of non-verbal mediums, for example paint, collages, puppets, or clay to tell their story. As children create their art work they are encouraged to explain how and why their relative died. During this process team leaders will try to identify any issues which may benefit from clarification. These issues are then written down and posted (anonymously) in Winston's Post-box to be answered in the 'Questions for the Doctor' session which takes place later that afternoon. (Stokes and Crossley 1995, pp.179–80)

This example is taken from a residential camp where children are invited to focus on bereavement in an especially constructed environment of attention, activity and protection.

Life-story books including plenty of photographs can help dying children to encapsulate their own lives, and assist children who have been bereaved to place the dead person (or pet) within the family and the chronology of the child's experience. 'Joe' (see Chapter 13), whose parents had separated, and whose grandmother and half-brother had died, was helped to make a wall display of photographs of family members (dead and alive) to identify his own place in his confusing family.

Tony Walter (1996) (a lecturer in sociology) emphasises the importance of talking about people who have been lost through death – a concept of equal relevance when the lost person is still alive but has left the child. He suggests that the focus for people who have been bereaved should be 'permission to *retain* the dead person', which can best be achieved through opportunities to talk, to tell stories, to construct a personal biography: 'Members of modern Western societies need to know that they can keep those they have lost, and that one way to do this is to talk honestly about the dead with family, friends and neighbours who knew them' (p.23).

Maureen Hitcham (1993) comments: 'Inside every child there is a story waiting to be told but when that story involves difficult issues such as death and dying, it is neither easy to tell nor to listen to' (p.21). She finds that 'Life Story Books and Video Diaries have proved very successful in helping children understand their worlds and where they fit in relation to the family, the illness, the hospital and medical personnel'; feelings, which may not be articulated, can be 'safely retained in the life book to be used over and over again as and when [children] are ready – verbal communication often follows very quickly and with surprising fluency' (p.32).

As this comment suggests, communication recorded in a life-story book may be, at least in part, non-verbal. For example, a young teenage girl drew two tombstones, one with the name, age and date of death of her sister. The picture illustrated not her actual death, but the fear that she might die. The girl 'had previously been unable to share this with other members of her family but after writing about it in her life-story book allowed them to read it' (p.33).

When Graeme developed a potentially fatal illness which caused much severe pain, he became 'depressed and irritable and withdrew from everyday activities'. His distress could be relieved in one of two ways: increase of pain control, or reduction of 'emotional stress by giving him adequate explanations of his experiences so that he was able to make sense of what was going on and begin to anticipate the future without despair'. His social worker helped him to produce some work which was incorporated in his video diary, and found that 'Apathy and irritability were quickly replaced with energy, enthusiasm and excitement.' Graeme 'did not easily share thoughts and feelings and was not well enough or interested enough to undertake traditional life story work'. This method of communication 'provided him with an opportunity to ask questions and clarify thinking', and 'his response was amazing' (Hitcham 1993, pp.39, 40 and 41).

Children may also keep written diaries, which are important as private documents, but may in time be available to adults to learn about past feelings and experiences. For example:

> After our 18-year-old son died, we discovered a diary he had kept at the age of 11, when his 5-year-old brother died. Here is an excerpt: 'About 1pm, something told me to pray for Danny. When I got home from school, I discovered that he had died just then! Debbie and I went up to the bedroom and saw him. We went and looked at a burial ground for four of the family. After we all ate (Daddy arranged for the funeral), a lot of people came over and we read the Bible, sang and prayed.'
>
> Two days later his diary entry was this: 'Today we had Danny's funeral. The coffin was white. The service was a blessing. Then we went to see the grave. It was very unhappy but Danny is with God. After we got home, Jerry Sterrett and I played ball in the yard.' (Bayly 1984, p.103)

While individual creative story-telling is ideal, children may be helped by published materials. Well recommended is *Badger's Parting Gifts* (Varley 1985), which describes Badger's sensations as he dies, gently and painlessly, in old age, and acknowledges the sadness of his friends, who remember all his gifts to them in the form of skills learnt from him: 'Using these gifts they would be able to help each other.' Although they become less sad, the friends never forget Badger and his gifts: 'Whenever Badger's name was mentioned, someone remembered another story that made them all smile.'

Water Bugs and Dragonflies: Explaining Death to Children (Stickney 1984) applies a Christian approach in a fable which may be used to illustrate how a dead child may live on in another dimension. It may also be useful for siblings of terminated foetuses, since the water bug seems to vanish completely from the pond and is not recognised in its transformation as a dragonfly: the children have never seen their dead sibling, but can think of the spirit released immediately into another form of life.

These books engage with spiritual aspects of death in different ways. *Badger's Parting Gifts* introduces ideas about survival through the memories of other people, but also suggests that Badger himself continues in some form: Mole wants to thank his friend for his parting gift: '"Thank you, Badger," he said softly, believing that Badger would hear him. And – somehow – Badger did' (Varley 1985). The water bug 'dies' as a water bug, but is reincarnated in a new (and superior) form.

Further suggestions about published material for children can be found in Hitcham (1993, pp.72–5) see also Chapter 15.

Play

Practitioners often encounter bereaved children in situations whose main focus is not the bereavement. 'Terry' (aged 9), for example (in Carroll 1995), was placed in foster care because his mother was unable to cope with his difficult behaviour (his father had died when Terry was 3):

> He was offered play therapy to help him express feelings about the loss of his natural mother; in his session it became clear that this recent loss had awakened feelings which he could not express when his father had died ...
>
> Terry was enthusiastic at the prospect of playing with me; he was told that this would make him feel less muddled about all the changes in his life.

Most of his play was very violent but:

> there were occasional glimpses of more vulnerable feelings, and infantile games such as 'peek-a-boo', but he was unable to sustain these for long and returned to more aggressive play. However, these brief returns to the comforts of infancy were the first indications I had that feelings about the early loss of his father remained unresolved.

After three months Terry introduced his father into play as a dinosaur, who first ate but later nurtured and protected a baby dinosaur:

> Initially he perceived his father as fierce and aggressive, following this with a wish that his father was still alive and would one day return to care for him, and he clung to this belief in the context of subsequent loss.
>
>   This play gave Terry great relief. Before he left he turned to me for a hug: the first I had had from him. He looked directly at me, and mumbled 'thanks'. Having been able to face the feelings associated with this initial bereavement, and have those feelings validated, enabled him to move on in subsequent sessions to think about more recent disruptions to his life. (pp.79–80)

Without attention first to Terry's feelings about the loss of his mother, the deep-laid distress and confusion about his father's death might never have been reached. At 9, two-thirds of his entire life had already been dominated by those feelings, which could be expressed only in behaviour regarded by his remaining parent as unacceptable, which led to rejection and thus further loss.

This boy's evident relief, once he was able to express feelings previously unrecognised by either child or adults, may encourage practitioners to create opportunities for other children to receive such patient and ultimately fruitful – and essential – attention. One might, for example, speculate about the development of his aggression and sometimes uncontrolled violence if he had never encountered his father through dinosaur play.

Hitcham (1993) describes experiences of using 'special' play techniques with dying and/or bereaved children. Although working within a specialist clinic, her work demonstrates needs of children which may be encountered in other settings, such as foster care. With Nicola, for example, she used loving and caring water play (demonstrated in her video, *Somewhere over the Rainbow*). When Nicola's brother, Michael, died, the girl could not, or would not, show emotion, and:

> presented to her parents as cold, distant, uncaring and indifferent about Michael's death. She even stated, 'better not to get too close to people then it doesn't hurt so much when they die'. Nicola genuinely believed she was the only one hurting. She felt her parents didn't understand and that they had one another so they were alright, but she was on her own. This technique helped to build bridges and open up a level of communication that proved very successful. (p.35)

The social worker also used candles to help Nicola, whose 'greatest wish was to be able to spend half an hour with Michael. She was convinced that … then she would be able to get on with her life', and now 'feels she has done just that':

The worker lights the candle and describes the flame as representing 'life' itself and that within 'life' there is 'love'. The worker holds the flames together, 'when two lives meet and fall in love, the flame gets bigger. Life is fuller and there is more room for love to grow. Often children are the result of this love.' 'When mum and dad met they fell in love, then you and Michael were born.' Holding the two flames together, the worker talks about 'when you meet someone special, they touch your life in such a way that it can never be the same again. At this point your life becomes one so that when you separate you each take part of that big flame with you.' One candle is then blown out. 'When Michael died he took part of you with him, but part of him goes on living in you.' (pp.36–7)

Nicola was enabled to talk about 'the mystery of Heaven', saying that 'she could understand and accept Life after Death and heaven, in terms of "that part of Michael that lives on in my heart" (p.37). Candles are also used symbolically in the Camp Winston candlelight ceremony (Stokes and Crossley 1995, pp.182–4) see also Chapter 13.

Through this and other activities during the session, Nicola demonstrated both physical and emotional change, becoming 'relaxed, bright eyed, happy and excited', and saying: '"it really feels like I have been talking to him"'.The session was followed with 'a visit to Michael's grave where Nicola buried a letter she'd written to him. Only she knows its contents' (Hitcham 1993, p.37).

Although this worker's aim was not, it seems, to engage with spiritual aspects of Nicola's responses to her brother's death and sense of neglect by her parents, the girl was enabled to explore ideas about death and continued existence, and to escape from her sense of guilt and anxiety. Hitcham's work released Nicola from the suppression of emotion and withdrawal from relationship which had developed during her brother's long illness, when her parents' attention and energy focused on Michael. Through this kind of play, Nicola could learn the dynamics of behaviour of all members of the family, gaining new understanding and strength – cognitive, emotional and spiritual – and through this, an enriched relationship with her parents. She learnt also to grow through sadness. Without the intervention of the social worker, Nicola might all too easily have become imprisoned in withdrawal, increasingly inhibited from forming loving, trusting relationships and from exploring experiences of spirituality. These and other methods are fully described in Hitcham (1993).

The deaths of children are not always caused by illness. For many, death comes violently: for example, in war, famine or natural disaster. It is sometimes the task of caring adults to enable children to live fully while under the shadow of inevitable, terrible death. In the Warsaw ghetto, during the Nazi occupation, Janusz Korczak (a paediatrician and writer) and his staff maintained the Jewish Orphans' Home under appalling conditions. By summer 1942 it was clear that the children could not be saved, and although Korczak always held on to some hope, he understood that the children must be prepared to face death. In July 1942 the Orphans' Home presented a play (by Rabindranath Tagore) in which a bedridden boy 'longs for life, nature, entertainment and … liberation. Calmed by the promise of freedom – he dies in waiting.' After the performance, Korczak was asked why he had chosen this play (which was on the Nazi censors' blacklist); he answered: 'that one must finally learn to accept the angel of death in peace' (Szlązakowa 1978, pp.122 and 124).

QUESTIONS

- If you are working with a child who is dying or bereaved, can you hear, and tell, the truth about death? If not, why do you find this difficult?
- Do you think that sharing the truth with children is important? If so, why? If not, why not?
- If you have to share the truth with children who are dying or bereaved, how can you communicate?
- How can you manage your own sorrow?

SUGGESTIONS

With colleagues and children:

- Discuss one another's ideas about the questions above.
- Which method of communication described in this chapter would you find most helpful if you were dying or bereaved? Why?
- Which method would you find least helpful? Why?
- Identify some other ways in which you could communicate, and describe what you would do. What materials would you need?
- Consider the story of Terry, and discuss how you think the death of his father influenced his behaviour. Identify how play helped him to engage with his feelings and change his behaviour. Imagine his possible feelings and behaviour if he had not had the chance to play in this way.
- Consider the story of Nicola and discuss how you think the illness and death of her brother, Michael, influenced her behaviour. Identify how play helped her to engage with her feelings and change her behaviour. Imagine her possible feelings and behaviour if she had not had the chance to play in this way.
- Considering all the examples of children's experience in this chapter,

identify links between responses to dying and bereavement and spiritual well-being or distress (see Chapters 13 and 14).

- Compile a resource file for your establishment containing ideas about and examples of communication with children who are dying or bereaved; you will find this a useful general resource for communication.
- Compile a list of books for children.

Summary

This chapter had briefly discussed some ideas about communicating with children who are dying and/or bereaved. While non-specialist practitioners may consider that they do not, or will not, have contact with children who are engaged in these experiences, it is likely that such encounters will occur in everyday care and practice, bearing in mind the impact of deaths of schoolmates and teachers, even when immediate family members are not involved.

Encounters with death often lead to heightened awareness of matters which may be described as 'spiritual', and with religious belief. Spiritual well-being may be enhanced or threatened, according to not only the nature of the experience itself, but also the attention and care available from adults. The needs and responses of siblings, for example, can all too easily be overlooked, possibly leading to experiences of spiritual distress.

It is hoped that these illustrations will encourage practitioners to become alert to the spiritual well-being of children, and to develop their own methods and aids to communication.

Spiritual and religious well-being

The spirit of children

On 1 April 1942, the Passover *seder* was shared, for the last time, in the Jewish Orphans' Home in the Warsaw ghetto. The father's place was taken, as always, by Janusz Korczak. An account of that last supper was written for the *Jewish Gazette* by a guest, Herman Czerwinski, quoted in Betty Lifton's (1988) description:

> The long tables, covered with spotless tablecloths, were lit by the 'beaming' faces of one hundred and eighty orphans, who were 'not abandoned, but joined by the spirits of their mothers and fathers'. Korczak sat at the head table with sixteen of the older choir members, 'who burst into a Zionist song whenever something in the Haggadah referred to Palestine. The seder guests were seated in the rear. When the youngest child asked: 'And how is this night different from all other nights?' Korczak responded with a few words that 'moved' everyone. After the service, 'plates, mugs, bowls chimed. Women came with food from all directions. Joy reigned at this Passover celebration.' (p.298)

What were those 'moving' words with which Korczak answered the child's question? Lifton suggests that Czerwinski may have omitted them from his account: 'lest the Nazis read them. For the same reason, he may have felt it best not to report that, during the Haggadah reading, Korczak walked to the window and raised his fist, as if crying out to God in rage and despair to account for the suffering of his children' (pp.288–9).

In the midst of his despair, the father of the orphans ensured that they experienced delight, sharing a traditional meal, fulfilling a religious obligation, worshipping their deity, expressing and receiving affection, celebrating spiritual abundance. On 6 August 1942, Janusz Korczak accompanied his children to the concentration camp at Treblinka.

On a sunny day in May 1997, half a century after those Jewish orphans died in the gas chamber, as I write these last words of this book, I hear on the radio that half the casualties of wars are children; a boy describes the despair of young people who routinely cut themselves because they feel inadequate, ugly, unworthy, because they are not heard, because they have no vision of hope; children who have committed serious crimes are described as 'evil', 'monsters', 'less than human'.

The real test of religion, of spirituality, is response to despair, whether experienced by children or adults. Jane Newsome (an independent representative of Voice for the Child in Care) describes young people who: 'feel that it doesn't matter what they do because they are not worth much and anyway no-one bothers about them' (cited in Crompton 1996, 4/45). This leads to the belief that 'If they are worthless, less than human, then they have no responsibility to behave as human beings, with all the dignity, responsibility and thought that requires' (Crompton 1996, 4/46).

But she adds, in hope:

> I have observed many young people in secure accommodation whose behaviour has changed because of the patience, care and imagination of good members of staff. Sometimes they have been helped to recover a sense of self-worth by being encouraged to explore a gift such as painting or writing poetry, or else it is simply that a member of staff has been prepared to take an interest and listen to them.
>
> This good practice could sow seeds to help in later life if a spiritual dimension could be recognized, showing that they are precious and important, together with every other human being, simply because of their humanity. (cited in Crompton 1996, 4/45–6)

When humanity and spirituality are not recognised, when children are dehumanised and demonised, it is not far to the ghetto and the gun.

Part 1 of this book introduced the Convention on Children's Rights promulgated by the UN in 1989, ratified by the UK Government in 1991, and still, in 1997, not fully implemented. As a children's advocate, Janusz Korczak 'spoke of the need for a Declaration of Children's Rights long before any such document was drawn up by the Geneva Convention (1924) or the United Nations General Assembly (1959)' (Lifton 1988, p.355) – and even longer before 1989. Basing her ideas on Korczak's writings, Betty Lifton compiled a list of 'the rights which Korczak considered most essential', drawing material from *Jak Kochać Dzieci, (How to Love a Child,)* parts I, II, III (1919–29); *The Child's Right to Respect* (1929) and other works.

From this list, I have selected a Declaration of Children's Spiritual and Religious Rights, with which I end my own writing at this time. It is based on Lifton (1988, pp.355–6), and the quotations it contains are taken from Korczak.

It is my hope that this book will link the children and practitioners introduced herein with practitioners who read these pages, and encourage attention to the well-being of the whole child – body, mind, emotions and spirit.

Declaration of Children's Spiritual and Religious Rights

- The child has the right to love. ('Love *the* child, not just your own.')
- The child has the right to respect. ('Let us demand respect for shining eyes, smooth foreheads, youthful effort and confidence ...')
- The child has the right to live in the present. ('Children are not people of tomorrow, they are people today.')
- The child has the right to be himself or herself. ('A child is not a lottery ticket, marked to win the main prize.')
- The child has the right to be taken seriously. ('Who asks the child for his opinion and consent?')
- The child has the right to be appreciated for what he or she is. ('The child, being small, has little market value.')
- The child has the right to resist educational influence that conflicts with his or her own beliefs. ('It is fortunate for mankind that we are unable to force children to yield to assaults upon their common sense and humanity.')
- The child has a right to respect for his or her grief. ('Even though it be for the loss of a pebble.')
- The child has the right to commune with God.

(from Lifton 1988, pp.355–6)

Useful organisations

Article 12, 8 Wakley Street, London EC1V 7QE, tel. 0171 843 6026, fax 0171 278 9512.

British Humanist Association, 47 Theobald's Road, London WC1X 8SP, tel. 0171 430 0908.

Children's Rights Office, 235 Shaftesbury Avenue, London WC2H 8EL, tel. 0171 240 4449, fax 0171 240 4514.

Christian Survivors of Sexual Abuse, BM, CSSA, London WC1N 3XX.

Cult Information Centre (CIC), BCM CULTS, London WC1N 3XX, tel. 0181 651 3322.

INFORM, Houghton Street, London WC2A 2AE, tel. 0171 955 7654.

Ritual Abuse Information and Network Support (RAINS), tel. 01483 898600.

UNICEF, 55 Lincoln's Inn Fields, London WC2A 3NB, tel. 0171 405 5592, fax 0171 405 2332.

Voice for the Child in Care, Unit 4, Pride Court, 80/82 White Lion Street, London N1 9PF, tel. 0171 833 5792, fax 0171 833 8637.

Bibliography

Ahmed, S. (1986) 'Black children in day nursery: some issues of practice', in Ahmed, S., Cheetham, J. and Small, J. (eds) *Social Work with Black Children and their Families*, London: Batsford, pp.40–50.

Ahmed, S., Cheetham, J. and Small, J. (eds) (1986) *Social Work with Black Children and their Families*, London: Batsford.

Allan, J. (1988) *Inscapes of the Child's World: Jungian Counseling in Schools and Clinics*, Dallas, Texas: Spring Publications.

Allen, C. (1991) 'The inner light', *Nursing Standard*, 5(20), pp.120–7.

Al'Qalqili, A. (1982) 'Fatwa on family planning in Islam', in Donohue and Esposito (eds) *Islam in Transition*, Oxford: Oxford University Press.

Al'Qaradwi, Y. (1960) *The Lawful and the Prohibited in Islam*, American Trust Publications.

Armstrong, H. (1991) *Taking Care: A Church Response to Children, Adults and Abuse*, London: National Children's Bureau, revised edition 1997.

Aylett, J.F. (1991) *The Muslim Experience*, London: Hodder and Stoughton.

Aylett, L. (1992) *The Hindu Experience*, London: Hodder and Stoughton.

Baker, A. (1985) *The Complete Book of Problem Pregnancy Counseling*, Granite City, Illinois: Hope Clinic for Women.

Bayly, J. (1984) 'The suffering of children', in Shelley, J. et al. (eds) *Spiritual Needs of Children*, London: Scripture Union, pp.101–7.

Beardsworth, T. (1977) *A Sense of Presence*, Oxford: Religious Experience Research Unit, Manchester College.

Bennett, O. (ed.) (1990) *Listening to Sikhs*, London: Unwin Hyman/Glasgow: Collins Educational.

Berryman, J.W. (1985) 'Children's spirituality and religious language', *British Journal of Religious Education*, 7(3), pp.120–7.

Bettelheim, B. (1978) *The Uses of Enchantment: The Meaning and Importance of Fairy Tales*, Harmondsworth: Penguin.

Bhaduri, R. (1990) 'Counselling with Karma', *Social Work Today*, 21(33), p.17.

Bird, G. (1996) *'East Meets West: Secular Individualism in Western Social Work Values and Practice, and its Interface with the 'Collective' in Asian Faith Perspectives'*, unpublished thesis, Leicester: University of Leicester School of Social Work.

Blue, L. (1986) *Thoughts for the Day*, London: BBC Publishing.

Bradford, J. (1989) 'Spiritual rights and religious rights in the 1989 convention', in *Children Worldwide*, Geneva: International Catholic Child Bureau, pp.41–3.

Bradford, J. (1995) *Caring for the Whole Child: A Holistic Approach to Spirituality*, London: The Children's Society.

British Humanist Association (undated a) *BHA Briefing: Abortion*, London: BHA.

British Humanist Association (undated b) *The Human Spirit: The Humanist Perspective on Spiritual Development in Education: BHA Briefing*, London: BHA.

Bunyan, J. (1954), (1st pub. 1678) *The Pilgrim's Progress*, London: Dent.

Cairns, K. (1990) 'Climate for learning', *Social Work Today*, 21(38), pp.26–7.

Carroll, J. (1995) 'Non-directive play therapy with bereaved children', in Smith, S. and Pennells, M. (eds) *Interventions with Bereaved Children*, London: Kingsley, pp.68–86.

Cattermole, F. (1990) 'Foreword', in Garrett, B. *Spiritual Development of Young People: NCVYS Briefings No. 10*, London: National Council for Voluntary Youth Services, pp.ii–iii.

Chadwick, R. (1973) 'Awareness and preparedness of nurses to meet spiritual needs', *The Nurses Lamp*, 22(6), pp.2–3.

Charleson, N. and Corbett, A. (1994) 'A birthday to remember', in Sinason, V. (ed.) *Treating Survivors of Satanic Abuse*, London: Routledge, pp.164–9.

Clark, V. (1996a) 'Bereavement and Moral and Spiritual Development: An Exploration of the Experiences of Children and Young People', unpublished PhD thesis, Plymouth: University of Plymouth.

Clark, V. (1996b) 'Bereavement and Moral and Spiritual Development: An Exploration of the Experiences of Children and Young People', *Spes*, 5 November, pp.37–40.

Clarke, S. (1993) 'Spirituality: A Buddhist Perspective – Cause and Effect in Education', unpublished paper, Plymouth: Plymouth University Centre for Research into Moral, Spiritual & Cultural Understanding and Education.

Coleman, J. (1994) 'Satanic cult practices', in Sinason, V. (ed.) *Treating Survivors of Satanic Abuse*, London: Routledge, pp.242–53.

Coles, R. (1967, 1972, 1978) *Children in Crisis* (5 vols), Boston, Massachusetts: Atlantic-Little, Brown.

Coles, R. (1984) 'Foreword', in Matthews, G., *Dialogues with Children*, Cambridge, Massachusetts: Harvard University Press.

Coles, R. (1986a) *The Moral Life of Children*, Boston, Massachusetts: Atlantic Monthly Press.

Coles, R. (1986b) *The Political Life of Children*, Boston, Massachusetts: Atlantic Monthly Press.

Coles, R. (1992) *The Spiritual Life of Children*, London: HarperCollins.

Collinson, C. and Miller, C. (1984) *Milestones: Rites of Passage in a Multi-faith Community*, London: Hodder and Stoughton.

Collinson, C. and Miller, C. (1985) *Celebrations: Festivals in a Multi-faith Community*, London: Hodder and Stoughton.

Compton, A. (undated) *Religious and Values Education in a Plural Society: A Guide for Teachers*, Hull: University of Hull Social Values Research Centre.

Cooklin, A. and Gorrell Barnes, G. (1994) 'The shattered picture of the family: encountering the new dimensions of human relations, of the family and of therapy', in Sinason, V. (ed.) *Treating Survivors of Satanic Abuse*, London: Routledge, pp.120–31.

'Coolidge, S.' (1872) *What Katy Did*, first edition.

CRDU (1994) *UK Agenda for Children*, London: Children's Rights Development Unit.

Crompton, M. (1990) *Attending to Children: Direct Work in Social and Health Care*, Dunton Green: Edward Arnold.

Crompton, M. (1992) *Children and Counselling*, Dunton Green: Edward Arnold.

Crompton, M. (1994) '"When I was a child ..."', *Friends' Quarterly*, 28(4), pp.145–53.

Crompton, M. (1995) 'Individual work with children', in Wilson, K. and James, A. (eds) *The Child Protection Handbook*, London: Ballière Tindall, pp.334–53.

Crompton, M. (1996) (ed.) *Children, Spirituality and Religion*, London: CCETSW.

Csikszentmihalyi, M. and Csikszentmihalyi, I. (1988) *Psychological Studies of Flow in Consciousness*, New York: Cambridge University Press.

Cupitt, D. (1991) *What is a Story?*, London: SCM Press.

Daly, B. and Vaughan, J. (1988) *Children at War*, London: Macdonald.

DSRU (1996) *Matching Needs and Services: The Audit and Planning of Provision for Children Looked After by Local Authorities*, Dartington: Dartington Social Research Unit.

Davies, D. (1994a) 'Introduction: raising the issues', in Holm, J. and Bowker, J. (eds) *Myth and History*, London: Pinter, pp.1–7.

Davies, D. (1994b) 'Introduction: raising the issues', in Holm, J. and Bowker, J. (eds) *Rites of Passage*, London: Pinter, pp.1–7.

Davies, D. (1994c) 'Introduction: raising the issues', in Holm, J. and Bowker, J. (eds) *Sacred Places*, London, Pinter, pp.1–9.

Davies, D. (1994d) 'Introduction: raising the issues', in Holm, J. and Bowker, J. (eds) *Worship*, London: Pinter, pp.1–8.

DES (1977) *Supplement to Curriculum*, pp. 11–16, London: HMSO.

DoH (1989a) *Guidance Notes*, London: HMSO.

DoH (1989b) *An Introduction to the Children Act 1989*, London: HMSO.

DoH (1992) *The Report of the Inquiry into the Removal of Children from Orkney in February 1991: Part 2*, London: HMSO.

DoH (1995) *Looking After Children*, London: HMSO.

Donahue and Esposito (eds) (1982) *Islam in Transition*, Oxford: Oxford University Press.

Donaldson, M. (1992) *Human Minds*, London: Allen Lane.

Drury, B. (1991) 'Sikh girls and the maintenance of an ethnic culture', *New Community*, 17(3), pp.387–99.

Erikson, E. (1965) 'Eight ages of man', in *Childhood and Society*, Harmondsworth: Penguin.

Fowler, J. (1981) *Stages of Faith: The Psychology of Human Development and the Quest for Meaning*, New York: Harper and Row.

Fowler, J. Nipkow, K.E. and Schweitzer, F. (eds) (1991) *Stages of Faith and Religious Development: Implications for Church, Education and Society*, London: SCM Press.

Frances Dominica, Mother (1996) 'Understanding death and dying', *The Spirituality of Children: The Way Supplement*, 86, pp.101–12.

Ganeri, A. (1994) *Out of the Ark: Stories from the World's Religions*, Hemel Hempstead: Simon and Schuster.

Garrett, B. (1990) *Spiritual Development of Young People: NCVYS Briefings No. 10*, London: National Council for Voluntary Youth Services.

Gendlin, E. (1963) *Focusing*, Toronto: Bantam Books.

Godden, R. (1989) *A House with Four Rooms: Autobiography*, Vol. 2, London: Macmillan.

Goodall, J. (1984) 'Foreword', in Shelley, J. et al. (eds) *Spiritual Needs of Children*, London: Scripture Union.

Goodall, J. (1994) 'Thinking like a child about death and dying', in Hill, L. (ed.) *Caring for Dying Children and their Families*, London: Chapman and Hall, pp.16–31.

Goodwin, J.M. (1994) 'Sadistic abuse: definition, recognition and the power to heal', in Sinason, V. (ed.) *Treating Survivors of Satanic Abuse*, London: Routledge, pp.33–44.

Goodwin, S. (1991) *Stories from India*, London: Hodder and Stoughton.

Goonewardene, A. (1994) *Buddhist Scriptures*, London: Heinemann.

Goudge, E. (1974) *The Joy of the Snow: An Autobiography*, London: Hodder and Stoughton.

Hamilton, C. (1996) 'Rights not rhetoric', in *Children's Rights*, supplement to *Community Care*, 26 September, p.1.

Hanks, H. and Stratton, P. (1995) 'The effects of child abuse: signs and symbols', in Wilson, K. and James, A. (ed.) *The Child Protection Handbook*, London: Ballière Tindall, pp.84–107.

Hanna, D. (1996) 'Rastafarianism', in Crompton, M. (ed.) *Children, Spirituality and Religion: A Training Pack*, London: CCETSW, pp.3/70–82.

Harris, R. (1995) 'Child protection, child care and child welfare', in Wilson, K. and James, A. (eds) *The Child Protection Handbook*, London: Ballière Tindall, pp.27–42.

Hay, D. (1995) 'Children and God', *The Tablet: Educational Supplement*, 7 October, pp.1,270–1.

Hill, K. (1995) *The Long Sleep: Young People and Suicide*, London: Virago.

Hill, L. (ed.) (1994a) *Caring for Dying Children and their Families*, London: Chapman and Hall.

Hill, L. (1994b) 'The role of the children's hospice', in Hill, L. (ed.) *Caring for Dying Children and their Families*, London: Chapman and Hall, pp.177–83.

Hillman, J. (1988) 'Foreword', in Allan, J., *Inscapes of the Child's World: Jungian Counseling in Schools and Clinics*, Dallas, Texas: Spring Publications, pp.xiii–xx.

Hitcham, M. (1993) *All About the Rainbow: A Handbook to be used with the Video Somewhere over the Rainbow*, Newcastle: Social Work Department, Royal Victoria Infirmary.

Hobbs, C. and Wynne, J. (1994) 'Treating satanist abuse survivors: the Leeds experience', in Sinason, V. (ed.) *Treating Survivors of Satanist Abuse*, London: Routledge, pp.214–17.

Holm, J. with Bowker, J. (eds) (1994a) *Myth and History*, London: Pinter.

Holm, J. with Bowker, J. (eds) (1994b) *Rites of Passage*, London: Pinter.

Holm, J. with Bowker, J. (eds) (1994c) *Sacred Places*, London: Pinter.

Holm, J. with Bowker, J. (eds) (1994d) *Worship*, London: Pinter.

Howarth, I. (1994) 'Cult concerns: an overview of cults and their methods in the UK', *Assignation*, (Aslib Social Sciences Group Journal), 11(4), pp.31–4.

Hull, J.M. (1991a) *God-talk with Young Children: Notes for Parents and Teachers*, Birmingham/Derby: University of Birmingham and Christian Education Movement.

Hull, J.M. (1991b) 'Human development and capitalist society', in Fowler, J., Nipkow, K. and Schweitzer, F. (eds) *Stages of Faith and Religious Development: Implications for Church, Education and Society*, London: SCM Press.

Ipgrave, J. (1995) 'God and Guna: The Religious Education of Muslim Children', unpublished report.

Ironside, L. (1994) 'Psychotherapy with a ritually abused 3-year-old: deceptive innocence', in Sinason, V (ed.) *Treating Survivors of Satanic Abuse*, London: Routledge, pp.87–93.

Jacob, S. (1993) 'An analysis of the concept of grief', *Journal of Advanced Nursing*, 18, pp.1,787–94.

Jaffrey, M. (1992) *Seasons of Splendour: Myths and Legends of India*, Harmondsworth: Penguin.

Jansson, T. 'The invisible child' (trans. Warbuton, T.) (1973) in *Tales from Moomin Valley*, Harmondsworth: Penguin.

Jeffreys, A. (1996) 'Friends in need', in *'Children's Rights'*, *Community Care*, 26 September, p.5.

Kavanagh, M. (1994) 'Spiritual care', in Hill, L. (ed.) *Caring for Dying Children and their Families*, London: Chapman and Hall, pp.106–22.

Keane, F. (1995) 'Spiritual damage', *Guardian*, 27 October.

Kelsall, M. (1994) 'Fostering a ritually abused child', in Sinason, V. (ed.) *Treating Survivors of Satanic Abuse*, London: Routledge, pp.94–9.

Kennedy, M. (1995a) 'Perceptions of abused disabled children', in Wilson, K. and James, A. (eds) *The Child Protection Handbook*, London: Ballière Tindall, pp.127–52.

Kennedy, M. (1995b) *Submission to the National Commission of Inquiry into the Prevention of Child Abuse*, London: Christian Survivors of Sexual Abuse.

Kennedy, M. and Kelly, L. (1992) 'Inclusion not exclusion', *Child Abuse Review*, 1(3), pp.147–9.

Kharbach, N. (1996) *Working together in Westwood: The Single Regeneration Budget Bid for Oldham*, Liverpool: Barnardos.

Khattab, M. (1987) *Stories from the Muslim World*, London: Macdonald.

Korczak, J. (1919, 1920, 1929) *Jak Kochać Dzieci (How to Love a Child)* Parts I, II, III, Warsaw.

Korczak, J. (1929) *The Right of the Child to Respect*, Warsaw.

Kübler-Ross, E. (1983) *On Children and Death*, New York: Macmillan.

Kunin, S.D. (1996) 'Judaism', in Crompton, M. (ed.) *Children, Spirituality and Religion: A Training Pack*, London: CCETSW.

La Fontaine, J. (1994) *The Extent and Nature of Organised and Ritual Abuse*, London: HMSO.

Labun, E. (1988) 'Spiritual care: an element in nursing care planning', *Journal of Advanced Nursing*, 13, pp.314–20.

Lawton, F. (1993) 'Viewpoint – stale justice', *The Tablet Catholic Weekly*, 2 October, in Kennedy 1995b.

Lee, L. (1959) *Cider with Rosie*, London: Hogarth.

Lewis, R. (1967) *Michel, Michel*, London: Heinemann.

Lifton, B. (1988) *The King of Children*, London: Pan.

Matthews, G. (1984) *Dialogues with Children*, Cambridge, Massachusetts: Harvard University Press.

McClure. M. (1996) 'How children's faith develops', in *The spirituality of children: The Way Supplement*, 86, pp.5–13.

McCullers, C. (1962) *The Member of the Wedding*, Harmondsworth: Penguin.

McDermott, M.Y. and Ahsan, M.M. (1986) *The Muslim Guide*, Leicester: Islamic Foundation.

McFadyen, A., Hanks, H. and James, C. (1993) 'Ritual abuse: a definition', *Child Abuse Review*, 2, pp.35–41.

Mearns, D. and Thorne, B. (1988) *Person-centred Counselling in Action*, London: Sage.

Minney, R. (1993) 'Are There Stages in Spiritual and Moral Development?', unpublished paper, Plymouth: University of Plymouth Centre for Research into Moral, Spiritual & Cultural Understanding and Education.

Mollon, P. (1994) 'The impact of evil', in Sinason, V. (ed.) *Treating Survivors of Satanic Abuse*, London: Routledge, pp.136–47.

Moran, M. (1968) *Pastoral Counselling for the Deviant Girl*, London: Chapman.

Narayanasamy, A. (1993) 'Nurses' awareness and educational preparation in meeting their patients' spiritual needs', *Nurse Education Today*, 13, pp.196–201.

Needs, N. (1994) 'Through the eyes of a child', in Crompton, M. (ed.) *Children, Spirituality and Religion: A Training Pack*, London: CCETSW.

Newby, M. (ed.) (c. 1993) *Thinking about Actions, Attitudes and Values in the Primary Classroom: A Guide to the Use of Story in Spiritual Education*, Kingston, Surrey: University of Kingston.

Nigosian, S.A. (1994) *World Faiths*, New York: St Martin's Press.

Nurnberg, A. (1995) *Know Your Rights*, London: UNICEF.

Nye, R. (1996) 'Spiritual development', in Crompton, M. (ed.) *Children, Spirituality and Religion: A Training Pack*, London: CCETSW, 2/6–19.

Nye, R. and Hay, D. (1996) 'Identifying children's spirituality: how do you start without a starting point?', *British Journal of Religious Education*, Summer, pp.144–54.

O'Flaherty, W. (trans.) (1975) *Hindu Myths*, Harmondsworth: Penguin.

OFSTED (1994) *Spiritual, Moral, Social and Cultural Development: Discussion Paper*, London: Office of Standards in Education.

Oldnall, A. (1996) 'A critical analysis of nursing: meeting the spiritual needs of patients', *Journal of Advanced Nursing*, 23, pp.138–44.

Piaget J. (1969) *The Child's Conception of the World*, London: Routledge and Kegan Paul.

Pihlainen, M. (1993) '"Every Child is Potentially the Light of the World": Reflections on Spiritual Citizenship', unpublished paper, Plymouth: University of Plymouth Centre for Research into Moral, Spiritual & Cultural Understanding and Education.

Quaker Home Service (1996) *Safeguarding Children from Harm: Protecting Children from Abuse*, Britain Yearly Meeting London: QHS.

Robinson, E. (1977) *The Original Vision*, Oxford: Religious Experience Research Unit.

Roskill, C. (1996) 'Foreword', in Crompton, M. (ed.) *Children, Spirituality and Religion: A Training Pack*, London: CCETSW, pp.vii–viii.

Salo, E. (1990) '"Well, I couldn't say no, could I?" Difficulties in the path of late adoption', *Journal of Child Psychotherapy*, 16(1), pp.75–91.

Schutz, A. (1964) 'Making music together: a study in social relationship', in Brodersen, A. (ed.) *Collected Papers II: Studies in Social Theory*, The Hague: Martinus Nijhoff, pp.135–58.

Seden, J. (1995) 'Religious persuasion and the Children Act', *Adoption and Fostering*, 19(2), pp.7–15.

Sharpe, S. (1987) *Falling for Love: Teenage Mothers Talk*, London: Virago.

Shelley, J. et al. (1984a) 'Foundations for faith: the first five years', in Shelley, J. et al. (eds) *Spiritual Needs of Children*, London: Scripture Union, pp.27–36.

Shelley, J. et al. (eds) (1984b) *Spiritual Needs of Children*, London: Scripture Union.

Shengold, L. (1989) *Soul Murder*, New York: Yale University Press.

Sinason, V. (ed.) (1994) *Treating Survivors of Satanic Abuse*, London: Routledge.

Smith, S. and Pennells, M. (eds) (1995) *Interventions with Bereaved Children*, London: Kingsley.

Stevenson, Y. (1976) *The Hot-house Plant: An Autobiography of a Young Girl*, London: Elek/Pemberton.

Stickney, D. (1984) *Water Bugs and Dragonflies: Explaining Death to Children*, London: Mowbray.

Stokes, J. and Crossley, D. (1995) 'Camp Winston – a residential intervention for bereaved children', in Smith, S. and Pennells, M. (eds) *Interventions with Bereaved Children*, London: Kingsley, pp.172–92.

Suffolk Education Department (1991) *Suffolk RE Agreed Syllabus/Attainment Targets and Programmes of Study for Religious Education*.

Szlązakowa, A. (1978) *Janusz Korczak* (trans. Ronowicz, E.) Warsaw: Wydawnictwa Szkolne i Pedagogiczne.

Tal, A. (1975) 'Father and Son', in Zim 1975.

Tamminen, K. (1991) *Religious Development in Childhood and Youth*, Helsinki: Suomalainen Tiedeakatemia.

Tate, T. (1991) *Children for the Devil: Ritual Abuse and Satanic Crime*, London: Methuen.

Tate, T. (1994) 'Press, politics and paedophilia: a practitioner's guide to the media', in Sinason, V. (ed.) *Treating Survivors of Satanic Abuse*, London: Routledge, pp.182–94.

Thompson, M. (1993) *The Buddhist Experience*, London: Hodder and Stoughton.

Timms, N. (1964) *Social Casework: Principles and Practice*, London: Routledge and Kegan Paul.

Torrie, A. (1978) *When Children Grieve*, Richmond, Surrey: Cruse.

Towler, R. (1994) 'New religious movements: the fears and the facts', *Assignation* (Aslib Social Services Information Group Journal), 11(4), pp.22–4.

Tranströmer, T. (1983) *Det Vilda Torget*, Sweden: Bonniers.

Turner, V. (1969) *The Ritual Process*, London: Routledge.

Turner, V. (1982) *From Ritual to Theatre*, New York: PAJ Publications.

UNICEF (1995) *The Convention on the Rights of the Child (Information kit)* London: UNICEF.

Ure, J. (1987) *One Green Leaf*, London: Bodley Head.

Uttley, A. (1974) *Ambush of Young Days*, London: George Mann.

Van Gennep, A. (1960) (1st pub. 1908) *The Rites of Passage*, London: Routledge and Kegan Paul.

Varley, S. (1985) *Badger's Parting Gifts*, London: HarperCollins.

Walshe, J.G. and Warrier, S. (1993) *Dates and Meanings of Religious and Other Festivals*, Slough: Foulsham.

Walter, T. (1996) 'A new model of grief: bereavement and biography', *Mortality* 1(1), pp.7–25.

Wattam, C. (1995) 'The investigative process', in Wilson, K. and James, A. (eds) *The Child Protection Handbook*, London: Ballière Tindall, pp.170–87.

Wattam, V.W. (1993) *Islam: A Student's Approach to World Religions*, London: Hodder and Stoughton.

West, A. (1996) 'Crying out for more', in *Children's Rights*, supplement to *Community Care*, 26 September, p.8.

West, J. (1996) *Child Centred Play Therapy*, London: Edward Arnold.

Wild, N.J. and Wynne, J.M. (1986) 'Child sex rings', *British Medical Journal*, 293, pp.183–5.

Wilson, K. and James, A. (eds) (1995) *The Child Protection Handbook*, London: Ballière Tindall.

Younger, P. (1972) *Introduction to Indian Religious Thought*, London: Darton, Longman and Todd.

Yusuf, A.A. (1946) *The Holy Qur'an*, Jeddah: Islamic Education Centre.

Zim, J. et al. (eds) (1975) *My Shalom My Peace*, London: New English Library.

Further reading

Series

The following series may provide useful background reading. Free catalogues are available from the publishers.

Asians in Britain, Cambridge: Health Education Council/National Extension College. This series includes: Henley, A. (1982) *Caring for Muslims and their Families: Religious Aspects of Care*; Henley, A. (1983) *Caring for Sikhs and their Families: Religious Aspects of Care*; Henley, A. (1983) *Caring for Hindus and their Families: Religious Aspects of Care*.

Discovering Sacred Texts, Oxford: Heinemann.

Exploring Religion, Glasgow: Collins Educational.

Faith and Commitment, Norwich: Religious and Moral Education Press.

Listening to … Glasgow: Collins Educational/London: Unwin Hyman. This series includes: Bennett, O. (ed.) (1990) *Listening to Buddhists/Sikhs*; Jackson, R. and Nesbitt, E. (1990) *Listening to Hindus*.

Living Festivals, Norwich: Religious and Moral Education Press. This series includes booklets on individual festivals, plus: Ewens, A., Davidson, M., Fairburn, N. and Priestley, J. (1991) *Living Festivals Omnibus: Christmas, Shrove Tuesday, Ash Wednesday and Mardi Gras, Holy Week, Easter*. Gent, F. and Schofield, L. (1993) *Jewish Festivals Omnibus,*.

My Belief, London: Watts. This series includes Obadiah (1995) *I am a Rastafarian*.

Religions of the World, Hemel Hempstead: Simon and Schuster/Norwich: Religious and Moral Education Press. This series includes: Bancroft, A. (1992) *The New Religions, Seeking Religion*, London: Hodder and Stoughton.

Teach Yourself World Faiths, London: Hodder and Stoughton.

Words and Pictures, Norwich: Religious and Moral Education Press.

Individual texts

Hackel, S. (1994) *The Orthodox Church*, Witney: St Stephen's Press.

Magdalen, Sister (1991) *Children in the Church Today: An Orthodox Perspective*, New York: St Vladimir's Seminary Press.

O'Donnell, K. (1987) *From the Cradle to the Grave: A Multi-faith Journey Through the Life-cycle*, London: Hodder and Stoughton.

Patel, N., Naik, D. and Humphries, B. (eds) (1997) *Visions of Reality: Religion and Ethnicity in Social Work*, London: Central Council for Education and Training in Social Work (CCETSW).

Rausch, D.A. and Voss, C.H. (1994) *World Religion: A Simple Guide*, London: SCM Press.

Rose, D. (1992) *Home, School and Faith*, London: David Fulton.

Videos

Byrne, G. (1985) *Encounter: Garvan Byrne talks to Mother Frances Dominica*, Birmingham: Central Independent Television.

Hitcham, M. (1993) *Somewhere over the Rainbow*, Newcastle upon Tyne: Malcolm Sargent Team, Social Work Department, Royal Victoria Infirmary.

Resources

Articles of Faith, Bury Business Centre, Kay Street, Bury, Lancashire BL9 6BU, 0161 705878 (free catalogue, *Religious Artefacts, Books and Resources for Education*).

British Humanist Association, 47 Theobalds Road, London WC1X 8SP, 0171 430 0908 (leaflets on numerous topics).

Community Development Department, Thamesdown Borough Council, Civic Offices, Swindon SN1 2JH, 01793 526161, extension 4858. (*Multi-faith Calendar*).

Pictorial Charts Educational Trust, 27 Kirchen Road, London W13 0UD, 0181 567 9206 (Religious Education Charts, including: *Christianity Today, Places of Worship, Days of Worship, My Neighbour's Religion, Religious Festivals*).

Author index

Subject index